THE CAPTIVE AND THE GIFT

Prometheus Bound by Peter Paul Rubens. Philadelphia Museum of Art, purchased with the
W. P. Wilstach Fund, 1950.

THE CAPTIVE AND THE GIFT

*Cultural Histories of Sovereignty
in Russia and the Caucasus*

BRUCE GRANT

CORNELL UNIVERSITY PRESS
ITHACA AND LONDON

A volume in the series
Culture and Society after Socialism
edited by Bruce Grant and Nancy Ries

A list of titles in this series is available at www.cornellpress.cornell.edu.

First published 2009 by Cornell University Press
First printing, Cornell Paperbacks, 2009

Printed in the United States of America

Library of Congress Cataloging-in-Publication Data

Grant, Bruce, 1964–
    The captive and the gift : cultural histories of sovereignty in Russia and
the Caucasus / Bruce Grant.
        p. cm. — (Culture and society after socialism)
    Includes bibliographical references and index.
    ISBN 978-0-8014-4304-6 (cloth : alk. paper) —
    ISBN 978-0-8014-7541-2 (pbk. : alk. paper)
    1. Caucasus—Civilization.   2. Caucasus—Relations—Russia.
3. Russia—Relations—Caucasus.   4. Caucasus—Relations—Soviet
Union.   5. Soviet Union—Relations—Caucasus.   6. Sovereignty—
Social aspects—Caucasus.   7. Sovereignty—Social aspects—
Russia.   8. Sovereignty—Social aspects—Soviet Union.
I. Title.   II. Series: Culture and society after socialism.

    DK509.G724   2009
    947.5—dc22
                                                            2008052552

For Jean-Vincent

Enchainment is a condition of all relations based on the gift.

MARILYN STRATHERN, *The Gender of the Gift*

CONTENTS

PREFACE

"We gave them so much" (*Stol'ko my im dali*). A Ukrainian friend with whom I had once studied in Moscow wrote me a few years back to describe her return to a seaside resort in Abkhazia, in the Republic of Georgia, on the Black Sea coast. She had spent time there as a child in the early 1970s and was taken aback by the declining state of basic infrastructure after years of post-Soviet economic stress, exacerbated by the struggle between breakaway Abkhaz and central Georgian forces. "We gave them so much, and yet, everywhere you looked, you could see what they had done with what *we* gave them. It was clear how things turned once they decided that we were no longer needed."

She underlined the word "we" in a familiar and genuine turn of phrase that I heard spoken this way more than once in Russia, to distinguish the Slavic majority from a Caucasus region that seemed to show little remorse for the collapse of the USSR. Twenty years earlier, "we" signaled all Russians, Ukrainians, Abkhaz, and Georgians under a shared Soviet project. Yet for all its remarkable internationalism, it was a project that never entirely convinced most populations at the Abkhaz and Georgian ends of the list that they were full partners alongside the rest. The "we" in the letter I held in my hand was a different kind of iteration, casting as spurned givers those of purportedly superior civilization and economy, whose efforts to better the lives of others were no longer appreciated. Soviet political rule had ended, but for my correspondent, so too had the mandate for cultural supervision that went with it, a cultural supervision that was widely understood, as in this letter, as a form of generosity, a form of giving. For all the intense forms of belonging generated in the USSR, however, this kind of giving is one that has of course been regularly questioned by most non-Russian peoples.

In scholarship, Russia's relations with the Caucasus are most conventionally expressed through politics, in works that focus on how treaties were drawn up, wars were fought, and lands were surrendered or annexed. This is easy enough to understand, as rapid political shift in the Caucasus was the order of the day at both the opening and the close of rule by imperial Russia and its Soviet successor, from the opening of the nineteenth century to the close of the twentieth. But as so many cases of imperial rule and its reincarnations around the world have shown, individual leaders and those who follow them more often than not legitimate sovereign rule on grounds of altruism rather than pure force. Claiming sovereignty over another entails the burden of giving. This is the gift of civilization, or, in a phrase that I believe better captures the political importance of this gesture in the Russian nineteenth century, "the gift of empire."

The investment of Russian imperial and later Soviet centers in the Caucasus region may have been variously motivated, but no one disputes that the time, money, and soldiers committed to the cause were considerable. Investment and sacrifice in this context were clear. But as the letter in my hand reminded me, this kind of gift comes not only from calculated gain but from a self-perceived noblesse oblige. It is the gift of social advancement. Montesquieu was among the first to identify this as a *mission civilisatrice,* a civilizing mission. But in Russian this became better known as a *kul'turnaia missiia,* a cultural mission, a project of advancing those under one's dominion. "We gave them so much," and look at how things turned out. The effective message was, they never really understood what we were offering. Or perhaps, they took what we gave, but they took inappropriately.

As I sat with letter in hand, I thought about a remark made to me a few years earlier by one of the first people I had met in the small city of Sheki, a regional center of northwest Azerbaijan, where I had gone to do archival and field research on the experience of one mountain community across the Soviet period. This man was brushing off the garden-variety sympathies I had extended after hearing that all of the city's silk factories—the backbone of the local economy—had sat idle since the close of the USSR. "Naturally we would like to see everyone back at work," he said as we motored up the roadway to the Palace of the Khan, an obligatory stop for the visitor. "The only time our city ever boomed was in the ninth century, with all the trade from the Silk Road. We've been going downhill ever since." He could no doubt read the polite look on my face as I strained to picture a ninth-century paradise. He smiled broadly and drilled his finger into the air. "We were at our zenith in the ninth century, when Russia was just a glimmer in the eye of Kievan Rus'. But what will Russians tell you? That *they* were the ones who came to civilize *us!*" Indeed, just who was the more distinguished civilization in Russia's long encounters with the many peoples of the Caucasus was a question laid before me more than once.

The Caucasus region, a diverse land mass of some 175,000 square miles stretching from the south of Russia to just north of Iran and wedged in between the Black and Caspian seas, has been home to dozens of civilizations over its extended history—others have gone further by arguing, in turn, that it demonstrates a shared civilizational structure of its own, one evolved from solidarities forged after years of conquest.[1] The Caucasus area is most commonly divided into North—encompassing Adygheia, Kabardino-Balkaria and Karachai-Cherkessia (which are the homelands of peoples commonly referred to in English as Circassians), alongside North Ossetia, Ingushetia, Daghestan, and more famously today, Chechnya—and South, embracing the contemporary territories of Armenia, Azerbaijan, and

---

1. This figure includes the three South Caucasus republics of Armenia, Azerbaijan, and Georgia, with the North Caucasus territories of Chechnya, Ingushetia, Daghestan, North Ossetia, Adygheia, Kabardino-Balkaria, Karachai-Cherkessia, Krasnodar Krai, and Stavropol' Krai. While the Russian Federation includes Rostov Oblast' in its North Caucasus Economic Zone, only small parts of Rostov Oblast' are traditionally included in the Caucasus, and those populations have not been factored in here.

Georgia.[2] Historically, when "the Caucasus" (in Russian, *Kavkaz*) has been spoken of most pejoratively, the reference is most often to *gortsy,* the highland peoples of the northern flanks of the Great Caucasus mountain range, whose allegiances to the Ottomans, to the Crimean khan, or more often, simply to themselves made them among the fiercest opponents of Russian annexation and some of the most difficult for the Russians to understand. The South Caucasus polities, by contrast, were relatively more accessible given the organization of small, centralized, semi-independent khanates that functioned through the decline of Persian rule after the death of Nadir Shah in the mid-eighteenth century, and thus were understood by Russian officials as relatively further along on civilizational scales.

My host in Sheki might well have responded to my Ukrainian correspondent that not all peoples of the Caucasus were eager to take what the Slavs were giving. But his comments also captured something all too often lost in broader discussions of colonial struggles and the competing logics of sovereign rules—that so much of sovereignty rests on languages of giving. For what so often gets lost in accounts of the gifts of civilization is that the givings—of religious salvation, of economic advancement, of cultural enlightenment—went very much in hand with the takings—of surplus value, lands, and bodies.

Scholars and political leaders alike have long known of the holding power of gifts. French ethnologist Marcel Mauss wrote in the 1920s that the gift "retains a magical and religious hold over the recipient. The thing given is not inert. It is alive and personified, and strives to bring...some equivalent to take its place" ([1925] 1990, 10). By striving to bring something back for having been given, the gift, in Mauss's eyes, already unsettles the more colloquial assumption that gifts are given selflessly, purely, without expectation of return. Mauss demonstrated that gifts very much create fields of social relations, languages of reciprocity, and expectations of time ahead to be shared.

---

2. Circassian (Russian, Cherkess; Turkish, Çerkez) is a term once used loosely to refer to all peoples of the northwest Caucasus, it more properly refers to the Adyghe-speaking peoples of that region and their diasporic descendants. Given nineteenth-century Russian usage of "Cherkess" to refer to peoples of the contemporary territories of Adygheia, Kabardino-Balkaria, and Karachaevo-Cherkessia, or even to all peoples of the North Caucasus more generally, I use the equivalent English term "Circassian" unless context makes the backgrounds of individual actors clear.

Can gifts really not be given selflessly, purely? Georg Simmel observed in 1907,

> Many peoples have the idea that one may accept a present only if one can requite it with a return present—a retroactive purchase, so to speak. This merges directly into regular exchange when it happens, as often occurs in the Orient, that the seller sends an object to the buyer as a "gift"—but woe to the buyer if he does not send a comparable "countergift." ([1907] 1971, 64)

Gifts may sometimes please, but they also provoke. Gifts, in this sense, are foremost "agonistic," evoking not only a sense of "agony" or struggle but the public nature of that struggle, where agonism takes its roots from the Greek *agora,* the public square or marketplace. The most powerful gifts, then, are those extended in the most public of ways, grand gestures demanding an audience.[3]

For all these insights into the agonisms of the gift, we have less often seen these languages of giving and taking extended to the study of broader political arenas, particularly in competitions over sovereign rule. *The Captive and the Gift* argues that to fully understand sovereignty and its many varied practices, one needs to consider how the taking of lives, lands, and resources could so quickly be narrated as forms of giving, indeed as gifts worth receiving. To do so I focus on the last two hundred years of Russian relations in the Caucasus, a world area that has long been distinguished for its own histories of exchange since the age of the Silk Road, and where "the exchange of bodies," as I suggest, deeply informed the imaginations of Russians about their own place in that region.

This book had its beginnings in fieldwork I began in the Caucasus in 1999, after ten years of work in the Soviet and later Russian Far East. Where I had earlier explored the Sovietization of an indigenous people on the Russian Pacific coast (Grant 1995), I became interested in comparative histories of the Soviet internationalist project, leading to research on a regionally famous mountain village in Azerbaijan (Grant 2004). In the

---

3. Simmel ([1907] 1971) is the most programmatic in emphasizing the role of the giver, while Herzfeld (1987) charts this unilateral field ethnographically for varied circumstances in Greece. Taussig (1995) uses the theme of unilateral giving in sovereignty through a discussion of debt peonage in South America. What all these studies have in common is an observation once made by Walt Whitman: "The gift is to the giver, and comes back most to him" (1980, 272).

transition from Siberia to the Caucasus, I was struck that there was relatively little scholarship about the Caucasus in English beyond the perennial
standards of military history, archaeology, linguistics, folklore, and more
recently, conflict studies, given that many of the armed conflicts in the former USSR have taken place in the Caucasus, with Chechnya being the best
known.

From the earliest Greek writers onward, what these literatures nonetheless have shared is the consistent rendering of the Caucasus as a "zone of
violence," home to mountain peoples naturally prone to belligerence. The
Caucasus somehow earned this reputation as a closed space despite centuries of recorded evidence to the contrary as a site of Silk Road trade and of
its occupation by a succession of foreign overseers: Greek, Roman, Turk,
Khazar, Arab, Mongol, Ottoman, Persian, British, and most recently, Russian. (The Germans, under Hitler, had plans drawn up for the area, too,
but never saw their advance.)

I became interested in what first seemed to be a paradox: the surprisingly
vital role played by the Russian captivity narrative in the Caucasus in the
early nineteenth century at a time when military command of these new
lands was distinctly growing. The most famous example of this tradition
came in Pushkin's narrative poem "The Prisoner of the Caucasus" from
1822, telling the story of an alienated Russian aristocrat who sets off for adventure and finds himself captive in the empire's south, only to be released
when a young maiden recognizes his true humanity and sets him free. In
Russia, Pushkin's lead was followed by Lermontov, Bestuzhev-Marlinskii,
and dozens of other writers who soon took Pushkin's aristocrat and more
popularly rendered him as a soldier in the imperial cause. The same fundamental plotline morphed across genre into opera, ballet, and later, one of
the USSR's greatest and most beloved motion picture comedies.

Rather than looking at these volunteered narratives of the Russian in
chains as another tale of the "conquering victim" (White [1947] 1991), I
tried to take these negative plotlines about captivity and consider instead
their positivities: what kinds of satisfactions have almost two hundred
years of varied Russian publics been taking in this still-popular captive
genre? From this, I entered the languages of gift and sacrifice. My main
approach has been to think of the gift—in the Russian case—as being
found both in the perceived act of giving in real-life instances of military
investment in the South (that is, in the southerly Caucasus landholdings of

the empire and later the USSR) and discursively in the tellings and retellings of how "our boy Ivan" got captured when all Russia was trying to
do was good. Without trying to overly rationalize or functionalize these
captivity narratives—which are, after all, works of art—I suggest that we
find a quite deeply patterned theme: how Russians gave of their own in a
civilizing cause to legitimate imperial, colonial, and later communist interventions. This is what I came to consider the gift of empire, found in tales
of sacrifice such as these, gifts of civilization that draw express attention to
the political contexts in which they were created.

A term such as the "gift of empire" narrates mainly the early Russian
ideology of rule in the Caucasus. It speaks to a vision of sovereignty that
opens with conquest and closes with victory, moving on to other affairs of
state and other mythographies. To fully map the kinds of local sovereignties at work in the Caucasus at the same time, including the ways in which
Russian practices themselves morphed over time, I look ethnologically
at the considerable archival and print resources documenting alternative
readings of purloined objects and persons from across the many societies
of the Caucasus. In exploring these varied and often competing Caucasus
modes of power and authority, we necessarily are invited to look at sovereignty beyond the classic frames of state power, as I do here with particular attention to the trade in famous ancestors, bride kidnapping, and
the lone-wolf male actors in the Caucasus who take refuge to plan blood
vengeance or new thefts of their own. I take up these widespread practices
precisely because they have normally been understood by Russian officials
and Caucasus scholars alike as aberrant forms of violence, signs of the Caucasus' resistance to modernization. By taking these seemingly solely negative practices as seriously as other scholars have taken captivity narratives,
I argue that we find a remarkably porous Caucasus landscape of mobility,
border crossings, and sometimes even exchanges over painfully proximate
borders that are the objects of constant negotiation. These are zones of
regular challenge, arenas that are by no means closed if one looks historically at the near continuous ways in which they have been built, crossed,
and crossed again.

What does it mean to think of competing logics of sovereignty in the
Caucasus over time? Very often sovereignty is predicated by a finite scene
of conquest, beginning with struggle and closing with the establishment
of regularized means of political control of one party over another. Take,

for example, the debate among historians about the exact duration of the "Caucasus war." Did it start in 1801, when vanquished Georgian rulers first pledged fealty to the Russian crown, or in 1817, when the policies of the famously severe General Ermolov came into play? Did it end in 1859, with the capture of Caucasus rebel leader Imam Shamil, or in 1864, with the more decisive military victories over the last of the rebel forces? In this debate they appeal to a discourse of sovereignty that understands conquest to be finite and the question of sovereignty to be closed. Likewise, to ask simply whether the conquest of the Caucasus was somehow right or wrong, as so many Russian writers have done in the last two hundred years, leaves unquestioned the nature and status of sovereign logics themselves.

This misses the far more interesting question of what I consider "open sovereignties," found not only in the relatively porous political practices of Caucasus societies but in the later captivity narratives of Russian writers such as Pushkin, Lermontov, and Tolstoy, whose own early careers in the Caucasus made them keenly aware of the limits of imagined, closed-book sovereignties. Foreign overseers might hold such idealized forms of sovereign rule from afar, but in the Caucasus, sovereignty has rarely been a settled question or a closed-book affair. What narratives of Russian aristocrats and soldiers held captive in the Caucasus tell us is that Russian publics learned a great deal about their southern lands through the language of the gift, in the act of sacrifice for higher causes. What is less often noted is that the same narratives showed a remarkable plasticity and openness toward widely circulated Caucasus practices of the exchange of persons. Over time the subjects of these many captivity narratives would become less and less "redeemed," to use the phrase of historian John Demos, whose work on captivity in the colonial Americas explores the scandals caused in settler society when some Puritan captives eventually favored their new, adoptive Indian communities over their own families (1994). Captivity was an active key symbol in Russian relations with the Caucasus for the very reason that the languages of giving and taking so well captured the complex moral vectors of sovereign struggle across the region.

By taking up the question of comparative sovereignties and the subjects of giving and taking in this manner, I aim to accomplish three things. First, by focusing on the language of the gift, I draw attention to the varied logics of sovereign rule extended over diverse and often unwelcoming subjects. Through the images of both real and fictional Russians held captive in mountain strongholds, I argue that the kidnapped body became one of the most prominent signs of sacrifice made for the advancement of newly captured lands. The Russian captive—real and imagined—was a remarkably powerful key symbol in the long-fraught relations between the political center and its southern territories.

Second, I reframe this fascination with captivity narratives—building steam in Russia at the very time when more famous captivity narrative traditions in the Americas, Europe, and the Ottoman Empire had lost their commercial audiences and moving across genres for the past two hundred years—by considering what an object of theft, a person or thing, could signify *outside* Russian frames of reference. I examine long-standing Caucasus practices of raiding, the exchange of human proxies during warfare, and bride kidnapping, alongside related experiences of voluntary self-abnegation and exile. This is intended to decenter the normally exclusive Russian perspective on events in the Caucasus since 1800. Taking up questions of sovereign bodies in this way suggests a rethinking of standard histories of nineteenth-century Russian colonial rule in recalcitrant lands. Russian officials appeared very much to be learning from Caucasus systems of exchange, exchanges that were themselves the historical product of many centuries of foreign incursions from at least the eighth century BCE onward. That is to say, to understand sovereignty in the Caucasus, one has to think historically not only about practices of Russian governance over time but with the equally historicized archive of the Caucasus' many social worlds. One has to recognize that among the many "peoples of the Caucasus," ethnologically speaking, Russians must be counted as indigenous, too, for at least the past 150 years. In unsettling these classic codes of colonizer and colonized, history and tradition, and guest and host, I am suggesting, we can start to see how mutually constitutive practices of captivity evolved over time in Russia's relations with the Caucasus and how this speaks to evolving codes of engagement.

Third, to the extent possible in any context where extant written records are heavily tilted in favor of the military victors, I consider reflections by Caucasians themselves on these records of cohabitation through contemporary interviews with Caucasus scholars and cultural figures who look back today on their reputations as brigands, as well as on some of the region's more distinctive collective efforts to write or portray on-screen Caucasus worlds beyond the world of official censors. What such reflections point to is that for better or worse, such captivities, thefts, and violent incursions have proven to be very communicative forms of engagement, fraught spaces of encounter that enjoy few luxuries of distance of the kind exercised more unilaterally in gifts of empire. To map early Russian imperial and more varied sovereign Caucasus practices over time in these ways is also to see their remarkable meldings through shared languages of kinship through conquest and later Soviet internationalist ideals.

Mountains and madmen, noble and cruel, closed to the outside world—these are just the beginning of patterned structures of knowledge about the Caucasus laid down in over two centuries of scholarly works, news accounts, children's primers, popular literature, and equally popular films. They not only describe a perceived world, but as "structuring structures," to think of the work of Pierre Bourdieu (1977, 63), they inform entire generations' relations to that world. To put this another way, it obliges us to consider the political through the realm of the cultural. By thinking through the languages of civilizing missions and of the many ways of being captive to the gift, I aim to locate this particular kind of giving more squarely in histories of colonialism, in Russian histories of the Caucasus, and in our understandings of varied Caucasian practices of exchange.

ACKNOWLEDGMENTS

The Daghestani writer Rasul Gamzatov once said of one of his works, "The idea for this book came to me the way a guest in the mountains does." He wrote, "In the mountains a guest always appears unexpectedly, but he is never unexpected, and never takes us by surprise, because we are always awaiting a guest, any day, at any hour, and at any minute" (1970, 22). Having had some experience of my own as a guest among patient Caucasus hosts, I took this to mean that an idea arrived with some hope, stayed longer than expected, and was significantly transformed along the way through the generosity of others.

While writing this book, I have been cognizant of my own status as frequent guest in both Russia and the Caucasus, so I foremost express my debt to the friends and colleagues there who gave me so much of their time.

Research for this book was sponsored by the American Council of Learned Societies, the National Endowment for the Humanities, the

National Humanities Center, the School of Social Science at the Institute
for Advanced Study, Princeton, and the research offices of New York University and Swarthmore College. I especially thank the ACLS and its late
director, John D'Arms, for their innovation in the creation of the Frederick Burkhardt Fellowship, without which this project would not have
formed.

I welcome the chance to thank kind colleagues who contributed to
this project through their advice, conversations, and generous readings.
They include Niyazi Abdullayev, Levon Abrahamian, Sergei Arutiunov,
Adam Ashforth, Jean-Vincent Blanchard, Angela Brintlinger, Jane Burbank, Indrani Chatterjee, Paulla Ebron, Alexei Elfimov, Robert Geraci,
Farha Ghannam, Rebecca Gould, Hikmet Hacizade, Cynthia Halpern,
Lisa Hajjar, Maya Iskenderova, Atiga Izmailova, Aidyn Jebrailov, Samira
Karaeva, Tom Keirstead, Charles King, Neringa Klumbyte, Susan Layton, Susan Lepselter, Byron Lindsey, Deidre Lynch, Paul Manning, Anne
Meneley, Fikret Mirkerimov, Rachel Moore, Kristina Nazimova, Brigid
O'Keeffe, Serguei Oushakine, Camil Quliyev, Harsha Ram, Doug Rogers,
Bryn Rosenfeld, Stephanie Platz, Hülya Sakarya, Rasema Samedzade,
Seteney Shami, Mateo Taussig-Rubbo, Kevin Tuite, Pauline Turner
Strong, Julie Taylor, Ol'ga Vainshtein, Robin Wagner-Pacifici, and Lale
Yalçın-Heckmann.

At Cornell University Press, Fran Benson, John Ackerman, and Peter
Wissoker have lent generous support for the series in which this book appears. Susan Barnett, Jamie Fuller, Ange Romeo-Hall, and Emily Zoss
sped production. For her editorial role, and especially for her friendship, I
am grateful to Nancy Ries.

Portions of an earlier essay, "The Good Russian Prisoner: Naturalizing Violence in the Caucasus Mountains," *Cultural Anthropology* 20, no. 1
(2005): 39–67, appear throughout this text. Portions of chapter 4 appeared
as "Brides, Brigands, and Fire-Bringers: Notes towards a Historical Ethnography of Pluralism," in *Caucasus Paradigms: Anthropologies, Histories,
and the Making of a World Area,* edited by Bruce Grant and Lale Yalçın-Heckmann (Berlin: LIT Verlag, 2007), 47–74. I thank both publishers for
allowing me to reprint this material here.

Russian transliteration follows the Library of Congress system, with exceptions made for established English-language spellings, such as Adyghe rather than Adyge, Chechnya rather than Chechnia, Daghestan rather than Dagestan, Dostoyevsky rather than Dostoevskii, and Tolstoy rather than Tolstoi. Azeri transliteration follows the Latin alphabet adopted by the Republic of Azerbaijan in 1991.

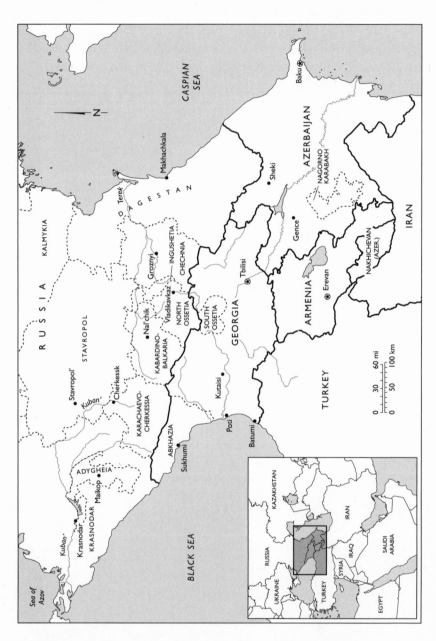

The contemporary Caucasus region.

THE CAPTIVE AND THE GIFT

1

PROMETHEAN BEGINNINGS

The conquest of the earth...is not a pretty thing when you look into it
too much. What redeems it is...an idea at the back of it; not a sentimental
pretence but an idea; and an unselfish belief in the idea—something you can
set up, and bow down before, and offer a sacrifice to.

JOSEPH CONRAD, *Heart of Darkness*

The classic political theory of Hobbes, Locke, and Rousseau long ago
focused on the kinds of social contracts inherent in sovereign rule, where
sovereignty itself might be thought of simply as "supremacy" with respect
to leadership—the established right to rule over others through force,
custom, or law. Talk of contracts invites consideration of broad, structural dimensions to which so many studies of sovereignty have confined
themselves—the absolutisms of collective good, the legitimacies and neces-
sities of monopolies over the use of force—yet as many scholars have noted,
we see less attention to how sovereignty actually operates, how such established rights come to be recognized. This is what Jens Bartelson has called
"the givenness of sovereignty" (1995, 21–35). In this light, sovereignty is
taken as given, in most instances, because it has already been given. Or to
paraphrase Pierre Bourdieu (1977, 167), the logics of sovereignty somehow
go without saying because they came without saying.

The language of social contracts such as Locke's is ultimately one of
compromise where contracts are needed to rein in individual bodies, whose

unrestrained drives to conflict should be held at bay for collective goods. Individual bodies have long been at the center of sovereign logics—as the focus of morality tales demonstrating the need for new forms of rule or the probity of old ones—especially at times when questions of power and authority are most in flux (Hansen and Stepputat 2006, 297). Bodies given for higher causes can be found at the cornerstone of histories of would-be rulers in the Caucasus. It is in the tale of perhaps the most famous suffering body ever known in the Caucasus that we find some of the earliest indications of what it means to *give* as a route to sovereign power. The eighth century BCE, when the Greek writer Hesiod introduced Prometheus, was, perhaps not coincidentally, an age of expansion for the growing Greek empire, as flotillas began to sail east across the Black Sea looking for grains, fish, fruits, and vegetables to feed their growing armies.

The Suffering Captive Giver

Prometheus's beginnings in the eighth century BCE tell a tale of exile and of minor characters who threaten to upset larger social orders. Prometheus was the son of Iapetos, who "was first to accept the virgin women [Klymene] fashioned by far-seeing Zeus" (Hesiod 1983, 26, line 511). Klymene bore Iapetos four sons: Atlas, Menoitis, Prometheus, and Epimetheus. In Hesiod's telling, Iapetos's other sons each meet burdensome fates for undisclosed reasons. Atlas, perhaps the best known, "supports the broad sky on his head and unwavering arms" (ll. 517–518). Prometheus's fate is more clearly causal. For his refusal to recognize the superiority of gods and for his theft of fire, Prometheus is assigned to his famous mountaintop prison.

> With shackles and inescapable fetters Zeus riveted Prometheus
> on a pillar—Prometheus of the labyrinthine mind;
> and he sent a long-winged eagle to swoop on him
> and devour the god's liver; but what the long-winged bird ate
> in the course of each day grew back and was restored to its full size.
> But Herakles, the mighty son of fair-ankled Alkmene,
> slew the eagle, drove the evil scourge away
> from the son of Iapetos and freed him from his sorry plight,
> and did all this obeying the will of Olympian Zeus,
> who rules on high, to make the glory of Herakles, child of Thebes,

greater than before over the earth that nurtures many.
Zeus so respected these things and honored his illustrious son
that he quelled the wrath he had nursed against Prometheus,
who had opposed the counsels of Kronos's mighty son.

(ll. 521–534)

But no sooner is he released than Hesiod's Prometheus, "a skillful crook"
(l. 546) sets about cheating Zeus by serving him white fat instead of meat in
a feast at Mekone and going on to steal fire from the king of the gods, spir-
iting it away "in a hollowed fennel stalk" (l. 566). No longer concerned with
Prometheus and mountains, Zeus wreaks a far deeper revenge on mankind for this trickery. He creates women, inaugurated in the form of Pandora, "the tempting snare." All men who would take wives from that time
forth would know the snare's meaning. Pandora was a beautiful woman so
fraught by her mix of good and evil that "even the man who does marry
and has a wife of sound and prudent mind spends his life ever trying to
balance the bad and the good in her" (1983, 28, ll. 607–610). When the lid
of Pandora's box is cast open, labor, sorrow, sickness, and a multitude of
plagues are let loose upon the world. And so, Hesiod tells his listeners,
had it not been for Prometheus, who provoked the gods to withhold from
men their means of living, "You would have been able to do easily in a day
enough work to keep you for a year, to hang up your rudder in the chimney
corner, and let your fields run to waste" (Thomson 1972, 317).[1]

There are many ways to read the life of Prometheus in Hesiod as the
story of a minor actor whose transgressions drew attention to the boundaries between gods and men, leaders and followers. According to Griffith,
for example, Hesiod's story "is designed mainly to illustrate Zeus' supreme
intelligence, and the futility of any attempt to outwit him" (1983, 1). In
this respect, Hesiod gives us the figure of the captive body that is held for
all to see who has the power to hold bodies and to punish them. Yet Hesiod's story already opens up a narrative element about gifts themselves. It
is because of Prometheus that tributary relations between gods and men,
parties who once associated freely, become firmly instituted. As Vernant
has observed, "Prometheus' failure [to outwit Zeus] not only makes the

---

1. See the parallel telling by Hesiod in *Works and Days* (1983, 68–69, ll. 47–109). For a longer
discussion see Athanassakis in Hesiod 1983, 1–9, 60–62; and T. Ziolkowski 2000, 28–31.

sacrificial rite into an act symbolizing the complete segregation of the two races [of gods and men], it gives this rupture the character of an irremediable and justified fall" (1989, 29). Hesiod's Prometheus points not only to the origin of the estrangement between men and gods but to the resultant need for sacrifice itself as a means of communication across sovereign lines. It is in Prometheus that gift and sacrifice take the political stage.

Many years later, by the fifth century BCE, the Greek writer Aeschylus recycled Prometheus's struggles with Zeus in ways that began to outline the gifts of empire when the story of Prometheus assumed a decidedly more benevolent plotline. No longer a minor actor whose calculated misdemeanors play out in a hundred lines, Prometheus becomes the subject of an extended trilogy, the second and best known of which, *Prometheus Bound,* offers us a generous hero of foresight, willing to suffer on a lonely mountaintop so that mankind may share in the gifts of civilization—skills such as hunting, healing, divination, and prophecy.[2] In Aeschylus, Zeus's authority has become almost entirely tyrannical, his realm "a harsh dominion" (1932, 59). Here the trickery at the feast of Mekone is omitted, and Prometheus's theft of fire takes center stage. Prometheus—whose name means "he who knows beforehand" (from the combination of the prefix *pro,* meaning that which comes before; the Greek verb root *manthano,* meaning to know; and the suffix of benevolence, *eus*)—signals that he is well aware of his objectives, if not the details of his anticipated punishment. When Prometheus steals fire, Zeus, tyrant and autocrat, condemns him to exile, chaining him to the summit of Mount Caucasus, where each day an eagle descends to devour his liver, only to come again the next and devour it once more.[3]

All things I foreknow
That are to be: No unforeseen distress
Shall visit me, and I must bear the will
Of fate as lightly as I may, and learn
The invincible strength of Necessity.
Yet of my present state I cannot speak,

2. "In these few words learn briefly my whole tale: Prometheus founded all the arts of man" (Aeschylus 1932, 87). For more on the authorship and sequencing of the trilogy, see T. Ziolkowski (2000, 33).

3. Bronevskii reasons that the "Mount Caucasus" mentioned by the Greeks in the tale of Prometheus can only be Mount El'brus because of its commanding height ([1823, 1996] 2004, 137).

Cannot be silent. The gifts I give to man
Have harnessed me beneath this harsh duress.
I hunted down the stealthy fount of fire
In fennel stored, which schooled the race of men
In every art and taught them great resource.
Such the transgression which I expiate,
A helpless captive, shackled, shelterless!

$$(1932, 57)^4$$

Through his offering of vital knowledge to Zeus in the defeat of the Titans and for his deliverance of man from destruction Prometheus has, in turn, bestowed upon man the tools of prosperity.

For long in darkness hid, I brought to light.
Such help I gave and more—beneath the earth,
The buried benefits of humanity,
Iron and bronze, silver and gold, who else
Can claim that he revealed to man but I?
None, I know well, unless an idle braggart.
In these few words learn briefly my whole tale:
Prometheus founded all the arts of man.

(1932, 87)

Only through a chorus of strophe and antistrophe do we meet the peoples of the earth whose lives are named by this giving. In a telling turn, they are the recent and soon-to-be conquests of the Greek Empire. Alongside the chorus themselves, those who lament Prometheus's suffering include "every land from Asia...to the Black Sea...Scythia...Arabia...and the Caucasus...in their whole-hearted expression of sympathy" (Griffith 1983, 156).

Antistrophe 1
And all the earth lifteth her voice in lamentation,
And all the mortals who on earth swell for thy lost splendour lament and mourn thy brethren's
Immemorial age of grandeur;

---

4. For all of Prometheus's knowing, he appears unaware of the bird that will greet him. "What again is the murmur I hear / As of birds hard by?" (Aeschylus 1932, 57).

And the peoples who inhabit the expanse of holy Asia
In thy loud-lamented labours do partake through grief's communion.

Strophe 2

Those who rule the coast in Colchis,
Maids in battle unaffrighted,
Ay, the Scythian swarm that roameth
Earth's far verges around the wide
Water of Lake Maeotis.

(Aeschylus 1932, 79)[5]

Antistrophe 2

Araby's flower of martial manhood
Who upon Caucasian highlands
Guard their mountain-cradled stronghold,
Host invincible, armed with keen
Spears in the press of battle.

(81)

In this context we can note that the mighty Caucasian highlanders, despite their strength, are cast as spectators in their own land. They receive the gifts of civilization, and what do they give in return? They give their thanks and their vigilance; they watch over the captive and weep for him. In a telling pattern that sets the stage for literally centuries of retelling this story, Prometheus is the good prisoner of the mountains who suffers for his generosity.[6]

As in the early episodes of Hesiod, Aeschylus's Prometheus is eventually freed. But in this revision, Prometheus reconciles with Zeus for good, and Zeus's reign is strengthened by the alliance. Never again in the Prometheus tale do we hear of the peoples of the Caucasus and central Asia. Yet their role is a central one. No mere stand-ins for all of mankind, they are of a very particular sort. They are the defiant peoples of the East, soon to be conquered more completely in the growing empire of the day. They

5. Lake Maeotis refers to the contemporary Sea of Azov.
6. The fullest template for this kind of study is Tuite's work on a "proto-Achilles" in the Caucasus (1998a). My reading of the Prometheus tale with regard to contemporary statecraft finds some kinship in Greenhouse's recent study of King Lear in a contemporary American legal order (2006).

make a cameo appearance long enough to make clear that Prometheus's gifts are, in effect, gifts of empire. But they vanish as quickly as they appear. In Aeschylus, Prometheus's giving is about the giver himself.

Prometheus knows what fate awaits him, but he gives generously to the conquered peoples and ultimately gives quite literally—with his time (thirty thousand years by one estimate) and his body in the daily capture of his liver.[7] It is this figure of Prometheus who presents us the kind of paradox that Richard White, historian of North American conquest, would later characterize as "the conquering victim" ([1947] 1991). Prometheus, the bringer of imperial gifts, ends up "a helpless captive, shackled, shelterless" (Aeschylus 1932, 57). He knows in advance of his suffering, but he gives generously all the same so that conquered peoples may grow. He is an earnest volunteer.

Between Hesiod and Aeschylus, many have tracked the "transformation of Prometheus into a true tragic hero and champion of the human race" (Griffith 1983, 4). From his initial status in Hesiod as "the amoral trickster whose deceitful ways set mankind on the slippery slope of moral degeneration" (Ziolkowski 2000, 31), he became, through Aeschylus, a model giver. In the pages ahead, Prometheus plays a key role for a number of reasons. Through his actions, in very practical terms, we find one of the earliest and most luminous examples of the structural confusion between giving and taking. In Hesiod, he gives fire to man but denies man his freedom as a result, burdening him with strife. In both Hesiod and Aeschylus, he gives fire to man but has stolen it from the gods. Yet despite this giving, we find only a blur of receiving. Through the tears of the mountain peoples, we learn briefly of their sympathy and their implied gratitude. But any formal recipients as such are studiously absent: no Caucasians or Scythians come forward with testimonials. Giving, in the end, earned Prometheus a place in the pantheon, according to Aeschylus. Giving conferred his ultimate status.

Prometheus and the Sovereign Ban

The story of Prometheus already tells us much about the gifts of civilization: to what kinds of persons they were given and the burdens imposed on

---

7. See T. Ziolkowski (2000, 70) on the subject of the time Prometheus spent atop Mount Caucasus.

both the givers and receivers. But the morality play in the Prometheus of both Hesiod and Aeschylus also hinges on Prometheus's fearsome removal from the company of the gods, his forcible exile from the greater collective. This focus on the exiled body is one that will be familiar to any reader of the Italian theorist Giorgio Agamben, whose work on sovereignty has drawn express attention to forms of power articulated in the right to take life but also to the act of banning specific persons from the world at large, in the taking of bodies out of social circulation. It is in the very act of exception, Agamben argues, at the very peripheries of social order as well as in its divine centers, that we find "the nucleus of sovereign power" (1988, 4). While core questions at the heart of Agamben's work are most often traced to the earlier work on political theology by Carl Schmitt (1985), the key idea for our purposes here might come instead from Jean-Luc Nancy's work on "abandoned being" (1993), which informed Agamben's thought on the body as site of exception. For Nancy, the centrality of the abandoned being comes up not only in the story of a captive like Prometheus but across human myth and history.

> Its figures pop up everywhere, a sickening whirl, Oedipus, Moses, Jesus, but also Roland, Robinson, Olympio, Phèdre, Tristram, Jean-Jacques, la Traviata, Josef K., and Hyperion, and the proletariat, and the sovereign. (42)

In Nancy's rendering, however, we are, as before, in a land of structured arrangement illuminated by the fates of archetypal actors whose bodies are held at bay by fate, by misfortune, or by their own willful estrangements.

In the work of Agamben, the ultimate sovereign act comes in the delineation of "bare life," the person or category of persons who may be "killed without being sacrificed." Almost every society of the Caucasus has known a variety of such means of banishment over time, foremost in the practice of ostracism (in Russian, *ostrakizm, izgnanie iz sem'i*). While the causes for ostracism could be diverse—murder, refusal of authority, or resistance to customary law (*adat*)—the resulting patterns of exile, physical or metaphorical, were strikingly similar. They constitute what Caroline Humphrey has referred to as localized forms of sovereignty. "Although nested within higher sovereignties," she writes, "these localized forms of sovereignty nevertheless retain a domain within which control over life and death is operational.... [They] construct the quasi-juridical terms in which exclusions can be made from their own body" (2004, 420). In eighteenth-century Daghestan among Darghins, for example, a typical notice such as the one below would be posted on the doors of the village mosque following a lengthy gathering to discuss the fate of the community's errant member:

> We, members of the X clan, cast out Y from our midst for his foolish behavior. From this point on, should he even be murdered, we take no interest in his whereabouts or will make no response upon his death. Should he be robbed, we take no actions toward the restoration of his property. Should any possessions remain unto him [after the act of ostracism], we renounce all rights to them, as he must to ours. From this day forth, he can no longer be considered a member of the clan and may not make claims to such. In affirmation of this, we swear on the holy Qur'an and make fingerprints on this page. (Anchabadze 1979, 139)

Among Mokhevs, for example, were any kin members to happen upon an exiled family member, there were strict prohibitions upon entering into conversation or even shaking hands (141). As across the Caucasus, exiled parties were expected to answer for their own welfare and safety. It was a form of severe social death that applied even to those who remained on the outskirts of natal villages and towns. If they were literally killed, their death would be followed without retribution or lament. These were sovereign forms entirely established through closure.

Yet the logic of Nancy's abandoned being did not rest on such bare lives alone, nor were all sovereign forms in the Caucasus the same. Mythology is full of situations in which sacrifice is very much part of a higher sovereign cause, as Prometheus tells us. So too are the archives of Caucasus social life, where young women could be released from their families for designs of alliance, men of wounded honor might take leave of their communities for the planning of vengeance or for renewal, or firstborn sons might be given over as valued objects held in safekeeping by enemies in wartime. These are far more porous sovereign practices, where bodies move across established social lines and where languages of gift and sacrifice very much narrate the making of new systems of power and authority.

In the more specific cases of kidnapping, we know that the act of holding a captive focuses attention on the ambitions and goals of the captor. But what should we make of fictional tales of captivity? What is the appeal for readers to learn of their compatriots held captive in alien lands? Are these no less morality tales of the gifts of civilization and the burdens of giving?

Promethean Gifts and Their Russian Narrators

The seemingly distant pedigree of Prometheus propels us to the contemporary Caucasus at its most paradigmatic: the narrative place that a number of Russian and European literary critics would later identify as a "literary Caucasus" or a "literary topos." It was at this very crossroads of the Caucasus' multiple and competing realities—the physical, the mythic, and the narrative—that one of its most legendary bards made his entrance. The first modern author of this prisoner story was the Russian poet Aleksandr Pushkin. Pushkin, an object of sovereign ban himself, was exiled to the South after printing one of his earliest poems. "Ode to Liberty," published in 1817, was a rare open criticism of tsarist autocracy that brought about Pushkin's exile from Petersburg just a few years later. With plans afoot to banish the poet to Siberia—the empire's harshest destination for political prisoners—Pushkin's advocates protested that the young artist still had a bright career ahead in the service of Russian culture. And so Pushkin was sent to the Caucasus to begin his six years of exile from the Russian capital (Sandler 1989). Of these years, Pushkin's actual time there was limited to just two months in 1822 spent at a hill-station spa where he penned his long narrative poem entitled *"Kavkazskii plennik"* ("Prisoner of the Caucasus").[8]

Six years of exile left a profound impression on the poet, who never ceased to bridle under the imperial censorship that followed him to his grave. It seems fitting, then, that Pushkin's tale is about another prisoner—an alienated cosmopolitan not entirely unlike himself—who finds himself at the summit of Mount Caucasus. Indeed, Pushkin's choice of the Caucasus as the setting for his political love poem, which was written at the height of the Russian military conquest of the Caucasus in the 1820s,

---

8. Critic Petr Morozov was more diplomatic when he wrote of Pushkin's stay in Piatigorsk, "Pushkin, by happy accident, was the first of Russian poets who managed to visit, if not the actual Caucasus, then its threshold" (1912, 392).

Пис: О. Кипренской. 1827.   Грав: Н. Уткинъ

Figure 1. Aleksandr Pushkin, engraving, 1827. N. Utkin, from an original by O. Kiprenskii.
Published in the almanac *Northern Flowers,* 1828 supplement.

should remind us that, as in Aeschylus, prisoners can sometimes be tricksters. For this poem introduces more than one imperial sleight of hand.

In Pushkin's tale, a young Russian aristocrat leaves his "fickle life" of high society for freedom and adventure in the North Caucasus. He is taken captive by cold-spirited Circassian highlanders, "tribes of robbers," as Pushkin calls them ([1822] 1997, 58). But a young Circassian girl falls in love with the Russian and angles to set him free.

> The moon above is shining clear
> But, in the deep peace, who comes here?
> What feet so stealthily have strayed?
> The Russian started, his eyes meeting
> A tender but unspoken greeting
> Here stands a young Circassian maid,
> Whom he, without a word, inspects.
> This is a false dream, he reflects,
> A mean trick which fatigue has played...
> And she would sigh and, now and then,
> Tears in her eyes would overbrim.
>
> (60–61)

In the dark of night the maiden brings the prisoner a saw and sets him free. They run to the edge of the river, where she halts at the shore.

> I know my future lot is picked;
> My father and my brother strict
> Would sell me, an unloving wife,
> For gold into some village other.
>
> (67)

The young woman may be held back by fate, but the young man takes the inspiration for freedom from the Circassians around him: he swims to the opposite bank and turns back to see his loved one, only to discover that she has apparently committed suicide.

> Then as the heavy waters smite
> There comes a distant moaning shout...
> Upon the wild shore he climbs out,

Looks back...
The shores are painted bright,
Foam-flooded, of refulgent white;
But the young girl is seen no more,
Not on the hillside or the shore...
The shores are sleeping; all is dead...
But for a light breeze in the ears.
As moonlight waters splash ahead
A rippling circle disappears.

(74)

As in Aeschylus, Pushkin heaped praise on Caucasian military might. As if inheritors of his earlier poems on liberty, Circassians became the first in a long line of peoples of the Caucasus to earn the ironic title of *vol'nye obshchestva* (free societies), a term invoked widely in Russian literature and historiography.[9] Hence from the beginning, this story was about a contradiction. Well-armed Russian forces had been routing Circassians, Chechens, and Daghestanis for decades; a concerted campaign of colonization had begun twenty years before the exiled poet took up his pen. Yet in Pushkin's tale the Russian protagonist is a captive, a noble victim. Indeed, it is the ultimate humanity of the captive—his attempts to wrestle with the tyrannies of the autocratic system to which he belongs and his efforts to love in a troubled setting—that earns him the admiration of the Caucasian woman, who, like her kinsmen portrayed in Aeschylus, vigilantly guards him and weeps for him.

Pushkin's Russian prisoner proved a sensation for reading audiences and a sturdy model for the long line of those who would go on to imitate, recirculate, reconfigure, or entirely repossess this Russian key symbol up to the present day. A popular and commercial success, the poem was almost immediately translated and reissued in French and German; within six months it had been rendered for the Russian Imperial Ballet. The poem was refashioned—in some passages almost word for word—by a youthful Mikhail Lermontov, and it appeared again as a short story by Lev Tolstoy in 1872. The genres employed by the great poet's admiring

---

9. For an extended discussion of the theme of *vol'nost'* in the Caucasus, see Bliev and Degoev (1994).

nineteenth-century imitators ran from high culture, as in the imperial opera composed in 1879 (Asaf'ev 1949), to low: appearing in circuit street fairs and cheaply produced bulletins circulating in Moscow and Petersburg (Barrett 1998; Mel'ts 2000; Zorkaia 1994). With each new iteration, the plot changed in small but significant ways. In his story "Prisoner of the Caucasus," Tolstoy made the more famous gesture of establishing that the captive was a Russian soldier, thus explicitly presenting the tale as an adventurous if reasonably critical narrative of Russia's colonial presence in the Caucasus. Published in a primer he designed for Russian schoolchildren across the empire, Tolstoy's story was reissued twenty-eight times and had sold more than 2 million copies by the time of his death in 1910 (Moores 1992, 29).

Beyond Tolstoy, the prisoner tale became the subject of a short feature film made at the dawn of Russian cinema in 1911,[10] another short story set on the battlefields of the post-1917 civil war (Ergushov 1929). and a socialist realist ballet (Bogdanov-Berezovskii 1949; Tarasenko 1938; Zakharov 1949). In a series of lectures on the poem, in 1946, Russian film director Sergei Eisenstein expressed his amazement at the prisoner's enduring popularity. "Pushkin's characters are flat, not rounded," Eisenstein told his students. Echoing semiotician Charles Saunders Peirce's observation that the most resilient symbols are often the most neutral—and hence more widely available to disparate audiences—Eisenstein continued, "They are more like signs, conventions" (Eisenstein 1998, 9).[11] "The greatness of Pushkin," the theorist of cinematic hieroglyphs wrote, "is not for the cinema. But how cinematographic!" (6). That is to say, for Eisenstein, how archetypal.

Despite Eisenstein's doubts that the prisoner cycle had any future beyond the ballet, it was in postwar cinema that the story would find its greatest audience yet. Pushkin's title was the model for the satirical blockbuster motion-picture comedy *Kavkazskaia plennitsa* (*Girl Prisoner of the*

---

10. Released by Timan and Reinhardt Studio, February 15, 1911. 385 meters. Vishnevskii (1945, 15) lists the director as Vitrotti, using the 1879 score by César Cui and the actor M. Tamarov in the lead role. By contrast, Likhachev (1927, 182–183) lists the director as Krivtsov. Though the film appears not to have been archived, it is also discussed in Savushkina (1988, 22).

11. Eisenstein did not lecture on the 1911 film but spoke approvingly of the ballet adaptations, for which he felt Pushkin's superficial characters were best suited.

Figure 2. S. P. Dubinin as the Russian captive and E. G. Chikbaidze as the Circassian maiden who sets him free, in the 1938 Leningrad Ballet adaption of Pushkin's "Prisoner of the Caucasus." Courtesy of the Mikhailovskii Theatre, St. Petersburg.

Caucasus) (dir. Leonid Gaidai, 1966).[12] Widely loved as a parody of Soviet social typecasting, the film, among its many legacies, became the inspiration for Moscow's upscale Girl Prisoner of the Caucasus Restaurant, decorated lavishly with photo stills and looping film clips. Since the 1960s, several other versions have appeared: an Armenian-themed prose version (Bitov [1969] 1992), a homoerotic prose version (Makanin 1995), and the Oscar-nominated film *Kavkazskii plennik* (released as *Prisoner of the Mountains*) (dir. Sergei Bodrov, 1996). These diverse cultural productions encompass almost two centuries of a very active prisoner symbol.

What does it mean that one of the most popular myths of the Russian colonial encounter repeatedly casts the victor/colonizer as captive? My aim is not to rehearse the conquering victim, in the sense used by White and many others but to analyze instead the remarkable persistence of the "good prisoner" symbol. Whereas the taste for colonial captivity narratives from the Americas and the Middle East waned among Euroamerican publics in the nineteenth century (Pearce 1947, 17), in Russia the popularity and ideological hegemony of such narratives have endured. How has this near epic folkloric staple sustained its power for so long, and why?

In this context, I look to examine the questions of captivity, theft, and gift in the Caucasus at a number of levels. By drawing on classical anthropological theories of exchange, I would argue that we need to see this myth as an "art of emplacement," one that generates a powerful symbolic economy of belonging in a highly charged setting. In contrast to the often-chaotic everyday violence in this region, popular understandings of this violence are strikingly patterned. Myths of the good Russian prisoner do not merely indicate the repercussions of violence in the Caucasus; they naturalize that violence in ways that enable diverse Russian publics to frame their government's military actions there as persuasive. In their earliest incarnations, such Russian captives were very much gifts of empire, generating recognition of givers in their own courts first and among recipients second, if at all. Such gifts of empire gave Russian publics many things: a mythic

---

12. The literal translation is "Female Prisoner of the Caucasus." I have glossed it as "Girl Prisoner" given the satiric genre of the film and the status of the heroine identified in the script as a *devushka,* a term which approximates "girl" in the youthful, unmarried sense in the film, more so than "woman" or "female."

cause for military expenditures in distant territories; a stronger place at the table with other imperial powers; and through the empire's enlightenment missions, a self-satisfying narrative of ongoing relations with the empire's newest constituents.

Yet rather than pausing to reflect solely on what the very active Russian captivity narratives of the last two centuries might say about Russian notions of power, selfhood, and exchange, I look to take the prisoner cycle one step further by placing it in the context of the longer-standing histories and ethnographies of theft, gift, and kidnapping in the Caucasus that have framed both this particular myth's reception and its ongoing relevance in a twenty-first-century retooling of the region as a whole. Indeed, the language of kidnapping did not spring unformed from the mind of Pushkin. Quite apart from the famous captivity narratives prevalent in Europe and the Americas in the seventeenth and eighteenth centuries, almost every society of the Caucasus has known practices of bride kidnapping, or bride capture, alongside a complex array of rituals of the taking and exchanging of men as proxies in blood feuds and larger-scale warfare.

In this way, Russia's particular mythography of the good prisoner entered a fertile landscape where idioms of the ritual lending, borrowing, and outright seizure of bodies had a long tradition. In short, where all societies of the Caucasus might share in the aphorism "Beware of strangers bearing gifts," we can also trace a long-standing history of what some have called "sporting theft" in the Caucasus (Colarusso 2002, 2), a means of circulating objects and persons that had the power to fundamentally recast social relations. In the zone of marriage, bride theft could upset social orders held back by the slower reciprocities of gift and countergift (Tuite 1998a, 306). In the zone of conflict, the exchange of male hostages or their outright transfer into neighboring, often feuding communities was a further way of keeping the peace (Kandelaki 1987; Khodarkovsky 2002).

The goal here is by no means to romanticize earlier forms of cultural interactions and conflicts: blood feuds commonly ended in generations of vengeance, and bride capture was as likely to be outright assault as the finely tuned recalibration of kinship categories accepted by many scholars. The Caucasus was once home to one of the world's most vigorous slave trades, with the capturing of bodies a standard practice there as in most of the world since ancient times. There is every reason to suppose that

Pushkin was familiar with such contexts.[13] But if the historical record is anything to go by, these were also forms of encounter that were not simply routinized but ritualized—that is to say, widely governed by codes of accepted conduct, or *adat,* and used sparingly. What attention to these forms offers is a look at the landscape of theft and gift into which Russians entered in the early nineteenth century—what some today have called the "frictions" of transnational exchange (Tsing 2005)—and from which Russian officers, in particular, took inspiration for their own habits of hostage taking. What were exchanged in the battlefields of the Caucasus of the nineteenth and twentieth centuries, then, were not only the bodies of men and women dislocated by the upheavals of conflict but multiple and competing understandings of giving and taking—the reciprocities of rule and the stealings that can undo them.

To connect such Promethean gifts to the Caucasus of the Russian empire, however, we need to first consider a history of Russian engagement in the region, with a particular emphasis on the spaces of encounter that these sovereign struggles generated.

---

13. Pushkin no doubt learned about the history of the region not only from his own extensive reading but also from discussions with the eminent Caucasus historian Semen Bronevskii in Feodosiia in 1820 (Pavlova 2004, 10).

2

HISTORIES OF ENCOUNTER, RAIDINGS, AND TRADE

Historians of the Caucasus have long labored to find just the right metaphors to suggest Russia's long series of encounters in the Caucasus region. The entrance of Russian forces into the diminished Persian realms of the South Caucasus on the heels of Peter the Great's decisive victory over Sweden was intended to constitute another Russian success story in the early eighteenth century. Yet it soon became known among Russian publics as the proverbial *kavkazskii uzel,* or "Caucasian knot," a tightly wound problem, hard to understand, harder to undo, and very man-made. "From the very beginning," the Russian historian Lazarev wrote, "Russia's encounter with an Asian Caucasus took place under the sign of Mars" (1990, 5). That is to say, it was a chronicle of events peopled by headstrong actors prone to using force and leading to stubbornly unresolved and rarely predictable ends.[1]

---

1. Sokolov (2005) creatively upgrades the *uzel* to a *zagogulina,* relying on the nearly untranslatable word most closely meaning a "distorted line" but more often used to signify an artifact of

When Russia entered the Caucasus in a formal drive to expand the sovereignty of Peter the Great in the early eighteenth century, there was indeed every reason to anticipate success. Since the collapse of Mongol and Timurid influence in the region, the main players had been Sunni Ottoman Turkey and the Shi'i Safavid rulers of Persia, with Muscovy and its Petersburg successors engaged in limited trading enterprises and episodic tribute relations, such as with Circassians from the sixteenth century onward. Peter's court viewed its particular manifest destiny in this context as a natural expansion of trade ties against a backdrop of lesser imperial rivals (Dzhimov 1995).

Peter the Great's concerted entry into the Caucasus field, led by an interest in creating trading links across the Caspian shores, began steadily with beachheads in Astrakhan' in 1717 and a growing network of commercial treaties across the lands of Daghestan further south (Atkin 1988; Zakharov and Nastenko 2000). But when Daghestanis began to launch attacks on Peter's holdings, Russian forces retreated from a landscape of competing Caucasian allegiances more complex than they had imagined. Likewise, in the late 1700s when Catherine launched her civilizing mission southward into Georgia with the intent of claiming Persia next, her commanders soon withdrew, not only because of the fierce resistance they met but because of Russia's unstable footing on what had first seemed to be sure ground. Though formal requests in the 1780s from a number of Caucasus principalities for protection from invading Ottoman and Persian forces had spurred Catherine to build forts, the forts themselves became the subject of attacks almost as soon as they were established.

This chapter explores the actual vectors of violence as Russian forces entered the Caucasus by considering key elements of Russia's late eighteenth- and early nineteenth-century engagements in the region with a view to the considerable traffic in bodies taking place there. These included slaves, captives, prisoners of war, and *amanats,* or human collateral who figured as proxy guarantors in warfare. The goal is not only to establish a historical setting for Russia's profile in the region but also to sort through the tangled vocabularies of sovereignty and captivity on which Pushkin and, in quick

---

irregular shape, such as an unreadable signature. Like its companion term, *zakoriuchka, zagogulina* is often used to suggest complicated, contradictory situations. See, for example, http://www.democracy.ru/library/publications/media/zagogulina.html.

succession, so many others drew in their offerings about the Caucasus to Russian reading publics. The idea, moreover, is not to contrast Russian "histories" with Caucasus "traditions" but to focus instead on how all parties found their political capacities and military practices transformed by mutual appropriations.

The chapter also explores the long-standing tendency of ethnologists and historians to single out *gortsy* (s. *gorets*), the highland peoples or "mountaineers" to whom the preponderant amount of Russia's vast chronicle of the Caucasus is devoted. The conventional history is a tale of peoples found high and low. Whereas "lowland" peoples, particularly in the many extant khanates of the South Caucasus (often but by no means exclusively designated *Aziaty,* Asians), were more openly in search of Russian protection and therefore less belligerent (Mamedov 1999; Zubov 1834), highland peoples of the North Caucasus such as Circassians, Lezgins, and Chechens sought no such protection and indeed vigorously rebuffed it. Charles King neatly framed this geopolitical paradigm when he remarked, "First the Russians conquered latitude, then they set out to conquer altitude" (2006; see also 2008).

The irony in this convention is that highland peoples were by no means the only active brigands on the Caucasus front, as the growing number of Russian sectarian settlers into lowland areas of Georgia and Azerbaijan, exiled from Russia after the decree of Nicholas I in 1820, would rapidly discover (Breyfogle 2005). Nor did all Circassian raiders, for example, live in the highlands. The very designation of *gorets,* alongside other famously plastic terms such as *Aziat* or *Tatar,* could at any given time encompass virtually any resident of the Caucasus, Christian or Muslim, living in mountain overlook or lowland city (Baddeley [1908] 1969, xxi; Bobrovnikov 2002, 5; "Perevernutyi mir" 1994, 19; Zubov 1834, 19).

Why, then, speak so loosely of such a diverse conglomeration of peoples? This oversized portrait of gortsy, painted most broadly, was the most spectacular from among a veritable array of Caucasus social structures in perceived need of civilizing. To be sure, the actual threat that Circassians and Daghestani highlanders posed to Russian garrisons, administrators, and settlers was very real. But at the same time, military officials' expansive perceptions of gortsy worked to ratify the very need for concerted advancement of the Russian mission. The overall principle is a familiar one, evinced in Adam Smith's eighteenth-century apothegm that if we did not have the poor, we could not have the ultimate experience—to give to them ([1759] 1790).[2] The gift of empire, in short, needs people to civilize.

Before arriving eighteenth-century Russian forces had significant truck with highlanders, they had to gain a footing in the lowlands of the North and South Caucasus alike, where sovereignty over lands and persons was in active shift.

Sovereigns and Slave Trades

After the fall of Nadir Shah in 1747, the suzerain khanates across the South Caucasus began to function more independently, conducting trade among themselves as well as with the numerous Ottoman, Persian, and Russian merchants active in the area. But Persian influence by no means entirely abated in the eighteenth century; it presented direct threats in a series of brutal attacks on the kingdoms of contemporary Georgia and the surrounding principalities. It was in this context, after the Georgian king and assorted khans requested protection, that Russia formally reentered the Caucasus. One of its first concerns in its efforts to stabilize and civilize was to put an end to the largely Ottoman trade in captives, together with the raiding on all sides that so readily produced these bodies for sale.

While the patterns of raiding and the capture of bodies that fed slave markets in the Caucasus significantly rose at the time of Russia's early eighteenth-century entry, practices of slavery and the slave trade itself had been evident in the region since the onset of written record, with the preponderance of activity in the areas directly under eventual Ottoman control.[3] Muscovy was no stranger to slave trading itself, as Richard Hellie (1979) has documented, with Russians undertaking the historically uncommon practice of drawing on their own communities for slave labor. Across the globe, the role of slavery in economic systems varied widely. In ancient Athens there was one slave to every three or four adult persons; in Moscow and Istanbul many centuries later (c. 1638), roughly 15 percent of the arms-bearing population were slaves; and in Crimea there

---

2. In a very different mountain context, Harkins (2004) advances a similar argument.
3. For an overview of perspectives on the history of slavery in the various regions of the Caucasus see Datsiuk (1955), Derluguian (1997), and Ramazanov (1961).

were reportedly twice as many slaves as Muslim free men and women (141; Toledano 1982).[4]

Slavery itself is not a phenomenon normally associated with the Caucasus, and to judge by extant sources, it was never a widespread indigenous practice (Bronevskii [1823, 1996] 2004; Derluguian 1997). But the *trade* in slaves, and the raiding that produced them, was another matter.[5] While historians of slavery have traditionally focused on ancient Greece, Africa, and the Americas, many have overlooked the extraordinary extent to which slavery existed in Europe and Eurasia more broadly (Buck-Morss 2000). Moscow was particularly vigilant in counting its losses and imposing a special ransom upon all Muscovite taxpayers as part of its legal code through 1679. Numbers are notoriously loose for actual bodies captured: victors over Russia could exaggerate to boast of their strengths, while Russian statisticians were expert at suggesting that the losses should motivate a strengthening of the imperial armies. In a single operation to invade the provinces of Moscow, Nizhnii Novgorod, Kolomensk, and Riazan' in 1521, the khanate of Crimea claimed to have taken as many as 300,000 to 400,000 Russian captives (Kuznetsov 1986, 50). A hundred years later, the Caucasian khanate claimed as many as 150,000 to 200,000 Russian captives. "After West Africa," Khodarkovsky has written of the era, "Eastern Europe—and Russia in particular—was the second largest supplier of slaves in the world" (2002, 21).

Across the eighteenth century, according to the distinguished historian Semen Bronevskii, Caucasus captives, obtained through a variety of domestic raiding systems, would be taken to Apana, Kods, Izgaur, Sogum Kale, Poti, or Batumi, where Turkish buyers would be stationed with their ships,

---

4. Peter Sugar (1971) has noted that in the sixteenth and seventeenth centuries, the Ottoman slave trade had grown so sophisticated that a caste of "professional prisoners" had arisen—men who would lease themselves out as placeholders for captives who would be freed on condition that they seek their ransom and return. The burden upon captives thus increased, requiring that they raise the funds not only for their own ransom but also for the fee to their proxy. The closest mention of something like professional prisonerhood in the Caucasus occurs in the memoir of Nikolai Shipov, who relied on a clause in the imperial legal code before 1861 that the person and family of any Russian held in captivity would be freed of the obligations of serfdom. His memoir is discussed in the excellent account by Brower and Layton (2005).

5. Derluguian makes the important point that while Russia sought to stem the trade of slaves in the Caucasus—effectively, the Ottoman slave trade in the Caucasus—its legislation indicated no objections to the institution of slavery itself (1997, 9).

ready to transport to Constantinople and possibly later to Egypt and the
Levant. The strongest men would be sent to Egypt to serve as Mamluks,
slave soldiers converted to Islam; the most attractive women would be sold
for a high price in Constantinople, and the remainder would traditionally
go to domestic service ([1823, 1996] 2004, 121). By 1830, however, the annual
export of slaves from the Caucasus had risen to as many as 4,000, despite the
fact that slave trading was by then a violation of Russian imperial law.[6]

The Ottomans may have been the main buyers, but who was raiding
whom was quite another question. When Adol'f Berzhe, a well-traveled
administrator in the offices of the Russian viceroy in the mid-nineteenth
century, was commissioned to assemble his magisterial twelve volumes of
Acts of the Caucasus Archaeographic Commission (*Akty sobrannye kavkazskoiu
arkheograficheskoiu kommissiei,* or *AKAK*) (1866–1904), he began in the
Tbilisi archives with a backlog of fraught correspondence between Georgian leaders and their merchant subjects. It is no coincidence that the first
rule of business should have been biopolitics or, to put it differently, the
ways in which state power makes itself known through myriad regulations
over bodies. For example, on June 19, 1747, Petr Avalishvili and a cohort of
fellow Georgian landowners made the following pledge to the Catholicos
patriarch Prince Antoni:

> You castigate us for malevolent activities on our estates, including the sale
> of captives, murder, pillaging, adultery and many other crimes. You, who
> sacrifice yourself for our people, cast aspersions on our house and, by dint
> of our title, obliged us to pursue new paths. Recognizing this injunction, we
> have made a pledge before God and the celestial sacred church from now
> forward to not become involved in the sale of captives, nor murder, nor any
> other malevolence arising between us, borne of bad habits against the path
> of God. (Berzhe 1866, 55)

The penitent Avalishvili hedged in an addendum: "Unless captives are
required by the government…[at which point] we will work to obtain

---

6. The Russian Empire was among the very first political bodies to abolish such trade in 1805
(Denmark was first in 1792). The United States and the United Kingdom followed in 1807 (Derluguian 1997, 9). Bronevskii lists the number of captives leaving the Black Sea coast at the time as
approximately two to three thousand per year, slowly declining with the early decades of the nineteenth century as Russia interrupted the traditional raiding circuits ([1823, 1996] 2004, 22).

them" (56). In 1795, the religious rivalry between Christian and Muslim took center stage in a letter from Manuchar Dadiani to the Georgian king Solomon.

> By the invasion of the devil upon our lands an ulcer to all Christians has come in the form of the sale of the unwilling [*prodazha nevol'nikov*], where the blood of Christians has been sacrificed for the sake of lawless Moham-medans.... We express our desire to bring this lawlessness to an end.... No one under my command shall further take part in the sale of captives. (61)

Certainly, between the constant small-scale raids and the struggles for sovereignty across the region, Ottoman slave traders were far from the only obstacle to Russian ambitions. On the eve of Russian protection in 1795, Persian armies took as many as 16,000 Georgian women in an assault on Tbilisi, never to return them (Zubov 1834, 33; see also Suny 1988, chap. 3). In 1798, in a mix of desperation and deft maneuver, Georgian king Georgi III pledged allegiance to the Russian crown. Over the course of the next decade, almost all the khanates of the South Caucasus followed suit, but the traffic in bodies, always at its highest when sovereign rule continued to be in flux, would not abate.

The "Caucasus War" and Cultures of Raiding

In colloquial terms, "the Caucasus war" (or "the Caucasus wars") conventionally dated from 1801 to 1864, signals one thing—struggles with *gortsy* in a fierce battle for mountain strongholds. But exactly when that battle began, when it ended, and who fought in it has become the subject of increasing debate.[7] It was a struggle that by no means took place exclusively in the mountains. Those who mark the outset of the war as 1801 trace it to the alienation of Georgian nobles who, having received firm assurances from their new Russian overlords that their titles and holdings would be respected under the new administration, soon found themselves expelled from their own lands and in fresh opposition to Russian power. Others

---

7. For a sample set of recent commentaries see the roundtable discussion in "Perevernutyi mir" (1994), as well as Gadzhiev (1998) and Gordin (2000).

trace the outset to 1817, when the famously aggressive policies of the newly installed general Ermolov came into effect. Did it end in 1859 with the capture of the legendary leader Imam Shamil? Or in 1864 with the more definitive defeat of Caucasus forces across the northwest? "The term 'Caucasus War' is sometimes modified by the epithet 'so-called,' " historian Vladimir Degoev has written, "because it has a number of features that differentiate it from classical wars" (2004, 69). His explanation goes a long way to explaining a conflict where, without clear borders, the possibilities for mixed allegiances and mutual transformations were considerable.

> It did not involve battles capable of predetermining the final victory of one side and the defeat of the other. The Russian troops did not always face an easily identifiable enemy; and sometimes they could not understand who their enemies were, who their friends were, and where they were dealing with neutral forces that were ready to swing either way depending on current circumstances. The mountaineers not only fought the Russians but also one another, settling old accounts and thus creating pretexts for new feuds with limited prospects of a swift resolution. (69)

Nor was it the case that all parties reacted the same toward Russian forces or did so with consistency across the first half of the nineteenth century. But what is widely shared is a view that this war was defined by the art of raiding.

With the entry of Georgia and neighboring khanates into a more formal Russian aegis at the turn of the century, the imperial court in St. Petersburg was extending a wide variety of terms of mutual engagement in the forms of protection, support, enticement, and varyingly, taxation. Caucasus khans and princes often sought Russian protection to ward off raiding Ottoman and Persian armies and sometimes even the aggressive property advances of growing local Russian populations themselves (Pavlova 2004, 17; see also Derluguian 1997, 137). But the empire also had long been proactive in cultivating loyalties through monetary rewards. As a rule, the longer the pledge of fealty, the greater the reward. When Tsar Pavel promulgated the Federal Union on December 26, 1801, the amounts tendered (*zhalovan'e*) varied widely. Mehdi Bey Shamxal Tarkovskii, whose forebearers pledged fealty in 1717, received the largest annual stipend, 6,000 silver rubles, whereas Saxrad Bey Masumu and Maxmud Bey of Tabasaran, who had not acknowledged Russian sovereignty until 1801, received only 450 rubles. That the Russian court extended this smaller sum at all is remarkable considering that neither of these two leaders from Tabasaran could be fully relied upon for support (Pavlova 2004, 17).[8] Whether these payments constituted gifts, bribes, or even barter arrangements depended, most likely, on whom you asked. Whatever the vantage point, the paradox is that, given the unsteadiness of early Russian rule in the Caucasus, the empire frequently had to pay in order to be able to extend its protections, the converse of contemporary protection rackets. In effect, officials had to give in order to be able to give some more, to give the gift of empire.

To maintain that there was a coherent rule of Russian engagement in the Caucasus throughout the first half of the nineteenth century would be to overstate a set of policies that were remarkably contingent on circumstance, to a large degree determined by competing leaderships, and taking place under regular siege. Thus the first of the legendary commanders of the Russian forces based in Tbilisi, Pavel Tsitsianov, himself of Georgian origin, made his reputation by ruling the peoples of the Caucasus according to what he considered indigenous terms of violence. It was an early sign of Caucasian practices being adapted to competing rule.

> These people's only policy is force, and their rulers' mainstay valor, together with the money requisite to hire Daghestanis. For this reason I adopt a system of rule contrary to that hitherto prevailing, and instead of paying, as it were, tribute in the shape of subsidies and gifts intended to mitigate mountain manners, I myself demand tribute of them. (Baddeley [1908] 1969, 65).

Demanding tribute rather than paying it as his predecessors had done, Tsitsianov took up a longer-standing Caucasus tradition of preemptive strikes made in the spirit of building ties rather than breaking them. These strikes came most often in the widely cultivated tradition of raiding that the Russians, too, soon found themselves emulating.

What was the raiding system in place that so bedeviled Russian efforts to conquer the South? In a small but growing literature that looks to elaborate the lesser studied logics of those who led assaults against the Russian

---

8. Khodarkovsky adds, "Continuing the old practice of paying tribute and taxes to the nomads was increasingly at odds with Moscow's own self-image of a sovereign Christian state." He remarks that Moscow had been aiming since the fifteenth century to reduce such payments (2002, 67).

garrisons, there is wide agreement on the extraordinary force of the attacks. One eighteenth-century Russian writer observed how, in a rural area outside of Tbilisi in 1754, there were over forty-three raids in a single six-month period, resulting in the loss of 350 captives, large numbers of cattle, and a wide array of other forms of property (Bliev 2004, 18; see also Lomsadze 1973). Raids at this time were not carried out by small bands but involved highly organized rapid strikes, anywhere from one thousand to twenty thousand strong. Writing at length of assaults by Ubykhs upon Abkhaz, Zvanba (1955) observes that preparation for any given raid lasted approximately two weeks, following a strict clarification of military hierarchy. Participation was voluntary. Women aided in all stages except the actual assaults, and all but the youngest and oldest men could take part, with parties numbering from eight hundred to three thousand. Virtually all aspects were carefully planned in advance, including extra food rations and multiple changes of clothing to allow for weather and hazardous circumstance. Raids usually took place in January and February, in part because of the relative quiet in the work season, because rivers would be at their deepest level of freeze to allow for faster passage, and because the reduced density of leaves in the forest offered greater visibility.[9] Raids took place only at night, usually half an hour before dawn, and just before a strike, front and rear guards would be further subdivided to cover all aspects of the attack as new contingencies arose. The most successful attacks rarely lasted more than forty minutes, but a vigorous defense could extend the fighting for days. Egress was just as carefully planned as ingress, with assigned spots for regrouping, the binding of captives, and resting. Following a successful assault, the top leaders would select one or two captives for their own household service, and the rest would be divided among all participants and their families, who often acted as shareholders in the monies earned from the captives' eventual ransoming or sale (43–54). The body count for this kind of trade was notoriously hard to track, but all estimates suggest that the sum we saw earlier—approximately four thousand captives sold to Ottoman merchants stationed along the Black Sea coast each year—was a modest one.[10]

---

9. One Russian writer made this observation about life along the Kuban' River in 1788: "An uncommon amount of snow, wind, and cold temperatures descended on these parts, bringing great harm to our troops and to the local population" (Anonymous 1898, 270). In other words, as temperatures fell, so too did Russians' ability to protect themselves from raids.

10. Bliev (2004, 128) states that over the course of the eighteenth century, Circassians annually included six thousand captives and as many horses in their tribute payments to the khan of Crimea

Russian forces subject to these raids naturally fought back, becoming quick studies in the most effective methods suitable to each terrain and location. General Aleksei Ermolov, appointed commander of the Caucasus forces after a successful career on the Napoleonic battlefields, routed a significant number of raiding parties, completely razing entire villages he judged to be complicit and cementing his reputation for merciless determination through a series of public executions.[11] But in spite of Petersburg's hopes that Ermolov's tactic of fighting fire with fire would calm the Caucasian dominions, raidings in fact did not diminish but increased. In turn, the more conciliatory stance of Ermolov's successor, Ivan Paskevich, did little to stem the tide. One of the more detailed reports of 1830, from inside Russian garrisons stationed in the area of the contemporary city of Krasnodar, describes how relatively small units of Russian Cossacks were routed in raid after raid by Shapsugs numbering in the thousands; such raids were taking place almost daily in the course of a single month. To some it appeared that every single Shapsug capable of taking up arms against Russians had done so (Tomkeev 1898, 198).

Far from being exceptional outbursts, raids and counterraids increasingly became the signature form of Russian engagement in the Caucasus in the late eighteenth and the first half of the nineteenth century, despite the well-recorded but lesser incidents of intermarriage and acculturation (Bondar' 1995, 127). Nor were Russians the only targets. "Not satisfied with brief raids," Bronevskii wrote,

> Some tribes [*plemena*] such as Kabards and Lezgins gained the glory of conquerors, pursuing almost constant battle with their neighbors: Cherkess with Abkhaz, Kabards with Ossetians and Chechens, Ossetians with Kists, Chechens with almost everyone around them, and Lezgins with Georgia and Shirvan. In a word, war is the normal state of affairs and a way of life for these peoples. ([1823, 1996] 2004, 39)

---

alone. Bronevskii ([1823, 1996] 2004, 122) suggests that there was a regular flow of two to three thousand captives traded up until 1800, when the numbers diminished because of Russian interventions. Derluguian (1997, 159) cites the higher rate of four thousand per month through 1830.

11. Breyfogle (2005, 189–201) observes how religious sectarian settlers in Azerbaijan in the early nineteenth century saw their own defenses as part of a broader culture of nomadic violence. "The sectarians generally reacted with extreme measures and frequently with greater violence than had been done to them. Descriptions of burning culprits alive, castrating rapists, hunting criminals, and setting upon thieves in large numbers to inflict beatings all reflect an approach to violence that was preemptive as much as retaliatory" (198).

Figure 3. Portrait of Aleksei Petrovich Ermolov, commander of Russian forces in the Caucasus, 1816–1827.

While not all would agree that war could ever be considered a normal state of anything (the Adyghe, for example, had their own divisions of labor for who took care of defense, thus designating war as a way of life primarily for the military classes), Russians had begun to enter and transform a landscape where, at least initially, raiding was done without special prejudice toward national character (Pokrovskii 1924, 199, 204).

Who was doing the raiding? History has again focused primarily on the gortsy of the North Caucasus, yielding the greatest number of chronicles, though evidence suggests that Russian garrisons and settlers in the lower altitudes of the South Caucasus had no refuge whatsoever from similar events (Breyfogle 2005). Bronevskii suggested that there were three fundamental types of indigenous rule across the Caucasus at this time: monarchic, aristocratic, and "democratic" (2004, 40). The last category is often glossed as "military-democratic" for the reason that these were the more egalitarian forms of social organization, relatively spare in their patterns of accumulation and therefore prone to large-scale raiding as a means of distribution and redistribution of wealth (Derluguian 1997, 41–48). But again, Christian or Muslim, highland or lowland, Spartan or satrap, all peoples of the Caucasus were more likely to be identified simply as *moshenniki* (swindlers), as the formal nomenclature in Ermolov's correspondence took root.[12] The next step up was gortsy, with particular attention given to the peoples of the northwest Caucasus, Daghestan, and Chechnya.

In recent years, Maksim Bliev, one of the foremost specialists on Caucasus raiding systems, set off controversy in Russian historical circles with a series of works on the nature and intensity of raiding practices in the Caucasus as the nineteenth-century Caucasus wars were under way.[13] Long

---

12. Umanets cites a passage from a letter to a superior officer as an example of Ermolov's epistolary style: "Permit me, your highness, to extract amanats from among the peaceful, known swindlers.... Permit me to announce to the peaceful swindlers...to convince them that we do not need peaceful swindlers" (1912, 46).

13. Bliev's inaugural essay on this theme was printed in the journal *Istoriia SSSR* in 1983 and drew widespread attention from a Soviet academy accustomed since the time of Stalin to viewing the raiding system as an anticolonial resistance movement (1983). These criticisms are reflected in a public dressing down in the same journal five years later (Ortabaev and Totoev 1988). For more comment on the Bliev controversy, see Avramenko et al. (1995); Akaev (2000); Bliev and Degoev (2004); Bobrovnikov (2002); Bryan (1992); Gadzhiev (1998); Kerashev (1991); and Reynolds (2005). Though I focus here on Bliev, given the high degree of constructive debate around his work, one

before Russian arrival, he writes, raids had an episodic character, provoked
by significant demographic disruptions occurring because of illness or poor
harvest, leaving communities no alternative but to compensate through
raidings and theft.

> In its early stages, when the mountain societies of Daghestan still led their
> localized, sedentary [*malopodvizhnaia*] way of life, raids served as a unique
> means of "redistribution" of property within various societies. Later, with
> the passage of these societies from egalitarian to hierarchical relations, raids
> acquired a special dimension and became an aggressive means of accumu-
> lating property. (2004, 16)

In a ginger side note, however, he added that from the eighteenth century
onward, with the increasing number of Russian arrivals and pressures to
dismantle clan structures, raiding took on a greater systematicity (17). Little else would be said by Bliev on the subject of Russian influence, for if
his argument about raiding was to work, the peoples of the North Caucasus had to find violence among their own cultural logics, all on their own,
without any help from the Russians.

Bliev's efforts to insist that Russia had nothing to do with increasing
waves of violence across the region ran counter to much evidence. In the
mid-eighteenth century, kidnappings of Russian soldiers and settlers were
in part what inspired the imperial army to construct the line of forts that
rimmed the North Caucasus to protect themselves from attack. Yet the ex-
istence of those same forts was seen as exceeding any welcome Russia might
have been extended in its early agreements with Caucasian peoples. As one
Kabardian chief wrote to Catherine the Great in 1782, "The newly built
forts on the Mozdok Line are the main cause of all the disturbances and
raids that we have carried out on Russia's borders" (Pollock 2006, 121).

Nor is the spirit of such mutual transformation without parallel in
other times and places. When they first arrived on the Canadian northwest coast, British officials were horrified by what they perceived as the
wasteful practices found in elaborate ceremonies of status recognition, or

---

could also point to the work of Iakov Gordin (2000), which has equally sought to diminish the
effects of Russia's role in the Caucasus, attributing the violence on all sides to simple human nature. Sultanov (2004) offers a brief critique of Gordin's work.

potlatch feasts, held by Kwakiutl, a subgroup of the people known today as Kwakwaka'wakw.

Possessed of an immense wealth in resources across land and sea, Kwakiutl were renowned among Amerindian peoples for their artistic creativity and highly complex social organization. Potlatch ceremonies to some degree were about ritual prestations, but they also frequently showcased the destruction, in whole or part, of valuables such as blankets and coppers (flat sheets of metal often beaten into the shape of shields and decorated) as a means of asserting social rank. British and later Canadian officials professed horror at what they perceived as the waste of commercial goods in such bacchanalian settings, and they saw such potlatch ceremonies as extraordinary examples of the backwardness of indigenous life (Bracken 1997). What many observers failed to realize, however, was that the potlatch was by no means an isolated example of timeless native custom but instead a practice very much changed by the historical moment in which it operated. Widespread epidemics and the seeming disregard for public health measures shown by the same authorities toward indigenous communities at the turn of the twentieth century had created a sharp drop in population. The result was demographic havoc in communities finely tuned to networks of exchange (Graeber 2001, 188–210; Kan 1989). In a social world that had become largely unhinged, the quantity of potlatches had escalated, and their purposes had shifted. If they were once geared primarily for consumption among Kwakiutl and the broader communities of Kwakwaka'wakw, well into British dominion they were just as often undertaken to assert their sponsors' preeminence in the eyes of government officials. As in the Caucasus, what government overseers perceived as shameful local practice was in fact largely a response to the very presence of the new government itself.

Raiding clearly existed in the Caucasus well before Russian intervention, but the intent of most non-Russocentric scholarship has been to assert its status as a ritual force, drawn upon when needed but foremost a performative act. Of the Adyghe, Dmitriev writes,

> Raids by gentry and princes were not only a way of life, but also a means of affirming the very existence of the aristocracy. What they acquired enabled them to meet their needs, clearly exceeding those of basic survival, but the harvest was considered to be an indirect, insignificant effect of the more

prestigious act of violence. The performance of the act itself (the raid) is what mattered; the spoils emerged only in the description. (2001, 343)

Dmitriev points out that traveling observers often confused the effects of raiding (theft) with the causes, seen in the affirmation of a greater social structure.

> Observers saw in this primarily a result—the spoils. Therefore in the memoirs of Russian and foreign authors these raids signaled a way of life based on thievery. In their descriptions, the common refrain to describe the characteristics of Adyghe behavior is: "They steal, and they respect those who know how to steal well." (343)

Dmitriev is therefore among those who look at the acts of violence by which the Caucasus has been so inflamed today—glossed by place names in ways that attach violent reputations to entire peoples: Chechnya, Nagorno-Karabagh, Abkhazia—and attempts to historically if not somewhat romantically redeem an earlier age of regulated balance that is not far off from Bliev's own imagined seventeenth-century sedentism. He continues:

> Without doubt, violence in Adyghe feudal society was integral to the social organization of society itself. It would have been impossible to maintain social organization or trade without it. In the days before the Caucasus war [of the nineteenth century], violence in this society was constructive and customary. Its use promoted the articulation of feudal classes, themselves advanced by this violence, and a monopoly held by leaders in this militarized way of life. (Dmitriev 2001, 34)

More positively speaking, Dmitriev's approach ratifies the essential ethnographic project of taking societies on their own terms but doing so in a manner that does not foreclose the intense effects of the economic and political tumult of which they are a part. Others have equally reflected on how the Adyghe were by no means a homogenous community but a highly stratified society where attacks would be carried out by both highlanders and lowlanders, by both pastoralists and petty traders, led by noblemen of the valleys and backed up by a professional class of warriors (Kerashev 1991). Such evidence clearly undermines the demonization of gortsy as the empire's sole opponents in a protracted campaign of pacification.

If Russian engagement in the Caucasus remained on an initially opti-
mistic footing throughout the eighteenth century, one reason for this mild
success may be that the Caucasus societies that the Russian forces were entering were relatively more prosperous than in previous eras. Derluguian
has persuasively argued that despite the ebb and flow of Ottoman and
Persian incursions, the eighteenth century was a period of relative quiet
for a Caucasus region that had been subject to near constant foreign invasion since the fourth century BCE. Corn had recently been introduced into
largely millet-based diets, making it easier to feed larger numbers who
required, in turn, more resources to support themselves and greater competition to secure them (1997, 60).[14]

By time of the concerted military battles of the early nineteenth century,
however, and the more draconian policies of Russian general Ermolov,
there can be little doubt about the havoc created by wide-scale conflicts
across the region. Meanwhile, efforts to insist on the natural belligerence of Caucasus peoples exclusive of Russian influence continued. As it
was becoming commonplace to associate the region with theft, Emperor
Nicholas I (r. 1825–1855) referred to the Caucasus as a "den of thieves"
(*razboinich'i vertepi*), while the poet Katenin was one of many who likened
the area to a "bandits' hideout" (*priton razboinikov*) "where thieves have
lived since ancient times" (*tam izdrevle zhili vory*) (Sultanov 2004, 24; see
also Bobrovnikov 2002, 20–22).

The Caucasus was sufficiently diverse that relations with Russians were
by no means uniformly negative. But in areas where Cossacks and sectarian settlers competed with or outright displaced local residents from their
land, as Enikolopov (1938) has shown for the North Caucasus, and Breyfogle (2005) has shown for the South, tensions were consistently high. In
this context, the bulk of raids by Circassians in the early nineteenth century
took place in response to challenges to their sovereignty and to their existing trade and political networks (Kerashev 1991, 171).

The result was a pattern of mutual misprision where questions of
cause and effect in the near-constant raids were becoming increasingly
difficult to answer. If Russians initially anticipated recognition of their
centralizing preeminence and generosity, they found themselves in a

---

14. One Russian captive held by Chechens in the 1830s recalls "the tall pyramids of corn"
that he sees for the last time as he loses his freedom and is taken into captivity (Ekel'n 1841, 92).

landscape where they were far from the only player. As Derluguian has remarked,

> The general scheme of "government" could be simply put as follows: the Russian commander addressed the local peoples and promised them protection and commercial advantages in return for their loyalty and peaceful behavior. An "accord" was signed with the potentates and elders, but sooner or later it was violated and, as a result of a raid, large numbers of people were killed and taken into captivity. A punitive expedition was organized and the cycle started all over again. Address, "treaty," raid, punitive expedition. (1997, 126)

In this context, what might Russian sovereignty have suggested for the Lezgins of Daghestan, for example, who had already concluded parallel arrangements with the Avar khans? The Lezgins swore allegiance to the Russian tsar, but circumstance suggests that it was a pledge that they most likely understood as a mere formality or payment of tribute at the very most. The Russians, however, understood the same document as a promise of absolute loyalty and obedience to the Russian administration (139).

While Russians may not have fully grasped the effect of their destabilization of Caucasus economies and societies, they were quite willing to engage in some direct practices of exchange along Caucasian lines, in the form of amanat. The word is derived from Arabic and means an object entrusted for safekeeping. In the Caucasus, it involved the election of a hostage who would move across enemy lines to minimize the potential for further violence. Long a practice in both the Ottoman and Persian realms, amanat was a practice in which Russians engaged from their earliest entries into the region.

> The Russian officials insisted that the hostages be chosen from the best families, and they sometimes refused to accept hostages whom they deemed to be from lesser native families. Most commonly hostages were members of the chiefs' extended family: sons, brothers, and nephews. The issue of who could be sent to Russian towns as a hostage was a source of numerous quarrels between the Russian authorities and the natives. The most valuable hostages were the sons of the local ruler, and particularly the ruler's potential successor. Even if a native chief submitted his eldest son from the first wife, the Georgian king Alexander had warned the Russian envoys in 1589

Figure 4. The surrender of Shamil, 1859. Print Collection, Miriam and Ira D. Wallace Division of Art, Prints and Photographs, The New York Public Library, Astor, Lenox and Tilden Foundations.

he could not be trusted, because "the shamkhal has as many sons as dogs." (Khodarkovsky 2002, 57)[15]

Perhaps the best-known example of the transfer of valued kin came in 1839 with the legendary Imam Shamil, one of the most charismatic and powerful of Caucasus leaders. Briefly subdued by the Russian general Pavel Grabbe, Shamil surrendered his twelve-year-old son, Jamalu'd-din, to an education and military future in St. Petersburg. To get him back by means of exchange fifteen years later, Shamil risked his own reputation by kidnapping two prominent Georgian princesses in return. The fact that they were female cost him considerable standing among compatriots, who considered

---

15. See, for example, Gudovich's insistence on acquiring amanat from North Caucasus communities in 1806 (Derluguian 1997, 97, 139–140). *Shamkhal* is a term that designates a range of hereditary rulers across the Caucasus.

such desperate acts beneath him.[16] "What it cost him to do so," Baddeley wrote, "may be best gauged by the persistence with which, long years after, he negotiated the return of one who had then become a stranger to him and his country, a uniformed servant of the Russian tsar" ([1908] 1969, 337).

Following the capture of Shamil in 1859, Russian officials retired him to Russia, where he went on to become a reluctant celebrity captive himself, yet one more body showcased in a display of sovereign power. His defeat was a watershed event in Russia's efforts to establish control over the mountains and valleys of the Caucasus' hundreds of principalities. The tide of Russian settlement—already significant with the flow of Cossacks, non-Russian Orthodox sectarians, and fugitives from the North—increased two years later in 1861 with the emancipation of the serfs and an imperial decree granting Cossacks land held by Caucasus nobility across the northwest. Between 1858 and 1865, as many as five hundred thousand Circassians were forced to emigrate, primarily along the very Black Sea routes that generations of captives had traveled before them, with many dying along the way or becoming captives themselves (Derluguian 1997, 221; Shami 2000).[17] The more definitive defeat of resistance across the northwest Caucasus in 1864 marked what is widely considered the end to the war. In the wake of such tumult, the Caucasus entered another period of relative quiet—excepting the Russo-Turkish War of 1877–1878, when Russia aimed to gain access to the Mediterranean and liberate Slavic peoples from Ottoman rule—until the more consequential unrest that began in 1905 and continued through the onset of World War I.[18]

Gift, Sacrifice, and Exchange

The Russian investment over the course of the Caucasus wars was indeed substantial, with estimates of the number of officers and lower-ranking

---

16. For more on the capture of Princesses Chavchavadze and Orbeliani, the canonic account is Verderevskii (1856). See also Layton (2004).

17. Bliev's inclination to see the Russian presence in the Caucasus as close to invisible, even at this stage in the annexation, is found in his explanation that Circassians were "drawn into mass emigration" because of the violence brought about by their own raiding systems, causing them to lose their "historical orientation" (2004, 11).

18. Baberowski makes clear that while the war might have ended, chaotic imperial legal and agrarian reforms across the Caucasus led to continuing spirals of violence in a situation still only very loosely under control (2004, 317).

soldiers lost between 1801 and 1864 ranging from twenty-five thousand to seventy-seven thousand. This was in a territory where it would be many decades before ready material gain would be realized (Tolmachev 2002, 17; Vedeneev 2000, 108). Other figures show sixty-five thousand wounded and over six thousand taken prisoner (Tolmachev 2002, 17). For earlier periods, Khodarkovsky has likewise commented,

> Russia's eventual success in expanding and stabilizing its southern frontier came at great human and material cost. One rough calculation may suffice to give an idea of some of the direct expenses incurred by the government along the frontier. In the first half of the seventeenth century alone, the Crimeans received from Moscow 1 million rubles in various forms of tribute and taxes. During the same time, they captured as many as 150,000 to 200,000 Russians. A conservative estimate of 100,000 people redeemed at an average price of 50 rubles per person would require a sum of 5 million rubles. Thus, over a period of fifty years, Moscow poured into the Crimea alone 6 million rubles. By comparison, 1 million rubles spent between 1600 and 1650 could have provided for the construction of four small towns annually. In other words, in the first half of the seventeenth century, Russia was short 1,200 small towns. That Russia was urbanized in comparison to its Western European neighbors is an undisputed fact, but that this shortage of urban centers may, in no small degree, be related to the nature of Russia's southern frontier is poorly understood. (2002, 223)

There is no question as to the difficulties endured by Russian military and settlers alike; they faced plague, famine, inadequate salaries, corruption, and uneven central government support to contend with an unstable environment throughout the early nineteenth century (Atkin 1988, 181). In contrast to the Americas, as other authors have observed, settlers in the northwest Caucasus found themselves as much the recipients of illnesses as their deliverers. Northern experience had first suggested to Russian arrivals that the lower-lying seacoasts and riverbanks would be not only the most aesthetically appealing sites but also the most expedient for purposes of travel. Yet they soon found themselves felled by cholera, malaria, scurvy, and typhus, unaware that their longtime Caucasian neighbors had left for the distant piedmont elevations precisely to avoid these swampborne illnesses (Barrett 1995, 583). Thus, ironically enough, the very elaborate spas for which so much of that corner of the Caucasus is famous today had their origins as centers of recovery from the effects of colonization.

In November of 1864, the new viceroy of the Caucasus, Grand Duke Mikhail Nikolaevich, shared familiar words in a proclamation to peasants marking their emancipation after Russia's own decree in 1861 to release all serfs:

> Village residents…I trust that you value the deep meaning of this day, one that opens a new life for you; that you understand the importance of the rights bestowed [*daruemykh*] upon you, that make you full masters of your own property, full sovereigns of your own labor. I trust that you understood to whom you are indebted for this kindness. The Emperor, providing for the well-being of all His subjects, would not exclude you from the circle of His great concerns. It is to Him that you are foremost indebted. (Strukov 1906, 286)

History showed that the day in question was not much of a break in the lives of most village residents, whose ties to land and the social relations that sustained them were far from simply contractual. Yet the grand duke's comments are telling in other ways: the tsar made a gift to Caucasians in the form of their rights to live under the tsar, a gift to which they were "foremost indebted." Their own sovereignty thus usurped and finding themselves in debt, they nonetheless were granted a loophole. They might become "full sovereigns of [their] own labor."

Looking back on the early nineteenth century, when the gift of empire proceeded with some force and acts of giving had little to distinguish them from acts of taking, it is key to remember that at the dawn of the age of Ermolov, there was more than one way to civilize. In an 1816 memorandum, Admiral Nikolai Mordvinov, an elder statesman writing from St. Petersburg, left no doubt as to Russia's mission in a perceived Asiatic South.

> Asia is young and uneducated, it can be more closely unified with Russia. All that signals the grace and superiority of enlightenment and labor will work to advance the power of Russia over this most spacious and important part of the globe. (Esadze [1914] 2004, 276)

How one would carry out such a mission was another matter. Remarking on his contemporaries' insistence on the need for violence in a fraught context that was by no means understood by many, Mordvinov objected that satisfying such calls had come only by enormous outlays of funds and great human sacrifice, yielding little tangible result. To bring peoples of the Caucasus closer into Russian lines of thought, Russian officials needed to be offering goods, such as schools, that Caucasians could use. Mordvinov then launched into what to the untrained eye might seem an almost whimsical logic of the gift. It was a decidedly more Jesuitical approach to imperial engagement and one that proved an early signal of Russian interest in learning from Caucasian practices:

> Asian peoples consider hospitality the foremost possible good deed.... This popular form of goodwill should be mobilized by all [Russian] leaders, administrators, and community elders. Russian commanders and their staff should keep guest rooms in their own homes—always at the ready, generously outfitted and supplied—in order to ensure the mountain visitor a pleasant, peaceful, and enjoyable stay. One hundred thousand rubles per year should be budgeted annually toward the maintenance of these networks of hospitality, as well as for gifts that can be extended at the ready. Such gifts should be of a sort that will instruct guests as to our ways and inculcate new needs in their own lifestyles on their own land. (277)

Mordvinov's idea was intended not only to appeal to the Caucasians' interest in organized hospitality but also to promote the kinds of dialogues and bilateral exchanges that were indeed wanting throughout the early Russian campaigns.

Over a hundred years later, the Soviet government followed the spirit of Mordvinov's advice far more creatively, establishing hospitals, schools, and houses of culture in remote locations long forsaken by their imperial predecessors and specifically formulating policies of *rastsvet* (ethnic flourishing) and *sblizhenie* (ethnic rapprochement) that went beyond pure appropriation or Russification. In the 1980s, one Caucasus writer attributed the relative success of the Soviet state in southern climates to these policies. "Without hosting and visiting we cannot imagine the Soviet Commonwealth of 130 peoples of the USSR. Sblizhenie through rastsvet, rastsvet through sblizhenie" (Mal'sagov 1989, 8).[19] Although hospitality on a federal scale may seem quaint, it attests to the use of state policies to achieve the goal of integration.

---

19. Kotkin (2007) pursues the same logic as Mordvinov in a consideration of practices of exchange in the Mongol and Russian empires, as well as the former Soviet Union.

The benevolence of the state, however pursued, was one largely advanced by the perceived brutality and unpredictable freedoms of Caucasus life. Were Russians the inventors of this mythology of martial mountaineers? Hardly. Recall Aeschylus's description of the Caucasians from the fifth century BCE: "Araby's flower of martial manhood / Who upon Caucasian highlands / Guard their mountain-cradled stronghold, / Host invincible, armed with keen / Spears in the press of battle" (1932, 81). By the time the Russians arrived, most societies of the Caucasus had known more than a few foreign overseers, leaders whose foreignness diminished as the deeply pluralist region transformed along with them.

3

Noble Giving, Noble Taking

She gives, and does not expect.
She can, but does not take revenge.
In giving back, she increases.
From the Ditchley Portrait of Queen Elizabeth I, 1592

With the flurry of decolonization and the rise of new states across the twentieth century, it became commonplace for scholars to look back and remark upon the depredations of imperial rule everywhere. Yet not all imperial forms of rule operated by the same logics, giving rise to a wide number of recent studies that reflect on how imperial rulers and their armies of administrators narrated and sustained the logics of conquest for themselves (Burbank and Ransel 1998; Calhoun, Cooper, and Moore 2006; Pagden 1995). While scholarship shows how civilizational hierarchies have been animated by the experience of difference, simply put—through travel, exploration, and discovery more or less from the start of human record—the varied logics by which empires and states have suggested the premises of their leadership are less well mapped. Yet "when sovereignty is identified within a particular configuration," as Caroline Humphrey has observed, "then sovereignty itself, which has to consist of practices, may be rethought not simply as a set of political capacities but as a formation in society that engages with ways of life that have temporality and their own characteristic aesthetics" (2004, 421). By thinking ethnologically and historically with questions of empire and gift and by considering how taking could be so frequently coded as giving, one sees that "empire" never signaled objective structures so much as it did patterned fields of contested relations. To explore this, I begin by considering a cornerstone of sovereign rule found in the languages of giving and taking: what it meant to extend (or impose) the gift of civilization or what I am calling the gift of empire.

By comparing a range of imperial settings over time, and locating the ways in which ideologies and practices of giving have guided imperial rule in the Caucasus specifically, the goal is not to focus on the particular gifts themselves—a silver bowl, a silken cloak—as this has been done often and to excellent end. Instead, the aim is to reflect on the performative labor of the act of giving itself. I argue that while the gift of empire may ultimately be unilateral, it sets in motion a remarkably effective means of establishing sovereignty over others, hinging on a language of reciprocity that requires little or no actual reception among the conquered. It is the logic of sovereign rule where the act of taking—of lands, persons, and goods—is enabled by the language of giving.

Consider one of the most famous images of England's Queen Elizabeth I, the Ditchley Portrait, commissioned by one of the queen's strongest supporters. Standing decisively astride the globe, the queen is flanked on the right by a sonnet, an ode to the sun in her honor, and below by three Latin inscriptions. The inscriptions read, "She gives, and does not expect. She can, but does not take revenge. In giving back, she increases" (Murray 2000, 55). First and foremost, the queen gives. But what does she give? Perhaps like the sun, she gives light—she is the Enlightenment itself—and her gifts enable growth and prosperity. She does not expect return, but the inscriptions make clear that return is already in play. How, otherwise, and for what would she contemplate revenge? If she is giving *back*, what, then, has she taken? The point, of course, is that the quite substantial taking is lost amid the language of giving, an apparently selfless giving that requires no return.

In these three canny lines, we see the language of imperial giving in full flush. The queen gives but does not expect. She need not expect, in fact, because she is already taking. In recognition of this taking, she gives back. In giving back to those around the globe she has claimed as her own, she increases. No doubt the idea is that she increases benefit to all, but as

Figure 5. The Ditchley Portrait of Queen Elizabeth I (c. 1592), by Marcus Gheerhaerts the Younger. Copyright the National Portrait Gallery, London.

other examples from the same period demonstrate, benefit to oneself was considered an equally fine end. In her book on the gift in sixteenth-century France, historian Natalie Zemon-Davis tracks the widespread popular belief that giving rewards the giver: "Qui du sien donne, Dieu luy redonne" (Who gives of himself, God gives back to him) (2000, 11).[1]

Although the imperial age may have reached its early heights in sixteenth- and seventeenth-century Europe, the role of the gift as a mediating element between competing forces was already a familiar one throughout the world. An extended chapter of the eighth-century Persian treatise, *Adāb al-ḥarb,* or *Customs of War,* reflected on "Sending envoys with gifts and presents and on the related rules of decorum," laying out the powerful leveraging of the gift in order to cultivate the will of the giver (Wiesehöfer 2001, 606). So, too, in his tenth-century epic chronicle of Persian history and legend, *The Shahnameh,* Ferdowsi (1998–2004) offers examples of gifts aimed more at provocation than at mutual prosperity.[2]

What, then, did the earliest Russian interventions in the Caucasus pledge to offer? From the time of Ivan's conquest of the Muslim city-state of Kazan' in the sixteenth century, official attention had turned to what a bulkhead in the Russian south could fulfill in terms of the empire's expansionist ambitions, as well as to what the Caucasus region itself might contribute to imperial coffers. Long after Greek, Roman, Byzantine, Mongol, Ottoman, and Persian rulers had conquered and claimed all or parts of the Caucasus as their own, Catherine the Great saw in the region's fertile valleys riches enough to conjure not only "a Russian Switzerland" (Umanets 1912, 44) but also a strategic location from which to expand Russian land holdings into Ottoman and Persian territories. This was Russia's "push to the warm seas" (Broxup 1992). It was also a key zone where the language of gift was extended from the outset.

Although it is Peter the Great (r. 1682–1725) who is perhaps best known among the tsars for his Westernizing drives, it was his francophile descendant Catherine (r. 1762–1796) who entered the Caucasus region with the

---

1. On the hall of mirrors that is giving and giving back, see the discussion of the etymology of surrender in Wagner-Pacifici (2005, 17–22).

2. For recent considerations of gift giving in the Persian and Ottoman realms, see Cutler (2000, 2001). I particularly thank Barry Flood and Shreve Simpson for sharing their papers from a panel on gift giving held at the annual meeting of the Middle East Studies Association, San Francisco, 2004.

strongest ideological drive. Catherine initially intended the conquest of the Caucasus as a stepping-stone to control over Persia and for greater access to trade across the Black Sea to the west and Asia to the south and east. But her concern with questions of civilizing mission set the stage for high hopes among elites in the late eighteenth and early nineteenth centuries that Russia's arrival would also bring light to dark corners (Baberowski 2004; Pollock 2006).[3] As the historian Romanovskii would write some decades later,

> Given the sacrifices that Russia was to bring to the Caucasus, there was no doubt that these sacrifices would find their deserved recognition, most of all because the triumph of Russia in the war with the Caucasus peoples was the triumph of civilization over the most tenacious barbarism.... As every person knows the obligation to labor not only for himself, but to use his life to bring greater good to society, so exactly does every great people have the obligation not only to advance itself, but to offer as much as it can for the development of other, more backward peoples. Can we deny the favorable influence of the West on our development? Are we not obliged to pay this debt of civilization by extending our influence to the East? ([1860] 2004, 29)

How imperial givers reflected on what they perceived as their civilizational largesse and how they directed such gifts were not constant over time. Early on the gift of empire in the Caucasus was the act of surety of a certain kind on the part of Catherine the Great. Early on, the gift of empire in the Caucasus reflected Catherine the Great's confidence that she could send General Zubov to capture all of Persia in the late 1790s. It was a gift rendered less steadily but more urgently as sacrifice when the battle tolls began to mount in the early decades of the 1800s. In the 1990s, during the height of the first Chechen war (1994–1996), historian Azamat Dzhendubaev paused to comment,

> Not long ago I came across a brochure with a title like "Speeches Made at the Meetings of the Caucasus Society" [from the early 1800s]...where

---

3. For a discussion of the roots of the European civilizing ideologies that influenced Catherine II, see Conklin (1997) and Fischer-Tiné and Mann (2004). For a discussion of nineteenth-century statements by leading historians and geographers on the Russian civilizing mission in the Caucasus and central Asia see Baberowski (2004); Hauner (1990, 38–48); and Mostashari (2006, 7–9).

members of the Russian elite were making toasts at public events, to the Caucasus, about the Caucasus, and so forth. In the full flush of war, there are still words about Russia's humanitarian role, how Russia should become a source of light, culture, and enlightenment in the Caucasus. Then, when the resistance began to grow, the toasts take on military notes: "As the bones of our hundreds and thousands of soldiers turn white in the hills, we cannot leave the territory for which we have paid such a high price." A little further on one begins to see disagreement over how to settle occupied lands. Who should be invited: Balts? Germans? Slavs? Note how the debate is no longer about how to "civilize" the mountaineers [*gortsy*], but how to settle on their land. ("Perevernutyi mir" 1994, 19)

Dzhendubaev's observation draws attention to the ease of the transition from taking to giving and from giving to taking in imperial contexts.

Reflecting on the eighteenth and nineteenth centuries of Russian engagement in the Caucasus, modern historians Bondarevskii and Kolbaia have set the bar of comparative generosity higher than most.

For all our criticism of tsarism's colonial policy in the Caucasus, we must at the same time acknowledge that nowhere else—not in the five centuries of Portuguese and Spanish colonial rule nor in the three-hundred-year history of the British and French empires—will we find such a reciprocally beneficial interaction between the culture of an imperial nation and that of the peoples it colonized. (2002, 11)

This is high praise for a violent colonial encounter. What were these benefits? Bondarevskii and Kolbaia see the Caucasus as having especially profited from accelerated modernization under Russian and later Soviet rule, a social advance that presumably would not have occurred had the Caucasus been left to the Turks, the Iranians, or the British—to mention only three possible alternatives in the scramble after 1917. An even more radical consideration would be to ask what it would have meant for the various societies of the Caucasus to have been left to their own devices.

The multi-faceted influence of Russian culture served to strengthen significantly the positive aspects of the national culture of the peoples of the North Caucasus, while weakening the impact of the feudal structure and blunting the hostility that existed among tribes and clans. (10)

The contemporary Russian historian Tolmachev also puts giving at the forefront. In his rendering, it was not Russian self-interest but a commitment to the defense of mountain freedom that obliged Russia to intervene in the fates of Georgia and Azerbaijan in the early nineteenth century.

> It goes without saying that in the historical context of the early 1800s the peoples of the Caucasus were not strong enough to defend their national independence.... Turkey and Iran, which at the time were even more economically backward than Russia, were constantly threatening to divide the khanates, principalities, and "free societies" of the Caucasus between themselves. Although Georgia was annexed in 1810 and Azerbaijan in 1813, those two territories were separated from Russia proper by Chechnya, Daghestan, and the northwest Caucasus, which were populated by courageous and freedom-loving mountain peoples who regularly made daring forays against lines of fortification in the Caucasus and hindered interaction with Transcaucasia. For this reason, in the nineteenth century it became vitally important to Russia, on both military and political grounds, to annex those territories as well.... From 1817 onward, therefore, the tsarist government was forced to begin the systematic conquest of the North Caucasus, which ended only in 1864. (2002, 16)

What Russia gave, by this reading and in the many readings we will see in the discussion ahead, was an investment not only in infrastructure but also in the lives of the empire's sons. In their efforts to "[allow] the Caucasus' peoples to overcome their economic backwardness, isolation, and political fragmentation" (18), Tolmachev focuses on the years 1801–1864, the height of the nineteenth-century campaign, during which he reports over twenty-five thousand Russian forces killed (17; cf. Khodarkovsky 2002, 223; and Vedeneev 2000, 108).

The Russian viceroys in the Caucasus were well conscious of this battle toll, so perhaps it is no surprise that not only the taking but also the giving of life figured in their calculus of battle plans. Early on in his administration, General Aleksei Ermolov, who served as military commander in the Caucasus from 1816 to 1827, vowed,

> No worthy officer will die under my watch without revenge.... Rebel villages will be torn up and burned, gardens and vineyards will be cut to the

root, and many years may pass before the traitors evolve to a primitive state. Extreme poverty will be their punishment. (Umanets 1912, 46)[4]

Likewise, writing to Prince Madatov, he advocated the need to

> convince the troops that any [highland residents] who surrender their arms or who likewise make no attempt to defend themselves should be spared directly; at the sign of the smallest resistance, destroy utterly as necessary, and along the way, do not become burdened with an excessive or weighty number of captives. (47)

In Ermolov we find the idiom of closed-book sovereignty, in the form of all-out conquest, at its most extreme in this setting. Where the question of rogue elements penetrating otherwise passive villages was concerned, Ermolov asked,

> Do residents defend themselves against rogue advances, or did they admit the rogues into their ranks? In the latter case, the village is to be razed, women and children are to be slaughtered [*vyrezyvaiutsia*]. (47)

But Ermolov's hard line against anti-Russian forces was in no way incompatible with his language of generosity.

> I highly approve of the return of female captives, to say nothing of the liberation of captives in general, for it is helpful to persuade others that Russians generously make a gift of life itself [*chto russkie velikodushno daruiut i samuiu zhizn'*] to those who do not put up resistance. (48)

Velikodushno darit' literally means to give by the grandeur of the soul. Ermolov gives back that which he has effectively already taken, the fate of his prisoners, in order to underscore his generosity. To fully appreciate this powerful but deeply paradoxical give and take, we turn to some of the influential studies on the concept of the gift and the ways in which they have absorbed famous archetypes of Russian character.

---

4. Ermolov was formally appointed *Komandir Otdel'nogo Gruzinskogo korpusa i upravliaush-chii grazhdanskoi chast'iu v Gruzii, Astrakhanskoi i Kavkazskoi Guberniiakh* in 1816. The forces became known as the *Otdel'nyi kavkazskii korpus* in 1820.

Grandeurs of the Soul

The mix of extremes that have long anchored discourses and practices of the mysterious Russian soul have been well mapped. Russia's most famous writers and critics have found in the "soul" a means of grasping everything from generosity to cruelty, conveyed with equal elements of gravitas and irony. Dale Pesmen has argued that what is at stake in modern Russian discourses of the soul is not only the "physics" of contemporary cultural practices but a metaphysics, a parallel plane that takes not just the lives of those who make up "Russia" but the sum of those parts as its referent (2000, 338). The physics may come in stories, gestures, dispositions, and fragments, but the metaphysics, in the ways deployed by their proponents, aim for a totalizing picture of Russian culture itself.

Long-standing literatures in gift giving and the gift have also followed such physical and metaphysical tracks. No small number of historical, literary, religious, and political studies have taken the physical exchanges of gifts among dynasts as their subject, where actual object-gifts figure as elaborately detailed signs of fealty, obeisance, or diplomatic parrying. But when language shifts from "gifts" to "the gift," a metaphysical dimension is introduced, one which invites consideration of how the circulation of such gifts can symbolize, if not directly produce the smooth functioning of social relations.

Anthropology's best-known scholar of the gift was Marcel Mauss (1872–1950). Born in the Lorraine in France, he studied briefly with E. B. Tylor at Oxford and later, at the age of thirty, took up a chair in the History of the Religion of Noncivilized Peoples at the University of Paris. Throughout his career, Mauss worked closely with his maternal uncle, the legendary French sociologist Émile Durkheim. It was from Durkheim that he took his most formative ideas in systems of "total social services" that best accounted for social health, as he saw it, in primitive societies, as well as for social reform in his native France.

In his 1925 *Essai sur le don: Forme archaïque de l'échange,* a study that drew widely on ancient Roman law and early non-European ethnology, Mauss's innovation was to ask whether long overlooked family contracts, sovereign treaties, and other broadly routinized forms of exchange might not evidence shared languages of reciprocity as the root of social prosperities. Writing against commonly held conventions that ancient or primitive societies followed "natural economies" based on simple barter for the sake of pure utility, Mauss saw in records of exchange, by contrast, systems of "total prestations," obligatory forms of giving that acted as a kind of social glue, binding friend and foe alike in the guise of mutually perceived social debt. Socially organized systems of giving, however primitive, Mauss argued, were not about exchange at all but about the making of persons and groups (1990 [1925], 68).

Mauss drew his most detailed examples from the work of two pioneering anthropological fieldworkers—Bronislaw Malinowski (1884–1942) and Franz Boas (1858–1942). Malinowski was an ethnographer whose Polish birth left him officially unwelcome on British territory upon the outbreak of World War I during a research trip to Melanesia; he was given permission from the British to effectively disappear, spending two years among Trobriand Islanders off the coasts of New Guinea. Boas was a German physicist whose study of geography and resource use in the Canadian North soon led him to the study of native social organization among peoples of the Northwest.

In his keystone monograph, *Argonauts of the Western Pacific* ([1922] 1961), Malinowski documented the complex flows of kula (ceremonial trade) exchange among influential leaders of Trobriand society. Across the islands of the archipelago they inhabited, Malinowski reported, kula leaders circulated two seemingly valueless trade goods. In clockwise direction, red necklaces called *soulava* passed from island to island, trader to trader; in counterclockwise direction, white bracelets and armbands known as *mwali* flowed along opposite routes (81). What fascinated Malinowski was that, valuable or not, the objects of the kula were traded with the utmost gravity. The most valued of the mobile kula collections were those objects that bore the marks of the kula's most accomplished masters. Some objects themselves had names, but it was the characters of the traders themselves—the most skilled of the givers and the canniest of the receivers—that were expressed in the objects traded. It was by these friendly but by no means voluntary forms of giving and taking of kula objects among trading partners, Malinowski reasoned, that reputations were made, sovereignties forged, and conflicts sublimated.

Indeed, a central operating premise of the kula was seen in circulation rather than possession. "It seems almost incredible at first," Malinowski wrote, but it is the fact, nevertheless, that one never keeps any of the Kula valuables for any length of time....A man who is in the Kula never keeps any article for longer than, say, a year or two." ([1922] 1961, 94)

Or to put it more directly, the greatest good one could possess was a character built on generosity. Thus, "to possess is to give," as Malinowski characterized Trobriand life. "*Noblesse oblige* is in reality the social norm regulating their conduct" (97). That is to say, giving confers nobility.

Mauss's own concern with contemporary European politics and their changing social security schemes led him to the Trobriand and a handful of other "historical" examples to revive what he understood as a near-lost European tradition of "noble expenditure":

> We are returning, as indeed we must do, to the old theme of "noble expenditure." It is essential that, as in Anglo-Saxon countries and so many contemporary societies, savage and civilized, the rich should come once more, freely or by obligation, to consider themselves as the treasurers, as it were of their fellow-citizens. Of the ancient civilizations from which ours has arisen some had the jubilee, others the liturgy, the choragus, the trierarchy, the syssita or the obligatory expenses of the aedile or consular official. Then we need better care of the individual's life, health and education, his family and its future. We need more good faith, sympathy and generosity in the contracts of hire and service, rents and sale of the necessities of life. ([1925] 1990, 66)

This drive toward seemingly "irrational" expenditure directed not toward personal accumulation but to greater social goods, he observed, "is still characteristic of a few of the fossilized remnants of our aristocracy" ([1925] 2000, 76).

The power of giving fascinated Mauss. It was the leverage of the gift that captured a system of "total social services," a panacea for a disintegrating modern community. As Malinowski had reasoned, the kula "welds together a considerable number of tribes, and it embraces a vast complex of activities, interconnected, and playing into one another, so as to form one organic whole" ([1924] 1961, 83). Even if Trobrianders themselves may "have no knowledge of the *total outline* of any of their social structure," Malinowski reasoned, totality was still the key (original emphasis). "Rooted in myth, backed by traditional law, and surrounded by magical rites," the kula was anything but "surreptitious and precarious" (85). It was, by contrast, a paragon of the well-functioning society.

If Mauss's interest in Trobriand life enabled him to portray the gift as a central mechanism of organic solidarity, the work of Franz Boas on the potlatch directed Mauss to see the agonisms of exchange in a more direct light. Boas worked among Kwakiutl, a subgroup of the larger people known today as Kwakwaka'wakw (introduced in the last chapter). Possessed of considerable wealth, Kwakiutl were renowned for their advanced artworks as well as for their highly complex social organization, formed in part on competitive giving. Boas's 1897 essay on the potlatch tracked Kwakiutl practices of the competition, which involved not only ritual prestations but also frequently the destruction, in whole or part, of valuables such as blankets and coppers as a means of asserting social rank. The very ability to give, Boas observed, and to an even more spectacular degree the ability to destroy even that which remains make the reputation of social actors. In giving, one humbles the recipient, laying down a gauntlet that invites either an even more remarkable return gift or a concession to the greater giver's greatness.

As in the Trobriands, the act of giving made the man. "Possession of wealth is considered honorable, and it is the endeavor of each Indian to acquire a fortune. But it is not as much the possession of wealth as the ability to give festivals that makes wealth a desirable object....[A] man's name acquires greater weight...as he is able to distribute more and more property" (Boas [1987] 1966, 80). But the question of redistribution was hardly without guile. In one of the many iterations of the potlatch, giving could also be called "flattening."

> I referred several times to the distribution of blankets. The recipient in such a distribution is not at liberty to refuse the gift, although according to what I have said it is nothing but an interest bearing loan that must be refunded at some future time with 100 per cent interest. This festival is called p'a'sa, literally, flattening something (for instance, a basket). This means that by the amount of property given the name of the rival is flattened. (81)

As with Mauss and Malinowski, Boas found that in the physics of exchange, the metaphysics of reputation, sovereignty, and the grandeur of the soul coincided.

Where later historians and anthropologists have added to Boas's work by showing how colonial contexts deeply transformed potlatch practices over time, Malinowski, too, has seen a range of successors. Perhaps none was more attentive than Annette Weiner, who followed in his steps some six decades later with a landmark work considering the value of objects produced by women and exchanged in the same Trobriand settings (1976). Though Weiner made her initial intervention by reminding readers how Trobriand women produced objects of exchange no less valued in trade circles—fine mats understood as fine cloth—her signal contribution came in showing how certain goods never in fact circulated at all. Where Malinowski had written in passing, "In the whole of the Trobriands there are perhaps only one or two specially fine arm shells and shell-necklaces permanently owned as heirlooms, and these are set apart as a second class, and are once and for all out of the Kula" ([1922] 1961, 24), Weiner emphasized those classes of objects that Trobrianders declined to share. In her book *Inalienable Possessions,* Weiner showed that certain forms of giving—such as the saving of a life, the lifetime of care that a parent renders a child, and the role of a famous ancestor in the building of a family name—could never be repaid. These relations and histories were crystallized in objects that often remained in private trust. Like Malinowski and Mauss before her, Weiner recognized that gifts are part of the identity of the giver. But *what* exactly is given is another matter. Weiner's contemporary, anthropologist Maurice Godelier, remarked on the "double substitution" at work in the circulation of "proxy" or "satellite" objects that circulated in the organized absence of the inalienable:

> The precious objects which circulate in gift-exchanges can do so only because they are substitutes twice over: substitutes for sacred objects and substitutes for human beings.... Unlike sacred objects, which do not circulate, these do. Not only in potlatches, in (competitive) exchanges of wealth for wealth, but also on the occasion of marriages, deaths, initiations; on these occasions they function as substitutes for human beings, "compensation" for a life (marriage) or a death (that of an allied warrior or even an enemy killed in battle. (1999, 72)

With these contributions in mind, consider at least four central innovations generated by Mauss so many decades ago. First, Mauss's wide-ranging comparative examples rapidly dispense with the possibility of the disinterested gift. All gifts have the potential for tyranny. As generations of readers have discovered, to plumb Mauss's slim volume and go forward without guile into any ritual exchange of gifts becomes a difficult task. Second, Mauss showed how the interests inherent in giving rapidly extend beyond individual or contracting parties to articulations and contestations of broader collective values, what I have been coding here as metaphysical but which constitute, of course, the essence of social life. Accordingly, third, the obligations to give, take, and reciprocate are rarely purely voluntary, taking place in existing fields of social relations and existing flows of power. Fourth and finally, giving is, at some fundamental level, agonistic.

To spend too much time on the agonisms of Mauss, however, can lead us to gifts that exercise only calculated functions toward desired ends. The philosopher Georges Bataille took the same works by Boas and read them very differently. What if the motivation on the part of Kwakiutl, Bataille asks, might have come not from mercantile ambitions to win friends and influence enemies but from a natural exuberance on the part of all life-worlds, an exuberance that expends its excess and finds intimacy in sacrifice? "Minds accustomed to seeing the development of productive forces as the ideal end of activity refuse to recognize that energy, which constitutes wealth, must ultimately be spent lavishly (without return)," he wrote. "For living matter in general, energy is always in excess.... [T]he choice is limited to how the wealth is to be squandered" (1988, 22–23). In the potlatch, then, Bataille saw the giving of gifts not for their utilitarian ends but as expressions of the exuberance of Kwakiutl leaders offloading their excess. Expenditure came in the form of those objects that, in Bataille's words, had been designated as "the accursed share, destined for violent consumption" (59, 67–69). Does this mean that all of Russia's investments in the Caucasus were, in Bataille's terms, something of a shopping spree? For Bataille, luxury was burdensome, and demanded to be spent (see also 1985). And in the Caucasus, Russian leaders would find that the burden of giving could be expensive indeed.

From Empire to Soviet Socialist Project

While comparative work into the shared experience of imperial practice has been among the strongest lessons of recent colonial and postcolonial histories, there are a number of reasons to consider the Russian imperial experience in the Caucasus as distinctive. Most concretely, the empire's newly acquired southern landholdings were contiguous with the central spaces of metropolitan Russia, in contrast to the traditionally overseas landholdings of Britain, France, and Spain. For Russia this created manifold scenes of encounter that created bridges across difference, promoting regular and frequent exchanges. Kinship through conquest became a hallmark of Russian intervention in the South, evidenced not only in the literal sense of intermarriage, of which there was a considerable amount beginning in the second half of the nineteenth century, but also in the cannier Russian military aphorism *stat' bratom zavoevannomu,* advising that the firmest political hold comes when one becomes "a brother to the conquered."

At a symbolic level, as so many Russian writers would remind the more confident of their countrymen bent on civilizing the South, the ancient pedigree of Caucasus civilizations invited the question of what a relatively younger state power such as Russia could offer its neighbors. What is the burden of giving, exactly, when it is not clear who is the superior giver? Race scientist Johann Blumenbach muddied these conceptual waters for Russian officials in the late eighteenth century when he chose the term "Caucasian" to signal phenotypically "white" persons of the highest physical order. For evidence, Blumenbach appealed not to his own German ancestors but to a shipment of skulls he had received from Russia, including that of a Georgian woman. In 1795 he writes,

> *Caucasian variety.* I have taken the name of this variety from Mount Caucasus, both because its neighbourhood, and especially its southern slope, produces the most beautiful race of men, I mean the Georgian; and because all physiological reasons converge to this, that in that region, if anywhere, it seems we ought with the greatest probability to place the autochthones of mankind. ([1775] 1969, 269; see also Baum 2006, 73–94; Gould 1994)

Skull color, symmetry, and a curious assertion of the beauty in bones did not last long as durable racial criteria, but for the Caucasus region the die was cast. Between a shared ancient heritage in general and one rather evenly round-headed Georgian woman in particular, Caucasians inherited the mantle of superior ancestor. Who were Russians to be offering anything to them?

In light of Russia's extensive incursions into Caucasus worlds and the physical contiguity with the imperial center, it is helpful to pause and ask: was tsarist rule in the Caucasus even "colonial"? At least until 1917, the considerable preponderance of Russian political reference was to the the the Caucasus borderland or frontier (*kavkazskii krai*), seen as an extension of the empire rather than its appendage. Spain, Portugal, the United Kingdom, France, and the Netherlands could have colonies, desirable ones located across warm seas. By this benchmark the contiguous Caucasus, like Siberia, did not qualify. Others have maintained that because the Caucasus was for so long a drain on Petersburg's coffers, the Russian court saw no benefit of the sort equated with colonial exploitation. "The enrichment of the Russian peoples at the expense of others did not take place," Vladimir Matveev has written.

> The "alien [*inorodcheskie*] territories" within Russia were always viewed, at least by most parameters, as provinces of equal rights, with tax burdens that knew no ethnic differentiations. Moreover, in a number of cases, for example, for Kalmyks, Bashkirs, Nogais, Crimean Tatars, and highlanders across the northwest Caucasus, taxes were significantly less "in recognition of need." In comparison to the central Great Russian regions, some of these areas were even in a privileged position, as they did not know serfdom or conscription, and were therefore afforded greater economic freedoms. (1995, 193)[5]

By this logic, the Caucasus could not be a colony because Russia was so generous toward it, suggesting that an army is not an occupier if it invests heavily in the occupation and the transformation of the political landscape in toto. As Velichko insisted at the close of the nineteenth century, "The Caucasus cannot be foreign to us: too much energy has been spent on it, it is too organically connected with Russia's great mission and calling in the world" (1904, 1). Pause to consider Velichko's logic. That the Caucasus should not be foreign has nothing to do with the Caucasus itself: Russia demands recognition for its generosity, and that generosity refuses the possibility of estrangement.

---

5. For similar positions see also Avramenko, Matveev, and Matiushenko (1995, 28); "Perevernutyi mir" (1994, 21); Zakharov and Nastenko (2000, 13); and Zubov (1834, 75).

Unalloyed generosity on the part of any imperial ruler seems a difficult path to pursue when ample evidence makes clear that, at least in Russia, from the reign of Ivan IV onward, officials explicitly sought a geostrategic platform from which to articulate rivalries with the Ottomans, Persians, and other regional economic powers. Others have recognized that the Caucasus was at least in part a colony with respect to the usual social, economic, and political senses of that term, but they hesitate to use the label given the genuine levels of social integration that took place, making at least some Caucasus elites and those who intermarried fuller civic members in broader Russian society (Lazarev 1990, 8).[6]

With the onset of the Soviet period, the Caucasus' status as colony, past and present, shifted significantly. In the 1920s, Soviet planners in the State Office of Colonization (*Goskolonit*) unequivocally embraced their role as colonizers inasmuch as colonization—a word that once signaled occupation of and resettlement to alien lands—now focused on the agricultural, industrial, and cultural development of challenged territories of the new USSR. This was in effect colonization without colonies, fed by a familiar enlightenment agenda that Francine Hirsch has succinctly cast as "state-sponsored evolutionism" (2005, 7, 89–92). From the 1930s onward, Stalin made it commonplace to view the Caucasus Wars not as the work of brigands and swindlers but as the liberation of peoples oppressed by colonial rule (Svirin 1934, 1935). While the political fortunes of specific episodes in Caucasus history subsequently rose and fell over ensuing years, the Caucasus' status as colony under tsarism remained more or less commonplace.

Whether we, as contemporary scholars, see the USSR as having been an imperial power is another matter, perhaps even a surprising one since even at the height of the cold war the Soviet Union was known as the communist regime or the bulkhead of socialism but rarely as the Soviet empire. After its end, however, the Soviet Union has increasingly come to be seen as just that. A great deal of the best work in Soviet politics and history, indeed, has included the USSR under an increasingly elastic imperial rubric given the ways in which the deeply internationalist Soviet Union managed to organize multiple layers of belonging beyond purely ethnic

---

6. Barrett (1995, 1999) is among the best in charting the degrees by which North Caucasus Cossack communities inserted themselves into, and were transformed by, the frontier encounters.

lines.[7] Clearly many scholars in the former Soviet Union are comfortable with such an imperial rubric. As the Caucasus historian Rustem Shukurov has observed,

> Although modern ideology distances Russia from its imperial past, Russia nonetheless remains an empire: the population of the Russian Federation, in essence, is divided into Russians and everyone else (Tatars, Bashkirs, peoples of the North Caucasus, and so forth). Russian entitlement begins with the name of the state and is buttressed by traditional state symbols.... "Imperial" status here lies not in firm evidence but in the practice of "teaching" [*nauchat'*] its subjugated peoples. ("'Kavkazskii nerv'" 2000, 19)

What such modern-day enlightenment practices signal is not simply a garden-variety perception of superiority over others but an undertaking of the politically very savvy role of giver in uneasy circumstances. The tyranny of the gift again.

Looking back at the USSR, however, what we gain in comparisons with imperial rule in other parts of the world we can also lose in not fully grasping the stunning distinctiveness of the Soviet internationalist project, one that generated a surprising degree of federalism and social mixing over seven remarkably tumultuous decades. Where the Caucasus is specifically concerned, that attention to the high degree of mixing and mutual appropriation means taking the language of "center and periphery" that has characterized so many studies of the experience of Soviet and former Soviet "nationalities" beyond the binary frames of colonizer and colonized. It means taking the languages, cultural codings, and historical experiences of non-Russian peoples into account in any story of exchange (Garsoian 1996; Todorova 1997; Von Hagen 2004). But it also means making those exchanges the forefront of analysis, looking at the spaces of encounter—the bridges, as it were—as the primary subject of analysis rather than at the spaces of enclosure (states, nations, empires) that traditionally define them. In keeping with more recent work in cultural politics, this suggests the need to move "beyond identity" as a static, naturalized category and

---

7. Among the many programmatic English-language works in this emergent canon are Beissinger (2005, 2006); Hirsch (2005); Martin (2001); Suny (1993, 1995); and Suny and Martin (2001).

toward "identifications," processes that are much more the products of the political forces around them (Brubaker and Cooper 2000). This suggests forgoing a view of Caucasus worlds as cabinets of curiosities, as traditional ethnographies of the region have long done, and seeing them instead as "constantly in the making, historically rooted, open-ended systems which are continually transforming themselves, borrowing from their neighbors, and being inextricably caught up in historical processes much larger than themselves" (Kohl and Tsetskhladze 1995, 151).

The case of Russian relations with the Caucasus is remarkable for both the length and consistency of popular Russian acknowledgment of and interest in the gifts and sacrifices made toward its own stewardship. This perception of gift and sacrifice has crossed many genres over at least two hundred years, and has been most significantly illustrated in an abiding attention to both real-life and, perhaps more tellingly, imagined kidnappings of Russian men and women in the southern territories many years after captivity narratives as literary genre seem to have lost their hold in all other parts of the world. Yet it has to be emphasized that this particular art form is hardly confined to Russia and its political incarnations in the last two centuries. Contemporary statecraft all around us offers examples of the same kinds of passive aggression writ very large, with taking cast as giving and giving as the buttressing of taking. Consider the well-worn refrains, "We are not occupiers," "We are there to help," "We were invited to protect," and more tellingly, "We are there to help residents establish their own government." Middle Eastern scholar Fouad Ajami makes this point most ambiguously in his flattering study of twenty-first-century American involvement in Iraq, *The Foreigner's Gift* (2006), while critic Kennan Ferguson takes positions such as Ajami's in Iraq more acidly. Ferguson observes, "Iraqi freedom, argued Donald Rumsfeld (then the U.S. secretary of defense)... 'is a gift, selflessly purchased by the very best and brightest among us'" (2007, 46; see also Lakoff 2006). The gift of freedom and other such sacrifices made on behalf of others are all grounds for intended good. Yet what history makes abundantly clear is that they are also durable pretexts for sovereign ambitions in foreign lands. What local populations on the receiving end of such gifts make of these ambitions is, to put it mildly, quite another matter.

At stake in this kind of study is far more than the elucidation of cultural histories in a part of the world that observers have for so long "unconsciously set in a squint" (Garsoian 1996, 9) by dint of erratic source materials and inevitably partisan nationalist renditions of complex interactions. The goal is to think more broadly about violence as a medium of knowledge as much as a medium of interaction, a rubric that can be as rhetorically plastic as it can be fundamentally brutal and that touches on every part of the world, rather than just on one particularly situated mountain range wedged in between the Black and Caspian seas.

4

RITES OF ENCOUNTER

Brides, Brigands, and Fire Bringers

When I first began work on the Caucasus, an experienced colleague in Moscow offered some advice. "The problem with the Caucasus," she said, "is that social science fears that kind of place—as if it is all just too much. Too many peoples, too many languages, too much to take in. So everyone takes cover under their own roof, working in one village, with one dialect, maybe one century. When you study the Caucasus, you have to take it all as one." I nodded approvingly, but in truth, I blanched at the prospect of what I knew she meant—the sheer human record of language, history, and religion are enough to overwhelm the sturdy.

To survey almost any set of histories of the Caucasus popularly circulated in the region today, one sees boundaries that not only are drawn more firmly than ever before but are often actively exclusionary (Gadjiev, Kohl, and Magomedov 2007). Contemporary histories of the Caucasus often strive to demonstrate preeminence to such a degree that descent-driven doctrines of firstness (as in "We were here first and therefore...") are soon superseded almost hyperbolically by claims to what begins to approximate "pre-firstness," and even "proto-firstness." Nationalist ideologies in the Caucasus, as in so many parts of the world, with their tireless ambitions to lay claim to sovereign rule through historical record, have propelled such discourses of descent all the more. What gets sacrificed along the way is an attention, by contrast, to alliance, the means by which such pluralist societies bound themselves through rituals of recognition.

It was not long before I, too, took refuge in a small, monoglot mountain village, beginning in 1999, to write a cultural history of Sovietization from the perspective of a single community and its residents (Grant 2004). Even from this reclusive redoubt, however, there were constant reminders of what my Moscow colleague had in mind, how deeply invested all communities of the Caucasus have been in one another's histories. As I tracked accounts of the village's famous rebel past, the idea of a common Caucasus civilization came through most strikingly not in the benevolent language of sharing but in idioms of theft.

This small town of about four hundred, perched on a tall hillside about an hour away from the area's regional center, had no gas or running water and had since the close of the USSR lost its electrical connections for all but three hours after midnight each night. Deprived of the comforts to which they had become accustomed under Soviet rule, people shared in the somewhat hard-bitten humor that communism was the most rapid route from feudalism to feudalism. What struck me more as the visitor, however, was how historical depth seemed to infuse daily life. Crumbling but clearly once sophisticated clay water channels of no precise vintage ran through the hillsides, evidence of more solid infrastructures from an unspecified time. Plentiful flagstones were claimed to be from pre-Islamic (that is, pre-eighth-century) graves, and any number of rock formations were reputed to be—some more convincingly than others—startling works of sculpture from long ago.

As farmers would routinely dig up earthenware pots of significant vintage, once used for storing grains or wine in another age, neighbors complained to me, "Georgian archaeologists used to come here regularly in the 1970s and buy these from us. Then one year one of us went to visit a museum in Tbilisi and the same pots had been labeled 'Georgian.' Georgian pots! From our village!" No neighborly community was more suspect than that of the Armenians—enemy figures of baroque proportions, long resented for their administrative prowess during the Russian imperial and Soviet periods and more recently for their hold over disputed lands in Nagorno-Karabagh, where a catastrophic, decade-long war offered no promise of end. When I had the spectacularly poor judgment one day to remark that the unleavened, brick-oven *tendir* bread seemed to be more or less of the same provenance as Armenian *lavash,* news of my treason spread fast. "Lavash is our tendir—they stole it from us!" was the universal refrain that lasted for days until my complete and irrevocable surrender could be established, readmitting me to unfettered conversation. I thought of Lévi-Strauss's famous line from *Totemism,* "If we may be allowed the expression, it is not the resemblances, but the differences, which resemble each other" (1963, 77). That is to say, how people assert their differences can indeed follow remarkable patterns, especially among peoples whose geographies and histories have left long legacies of borrowings, stealings, and sharings.[1] I learned to hold back on the subject of stuffed grape leaves and the Greeks, on Azeri literature and the Persians, and so forth. Regardless of how scholarship might choose to frame such exchanges, passages, and borrowings, it was plain to most people I met that everyone had been stealing from everyone (or at least from *them*) for quite some time.

In this context, the ultimate trick about theft is not what it denies but what it generates—rites of encounter, a means of suturing one history to another, however negatively. In a purely performative sense, the theft of significant objects and particularly of significant persons enchances the reputation of the taker at the expense of the loser. But in a subtler sense, constant reminders of theft centered on who stole what from whom implicate all parties in a single narrative. Marshall Sahlins seemed to have this in mind when he offered the concept of "negative reciprocity." Beyond the more intuitive senses of "balanced reciprocity" (where A gives to B, and B gives to A), or "generalized reciprocity" (A gives to B, B gives to C, and so forth in the belief that all good turns are returned through a collective good), Sahlins pointed out that acts such as stealing could generate their own reciprocal dimensions. He calls negative reciprocity "the attempt to get something for nothing with impunity, the several forms of appropriation, transactions opened and conducted toward net utilitarian advantage" ([1978] 1996, 32). Regardless of whether one finds express utility in the takings, what this draws our attention to is that one can find reciprocity in

---

1. Harrison (2003) is one of the best treatments of this argument. See Kobychev and Robakidze (1969, 21) for further comment on shared Caucasus histories.

even these unlikely scenes. The overall idea that we might take from this is that unlawful gains can be just as much about building relationships as about seemingly ending them.[2]

In his studies of the twentieth-century rural Greek community of Glendi, Michael Herzfeld took this idea a step further when he found striking patterns of reciprocal animal raiding that surprisingly paralleled subsequent alliance formations.

> Many Glendiot men claim that the origins of the hospitality for which their village is famous (as in Crete in general) lie in animal-theft. Men would go in search of their missing livestock, or perform this errand on behalf of co-villagers and kin, and would need places to stay in the villages they visited. Usually, they would be entertained by their own spiritual kin, themselves perhaps the end product of some earlier raiding cycle, and would be expected to reciprocate hospitality in due course. The connection with raiding is laden with meaning. When Glendiots raid other highland villages, they do so on the clear understanding that this is likely to prove a reciprocal business and to entail considerable danger before a suitably daunting impasse causes the protagonists to accept mediation and eventually to become spiritual kin and allies. (1987, 79)

While extant evidence from the Caucasus may not volunteer such neatly tied logics, Herzfeld's insights are key here in reminding us how theft can be socially generative. This chapter returns to the contrast suggested at the outset between ideal-type, closed-book sovereignties and the relatively more porous practices found across the Caucasus. In this context, it examines these ethnographic, historical, and oral-epic sources on the exchange of persons across the Caucasus in order to consider alternate readings of captivity, violence, and sovereignties in this repeatedly conquered region. What emerges is a deep archive on the subject of theft and captivity that suggests ends that are as performative as they are instrumental: concepts of "detachable persons" in the forms of men and women as they move across lines of kin, clan, and region as boundary-negotiators, and sovereignties

---

2. In more contemporary contexts, Anna Tsing (2005) has glossed these border-crossing agonisms as "friction"—the global sites of interaction that mutually constitute all involved. With a more direct focus on violence, Ashis Nandy takes up the same communicative theme in his essay "The Discreet Charms of Indian Terrorism" (1990).

that are forged through micropractices such as the exchange of persons as much as by broader military interventions.

Looking to these alternate historical records—particularly through the keystone idioms of theft and gift, captivity and freedom—we can explore patterns that say as much about the forces exerting power in and around the Caucasus as they do about the region proper. Understanding these historical practices of the traffic in persons across the Caucasus provides insight into the kinds of equally deeply rooted imperial patterns of giving, and especially taking, in an area that has known continual foreign military invasion since the onset of written record. This invites us to broaden the scope of our investigations, to look not only within specific societies but also across these famous lines of contestation.

In this way, rather than considering the melodramas of captivity solely from the point of view of Russian soldiers and aristocrats, as so many Russians have done since Pushkin sparked popular imagination with "Prisoner of the Caucasus" in 1822, or relying on the languages of nationalist hagiography found in the non-Russian republics since the fall of the Soviet Union, let us consider the more open forms of sovereign rule spurred by very different kinds of recorded exchanges across the Caucasus.

The Trade in Famous Ancestors

In a considerable work of reconstructive scholarship, Colarusso (2002) tracks the epic legends of the Narts, a mythical people claimed as shared ancestors across the North Caucasus but especially among Circassians, as well as Abkhaz, Ossetians, Ingush, and others. Their shared status alone challenges the more conventional doctrine that the compartmentalized Caucasian kingdoms rarely interacted. But the more striking element is the "sporting theft" that emerges across the epic landscape. "Since social rank was inherited and prestige was measured by valor" across the North Caucasus, Colarusso writes, the possession of goods was less important than the means of their circulation. "In fact, a sort of sporting theft was common, so that goods tended to circulate outside the community" (2).[3]

---

3. Many sources from across the Mediterranean and the Middle East make clear that sporting theft was not limited to the Caucasus, even if it did not become as characteristic of those regions.

Colarusso's sources for the Nart epics are necessarily the extant print versions of these otherwise predominantly oral genres, most published in Russian and North Caucasus language editions in the age of Russian imperial and later communist censorship. Their relatively recent provenance helps explain some thematic confluences after centuries of distillation, not least after Prometheus became coded as a Greek classic of more prominent retellings, making these works all the more worth appropriating (or, depending on your perspective, stealing back). What emerges is a galaxy of narrative givings and takings. In one myth, the Circassian Sosruquo travels to a mountain fortress to steal millet from an ogre and distribute it to his people (2002, 202). In another, it is the nectar of the gods (216), and in still another, Sosruquo steals fire from a Cyclops in a cave in a ravine (222). In many stories, mountaintops are the homes of villains and horrors for captives (169–170, 200).

Since so many ancient tales of captives on mountaintops have long circulated across the Caucasus (Abrahamian 2007), the enduring and relatively greater fame of the Greek Prometheus outside the region has baffled many Caucasus residents. "Prometheus—they stole him from us!" is the classic refrain I have heard throughout Azerbaijan—as the topic has proven an easy one to solicit opinion on almost anywhere I have found myself. But this might be some news to Armenians, Georgians, or Adyghe, who are no less robust in their defense of what they understand as their own purloined intellectual properties. Rather than trying to resolve just who thought up this particular captivity first, let us pause to consider what the abundance of captivity origin stories might tell us.

For French scholar Georges Charachidze, the debated provenance of the Prometheus myth recalls the once "ancient canvas stretched across all of eastern Eurasia" (1986, 341; cf. Duchemin 2000). Charachidze's most prominent spur is the cycle of retellings of the story of Amirani, a hero claimed widely under different guises across the Caucasus, from Armenia to Georgia to Ossetia and beyond.

As with Prometheus, Charachidze distills two key phases in Amirani's mythography. In his simplest renditions, Amirani, like Hesiod's Prometheus,

---

Lale Yalçın-Heckmann writes (personal communication) that the Turkish *talan,* meaning pillage, carries this connotation of sporting theft as well. For ethnographic examples of the extent of this practice, see Gilsenan (1996) and Herzfeld (1987). Karpov (1996) most extensively ties these questions of bravado to cultures of masculinity in the Caucasus.

enters punished. Rather than the sin, it is the performance of divine sovereignty through the exclusion of the limit-figure—the actor who is subject to estrangement or exclusion at or beyond the limits of society—that takes center stage. God punishes Amirani in three phases. First, he chains him to a post fixed deeply in the ground; second, he buries him under an enormous domelike structure on a mountaintop, opening the dome only once each year for air; finally, Amirani, still chained, is entombed in the belly of a monster (1986, 28–38). The trick, however, is that Amirani is not constant through these privations. Captivity makes him stronger: his strength grows rather than diminishes with each struggle (80). The story of Amirani, therefore, is about a struggle over human autonomy—about men capable of becoming as strong as or stronger than their overlords and about keeping potential usurpers to power in check.

In the second set of legends, according to Charachidze, tellers introduced Amirani's sins as a series of causal factors. Amirani suffers because of women and their idle talk. Nor is he a friend of the blacksmiths who chain him to his post, ironworkers whom Charachidze casts as representatives of an increasingly commercial social order, modern industry, and not least, the makers of cult religious objects (122). Like Prometheus before, after, or alongside him, Amirani's subversion of codes of rule lands him at the top of Mount Elbrus (the actually existing, tallest peak in the region, rather than the fictional Mount Caucasus of Hesiod's and Aeschylus's imagination).

Who came first, Prometheus or Amirani? Alongside Charachidze, Tuite has been among the most scrupulous in mapping the traffic in early Caucasus mythologies. In the kinship between Prometheus and Amirani, he finds "an imaginary world-order of abundance and unconstraint, in which one could live off the riches of nature without having to engage in labor or exchange" (1998a, 306). It is a world "marked by the absence of principal constraints imposed by civilization, settled life, marriage through alliance and exchange, the toil and risk of agriculture" (307). As with any legend of such proportions, provenance is a question little answered by scant written records that shift between myth and history.[4]

---

4. Tuite has elsewhere advanced the Caucasus' claims to putatively foundational Greek myths, in the case of a "proto-Achilles" (1998a, 331). Wilhelm (1998) offers an extended consideration of Charachidze's historical geographies, being somewhat more confident on the subject of the "significant colonization" of the Caucasus by the Greeks in the seventh century BCE.

The question is important for several reasons. In the cases of Prometheus and Amirani, what the evidence does show is the ready potential for mythographic borrowings and sporting thefts in all directions. Charachidze points out that well before Hesiod, in the ninth century BCE, a shared Mycenaean civilization crossed eastern Eurasia (1986, 326). Other records demonstrate how a century later, by which time Hesiod is understood to have penned the first Prometheus tale, Greeks had set out across the Black Sea, north and east to the shores of Colchis, driven by hunger in search of fish to supply growing armies (Ascherson 1995, 50). Was neighboring eastern Anatolia the "Ur-Heimat" of Indo-European civilization, as Tuite has asked (1998a, 289)? Charachidze equivocates.

> Indo-European groups similar to the Greeks of the future, perhaps their precursors, even their penultimate ones, found themselves in enduring contact between the Balkans and central Asia with peoples of other origin whose descendants now occupy the southern Caucasus and particularly the lands of ancient Colchis. Such a cohabitation implies a certain cultural community by dint of proximity, exchange, and war, manifesting itself in lifestyles, shared conceptual systems, and common lived experiences. This favors a practice of collaboration and of confrontation either deliberate or involuntary between the mythologies in motion. (1986, 326)

In this way, the riddle of ancient origins slowly untangles in light of gradual and increasing evidence of the mobilities and border crossings for which Caucasians later became known. The Caucasus today is rightly understood as a place of guarded borders, but in eras past this was by no means always the case. Remarking on early Christian Georgia, for example, Rayfield writes,

> From the fourth century Georgians were sent to monastic colonies in Jerusalem, Antioch, and Constantinople. From there, under Arab pressure, they spread to Saint Katherine's monastery on Mount Sinai, and by the tenth

---

He is also right to note that whatever the borrowings, "mythic entities are seldom if ever borrowed completely from one culture to another [with] name, personality, attributes, and exploits all in one package" (151). Abrahamian (2007) takes the question of a "wide proto-Caucasian context" most ambitiously by considering the chthonic origins of Prometheus as son of Iapetos, his relationship to rock formations, and the possibility of myths set in sky and sea having more in common than normally realized via the mediating status of the chthonic figure chained to a rock at great heights. Rather than comparing Prometheus to Amirani, Abrahamian looks to earlier Creto-Mycenaean sources on the Minotaur and the labyrinth as a holding zone.

century to Mount Athos. This brought them into contact with most of the nations of the near east and eastern Mediterranean: the resulting waves of translation thus far outweigh in quantity, if not in quality, the original litera-ture that was yet to come. Georgian was not merely a recipient, however, but very often an intermediary, as texts might be translated, through Georgian, from Arabic or Assyrian into Greek or Armenian, in endless permutations, frequently leaving only the Georgian version to survive barbarian or Islamic attack.... [Thus] some Georgian writers, such as the [fifth-century] prince Peter the Iberian... became purely Greek writers. (1994, 20)[5]

Beyond the worlds of Prometheus and Amirani, tales of captives every-where suggested a discourse of heroes forged in liminal zones.

Take, for example, the tale of Diandeko-Sevai. Kidnapped at birth by the enormous falcon Shamgur, Diandeko-Sevai, ancestor to a famous line of Circassian princes, was raised by this "feathery thief" on a mountain-top so high that it looked down with contempt on thunder and lightning (Khan-Girei 1893, 3). The falcon, Shamgur, turned to abduction not for holding the young prince permanently but to fold the future god into his own kin line. A paradoxical lesson thus emerges: captivity itself was not the narrative end point but the means to it in the form of realigning estab-lished orders. As happens so often in Caucasus legend, seemingly negative plotlines take distinctly positive directions.

Across the spectrum of these givings and takings, process rather than product makes the leader. When another Nart warrior wins his long-sought damsel,

> He is carrying her off not to be his bride but to prove his might. This is his way of seeking [in turn] a worthy opponent from among the Narts, a hero capable of defeating him. (23)[6]

In examples such as these we find the logics of Bataille most prominent: beyond pure utility, persons may be stolen foremost to perform sovereignty in an act of power as spectacle.

---

5. Dragadze, echoing Garsoian (1996) who speaks more broadly of the Caucasus as a whole, concedes that Georgians have had a long tradition of claiming kinship with the Greeks in order to suggest their superiority to other Soviet-era nationalities (1988, 9). For more examples of contested mythologies, see Arans and Shea (1994); Maksimova (1965); and Schulze (1999).

6. In her work on contemporary Kurdistan, Yalçın-Heckmann points out that when bride abduction was undertaken so publicly with the intent of dishonoring the bride's family or clan, the bride's honor could still be considered intact upon her release (1991).

If the Prometheus of Hesiod was a morality tale about autocracy, yielding to the Prometheus of Aeschylus as a morality tale about democracy,
the comparable Nart sagas shift the register to the moralities, in turn, of
individual valor, hearth, and clan.[7] Some might call this theft or brigandage; others called it a functional social order in the absence of durable state
structures. This does not give us cause to romanticize theft, genuine or
sporting. But it does give us ground to recall the basic messages of Lévi-
Strauss and Malinowski, that myth speaks to subjects unresolved, charters
for action not yet laid properly into habit and needing corrective guides.

We also find that captivity as such is a generative crucible that has to do
with overcoming tensions among neighbors, tensions that are never seen as
extinguished or even extinguishable. They are, instead, continually negotiated, never silenced. Caucasus variants of these myths dwell on questions of
sovereignty—collective and individual—because as historical record demonstrates, the political threshold for better and for worse has long remained
open to challenge. These localized forms of sovereign rule, to recall Humphrey's (2004) phrasing, could not in any sense be described as ideal types;
instead they are partial, open-ended, and subject to regular transformation.

Historically, the social question has been whether Caucasian societies
developed such elaborate codes of giving and taking because of a natural bellicosity. But centuries of invasion by colonizers and clansmen alike
should also invite us to ask how any society would not raise military systems to high art under such circumstances, making these practices central
to mythographies and other forms of historical knowledge. Rather than
contrasting European notions of sovereignty to those of the Caucasus, we
need to understand them instead as mutually constitutive over time.

The Traffic in Women

Thus far we have considered identity shifts of key mythic figures, literally,
across borders of time and space. But what of the known living persons
whose passages across identity divides created the kinds of functioning

---

7. The comparable Armenian cycles of Artawazd, retold as a redemptive project for the Armenian people at the hands of oppressors, is one significant exception where Nart sagas are closer
to the emancipatory visions of Aeschylus (Colarusso 2002, 102).

social wholes and more specifically the social levelings that were understood to keep these small societies of "mountain aristocrats" in check? Perhaps no persons have garnered as much attention as the women given and taken in marriage in virtually all societies of the Caucasus. Once the salacious focus of travel writers who saw erotic melodrama in young women's plights, the bride continues today at the center of debates over human rights, social reproduction, and rule by custom rather than by law.

The image of the limit-figure extends further when we explore the ways by which the marriageable woman—as central to any group's reproductive potential as any member can be—can be seen as "detachable" in the sense put forth by Marilyn Strathern in *The Gender of the Gift* (1988), a work on highlanders from a very different part of the world. To be detached from one known social sphere for transfer across perceived social boundaries both enforces borders and necessarily speaks to concerns over their very logics and durabilities. In some ways they are limit-figures in their equivocal positioning at the limits of social groups.[8]

In his foundational study, *Elementary Structures of Kinship* [1949] 1969, Lévi-Strauss contended that the exchange of women in early societies marked the center, if not the very genesis, of the culture concept. Following the earlier arguments of Freud in *Totem and Taboo* (1950) that the incest prohibition marked one of the earliest triumphs of culture over nature and thus the onset of civilization, Lévi-Strauss reasoned that the self-control shown by sons toward the women of their immediate family (in the form of out-marriage, or exogamy) rested on a generalized reciprocity whereby socially proximate but sufficiently distant kin groups would exchange their own women in return. As with Freud's work on the prohibition of incest, exogamy, in Lévi-Strauss's terms, made society.

> Like exogamy, the prohibition of incest is a rule of reciprocity, for I will give up my daughter or my sister only on condition that my neighbor does the same. The violent reaction of the community towards incest is the reaction of a community outraged. Unlike exogamy, exchange may be neither

---

8. My thinking on detachability has also been influenced by Strathern's other work on the exchange of women (1984), together with Shami's consideration of the biographies of two women of the Caucasus separated by a hundred years, whose imputed expendability as kin members made them practiced border crossers (2000).

explicit nor immediate; but the fact that I can obtain a wife is, in the final analysis, the consequence of the fact that a brother or father has given her up. But the rule does not say in whose favour the person shall be given up. On the contrary, the beneficiary, or in any case the beneficiary class, is de-limited in the case of exogamy. The only difference then is that in exogamy the belief is expressed that the classes must be defined so that a relationship may be established between them, while in the prohibition of incest the re-lationship alone is sufficient to define continually in social life a complex multiplicity, ceaselessly renewed by terms which are directly or indirectly solidary. ([1949] 1969, 62)[9]

By this logic, women were the primal gifts in human civilization, extended from one family to another by carefully drawn lines of relatedness and to functionalist ends of social advancement. "Thus," wrote Lévi-Strauss, "a continuous transition exists from war to exchange, and from exchange to intermarriage, and the exchange of brides is merely the conclusion to an uninterrupted process of reciprocal gifts, which effects the transition from hostility to alliance, from anxiety to confidence, and from fear to friendship" (68).

Several critics have shown up the limitations of such a neatly drawn origin story, yet another where the idiom of giving covers a vast range of events that more predominantly include takings and frequently assault. In a widely cited synthetic essay, Rubin agrees with Lévi-Strauss that

> [t]he "exchange of women" is a seductive and powerful concept. It is attrac-
> tive in that it places the oppression of women within social systems, rather
> than in biology. Moreover, it suggests that we look for the ultimate focus
> of women's oppression within the traffic in women, rather than within the
> traffic in merchandise. (1975, 175)

---

9. Women in early societies, therefore, were for Lévi-Strauss the earliest gifts: "The first stage of our analysis has been intended to bring to light this basic characteristic of the gift, represented by women in primitive society, and to explain the reasons for this. It should not be surprising then to find women included among reciprocal prestations; this they are in the highest degree, but at the same time as other goods, material and spiritual" (1969, 65). The point is that in Strathern's analysis, where persons are constituted not by bodies but by relationships (1988, 268), social rela-tions make the marriage, not the other way around. "In short, the system of prestations *results* in marriage" (Lévi-Strauss 1969, 67, original emphasis).

But Rubin's appreciation of Lévi-Strauss's intervention largely ends there, not least given Lévi-Strauss's definition of the exchange of women as the root of all culture via their "world-historical defeat."

> Exchange of women is a shorthand for expressing that the social relations of a kinship system specify that men have certain rights in their female kin, and that women do not have the same rights either to exchange themselves or to their male kin. (1975, 177)

Thus, Rubin observes, while taking women's status out of the clutches of biological determinism is a necessary first step, Lévi-Strauss does not go far enough. The goal is to see women's subjectivities and women's subjection in a series of comparative historical and political frames in order to track the very man-made nature of their social positions.[10]

Not all who have joined in Rubin's comparativist drive have come to the same conclusions. The problem remains that for all the gradations of voluntarism, custom, and coercion, some anthropologists have found that for at least some societies, the terms of debate that focus on subjects and objects in the respective forms of persons and property may well miss the point. Marilyn Strathern takes up the case of contemporary Daulo women living in the Mount Hagen region of highland New Guinea. The Daulo community where Strathern worked saw women as key producers of income in the coffee-driven cash economy where proceeds from women's labor, as well as the young marriageable women themselves, seemed to circulate at the sole behest of men. Yet Strathern points out that few women found this situation strange or directly degrading. At stake for Strathern is a realization of culturally specific ideals of "persons," gender, and property. She remarks,

> It is the western dichotomy between subject and object which informs the anthropological desire to make women the proper subjects for analysis, to treat them in our accounts as actors in their own right. We are terrified of rendering them as mere "objects of analysis" because this diminishes our own humanity. (1984, 162)

---

10. Cowie (1990) and Irigaray (1985) pursue similar lines of argument with regard to Lévi-Strauss.

In this vein, Strathern argues that Lévi-Strauss never meant to imply that because women were being exchanged they were less than persons. Instead, he invited us to think of how subjectivity is articulated in societies where persons—constituted by social relations in a myriad of ways—are not always coterminous with bodies. Thus "it is not the male or female persons who are exchanged.... What is exchanged is the sign they represent" (164).

> We should not be particularly disturbed if Daulo women are sometimes compared with shells or trade stores. To imagine they are being treated as objects is based on our own antithesis between persons and things, a false premise in the circumstances. (166)

In the case of the Daulo, Strathern argues that gender comes of social relations rather than fixed objects or bodies, such that all items exchanged can have male and female characteristics, as can bodies.[11] Thus, "gender is evinced through what Melanesians perceive as the capabilities of people's bodies and minds, what they contain within themselves and their effects on others" (1988, 182). What sets women apart in this context is their detachability, their capacity to circulate more widely than men, who are seen as more sedentary. In this way, Strathern invites her readers to look at capacities as well as constraints.

> Women as well as men have a male identity. They are nurtured clan members. Their efforts and achievements, however, are to different ends. Whereas men augment this maleness through their transactions, women make the increment detachable. In this metonymic sense men's "on the skin" attributes are female. Whereas some women are pre-eminently detachable, men become so only in specific contexts.... [Women's] very detachability points as a source of nurture and productivity separate from men's. (1984, 170)

---

11. This focus on the relative constitution of personhood is part of Strathern's larger project of looking not at "individuals" but at "dividuals," persons whose understandings of self are constituted across lines of social relations (1988, 13). Thus she writes, "To concentrate on the objectifications of Melanesian cultures appears to eliminate subjectivity. The acting agent is seemingly not required in my explanation of how people manage their affairs—and I write as though cultures proceed independently with their reifications, persons appearing only as the reflex of relationships. In fact, the individual subject has been present in my account all along; she/he just does not take the shape we are used to seeing" (1988, 268).

It is this idea of capable detachments that invites parallels between detachable heroes such as Prometheus and Amirani—whatever their delivered ends—and detachable persons in the form of those women who are thought most eligible to relocate upon marriage.

The goal in linking one intensely populated set of highland communities in one part of the world to another is not to diminish any of the efforts by contemporary activists to reduce human trafficking and to advance the status of women across the Caucasus. But it urges us to recognize that, whatever the vectors of power, justice, and potential humanity that adhere to any given scenario, certain widely entrenched codes of the movement of male and female bodies across social lines are to some degree read into each event. What Prometheus and brides have in common are qualities of detachability whereby border crossers become border makers.

Orthodox forms of marriage in the Caucasus vary as widely as do the languages, religions, and political systems of those who live there (Luzbetak 1951). But it becomes difficult to tell the orthodox from the renegade when such seemingly unorthodox a practice as the kidnapping of a young woman against her will for the purposes of marriage finds such long-standing currency in the histories and discourses of Caucasus life. However unevenly we might be able to map a tradition that rebuffs close scrutiny by design, marriage by capture today appears to have lost none of its force as a keystone in debates over social justice, gender equity, and the sovereignty of persons.

The capture of women in marriage dates back as far as legend and written record allow, not least in the oldest Greek, Roman, Aramaic, Arabic, Turkic, Mongol, and Persian-speaking societies of those people who conquered the Caucasus prior to the Russians. Börte, the wife of Genghis Khan, was twice kidnapped, and one of the best-known early sixteenth-century Russian explorers in the region, Stenka Razin, immediately set about abducting a local princess during his first trip down the Volga River. In the nineteenth and twentieth centuries, however, Russians and Caucasians alike generated a steady flow of kidnapping scholarship, not least for the same reasons that Engels, in *The Origin of Family, Private Property, and the State* (1902), and Morgan, in *Systems of Consanguinity* ([1870] 1997), later made clear: conquering nineteenth-century empires, abetted by increasing abilities to survey and appropriate their constituencies, took an aggressive interest in idioms of property and ultimately its transfer.

Consider the following account set among Abkhaz on the Black Sea in the early twentieth century, before the onset of Soviet power. In the village of Markula lived Khanifa, a beauty and master craftswoman. She was loved by Khazgerii, a young man from a neighboring village who was famous for his success in extended raidings. The couple was in love, but one day a more powerful suitor, Prince Ozbek, spotted Khanifa. Overwhelmed by her beauty, Ozbek asked for her hand in marriage, something her father urged her to submit to. Fearing for her future, Khanifa informed Khazgerii through one of his relatives, Khizan. But Khizan, having been paid off by Prince Ozbek, double-crossed his kin and told Khanifa that Khazgerii would come for her. Prince Ozbek instead came in disguise. The wily Khazgerii, however, followed her tracks, rescued her, and killed the prince. On the run, the young lovers took refuge far away in the estates of Prince Marshan. Khazgerii elected an alliance with his protector through milk kinship (technically, kinship established through nursing at the breast of a woman other than one's mother but also through ritually touching the breast of an elder female member of the clan one seeks to join), and lived there with his bride for ten years. Khazgerii eventually met his death at the hands of a relative of Prince Ozbek, thus setting up a long period of conflict between the kin of the two princes (Inal-Apa 1954, 47).

Russian officials might have seen in this story only blood vengeance, despite the fact that records show that most disputes ended not with blood but with the payment of simple fines following the usual codes of custom (Bobrovnikov 2002, 57). The important point is that whether such abductions were in fact consensual or semiconsensual elopements or outright assault, whether they ended in good favor or in grief, it is clear that throughout the region they were a constant source of negotiation, observation, and debate across well-known borders and boundaries. The negotiations often led, in turn, to the shifting and remaking of boundaries. Khanifa and Khazgerii, by their migration, forged new kin alliances, but their fate demonstrates that their former lives were by no means extinguished. In this way two Caucasus communities found themselves very much connected.

Leontovich's 1882 study of customary law in the mountains is one of the most extensive historical anthropologies in this context. Writing of the mid-nineteenth century, he observes that questions of *adat,* or custom, and their proper adjudication were not taken lightly anywhere in the Caucasus. Elder representatives of villages, churches, and mosques were constantly holding meetings and attempting to resolve these forms of marriage arrangements along mutual lines. No circumstances were perhaps better recorded than bride thefts between longtime rivals among Cherkess and Nogai of the Kuban' region in the North Caucasus. In one instance, a couple's attempted elopement led to the killing of both a Nogai woman and her Cherkess would-be suitor. An elder relative of the Cherkess man from Beslan, advocated a resolution on the basis of shari'a law that would have required that they make only modest financial reparations for the theft. Nogai princes from the wounded party shamed them, however, by making an appeal to perceived pre-Islamic adat, thus forcing a higher price. The Beslan Cherkess conceded but in the ensuing years, made no additional gestures. The Nogai, who historically considered themselves superior to the Cherkess, took offense that not a single Cherkess came to extend customary rites of apology to the injured family. Not until two full years later did the complex performances of financial tribute and retributive violence cease ([1882] 2002, 173–175; see also Kudaev 1988 for similar events).

Marriage by capture has of course never been limited to the Caucasus, yet as studies from around the world show, it has often been easier to theorize this secretive-by-design practice in the abstract (Ayres 1974; Barnes 1999; Kisliakov 1959; Maksimova 1965; Pershits 1982; Smirnova 1979) than it has been to document it in the concrete.[12] In a wide-ranging comparative study (1979), Dumézil has ventured that marriage by gift or dowry dominates in societies governed by clerics; marriage by capture dominates in societies governed by warriors; and marriage by bride-price dominates in protoindustrial contexts organized around more complex forms of production, exchange, and monetary systems (see also Allen 2000). Soviet-era scholars, by dint of ideology and inclination, have strained to argue the material determinants for all three of these forms of marriage, with special attention to marriage by capture as a means of social or class leveling, the overthrow of oppressive hierarchies. Their contemporary counterparts among Caucasus specialists, eager to suggest the overcoming of backwardness where bride theft as such might be recognized as a social good in itself, argued in chorus that its persistence was due solely to grounds

---

12. Some notable exceptions to this trend from beyond the Caucasus include work on central Asia (Amsler and Kleinbach 1999; Edgar 2004; Werner 2004), France (Haase-Dubosc 1999), and Turkey (Bates 1981; Sertel 1969).

of penury—by the inability to pay even a token bride-price or the more substantial expenses of a wedding to which residents of one or more entire villages might be invited (Alimova 1989; Babaeva 1964; Gagieva 1973).[13]

Though contemporary activists have labored to produce first-person accounts of all manner of human trafficking in the Caucasus, historically speaking, evidence is less clear. Dragadze observed that in the Georgia of the 1960s, it was the first rule of citizenship in any child's education that children were expected to

> 1) be secretive about certain domestic and other matters; 2) be persuasive towards all shop keepers to sell goods they say they do not have; 3) never say aloud that they do not take at face value what they are taught outside the home; and finally, 4) children must be taught the capacity to imitate an adult's ambivalence in those areas which fit only with difficulty into the richly woven mesh of beliefs and codes of behaviour described and taught with constancy and assurance. (1988, 137)

Thus,

> [t]hrough silence—you never tell anyone you have witnessed an abduction and you never say that a couple is matrilaterally (or in any other way) related after a wedding has taken place—stability can be maintained. (131)

Yet what is striking is that across nineteenth- and twentieth-century accounts, even those that in no way strain to minimize the violence inherent in any person's abduction, the vast majority observe that nonconsensual events—where the vectors of consent are foremost between a bride and her parents before, during, or after a woman's kidnapping, rather than between the bride and her suitor—were crimes pure and simple, against which all communities labored to protect their daughters (Alimova 1986, 1989; Gagloiti 1974; Inal-Apa 1954; Kudaev 1988; Leontovich [1882] 2000; Sandrygailo 1899; Smirnova 1983; Ter-Sarkisiants 1989). These accounts indicate that while these marriages were by no means free of the cultures of militarism and performative aspects of theft by which they took place, crimes recognized as such were strictly repudiated.

---

13. For contemporary English-language accounts of the strains presented to marrying parties in this hospitality-intensive part of the world, see Platz (1996) and Yalçın-Heckmann (2001).

One of the ironies in the historical record is that in many parts of the Caucasus the Russian imperial administration made a tacit but consistent policy of allowing pre-Islamic practices such as bride kidnapping, perceived as having originated before the Arab conquest in the eighth century and therefore referred to as adat, so as to combat what they considered to be the far better organized and thus more threatening rule by Muslim religious law, or *shariat* (from the Arabic *shar'ia*). In his study of Daghestan and Azerbaijan in the late nineteenth century, Sandrygailo observes that while Russian overseers took the question of bride kidnapping seriously enough to include it in their criminal codes, Russian officials rarely enforced these rules in order not to be seen as interfering in domestic (as opposed to religious) matters. Because practices of bride capture were deeply entrenched and could easily escalate into blood feud, it is not hard to see why local governments would have preferred to regulate rather than ban the practice outright. On paper, according to Sandrygailo, if a woman effectively eloped, then the man was obliged to pay only a 30-ruble fine, plus seven kettles of a 2-ruble value to every *turkag* (judge's deputy) in the *okrug,* or region. If the abduction was without the woman's consent, then the fine rose to 50 rubles. If the woman was married, then all the abductor's property was transferred to her husband (1899, 94). In some counties into which couples attempted to integrate themselves after nonviolent elopements, the man would be asked to produce as many as seven bulls as a community offering (119; see also Gagieva 1973, 20; and Smirnova 1983, 106 for comparable examples).

In the Soviet period, early Bolshevik activists rushed to condemn these backward and aggressive practices, producing rapid legislation that varied by region. In 1930, Akopov surveyed new legislation that had been introduced the year previous in a decree of the plenum of the Supreme Court of the RSFSR, "On judicial practice on matters of crimes of daily life" (*o sudebnoi praktike po delam o bytovykh prestupleniiakh*). The original penalty for attempting bride capture was set at two years, but in other areas such as the Bashkir SSR, where the struggle was seen as more intense, the term was five years (1930, 58–60). In the nine autonomous *oblasti,* or provinces, of the North Caucasus at the time (Ingush, Ossetian, Chechen, Adyghe, Kabardino-Balkar, Karachai, Oirat, Cherkess, and Kalmyk), 155 such "crimes of custom" were prosecuted between 1926 and 1927, and among the condemned, officials stressed that 80 percent were illiterate, thus suggesting that it was a practice that would be eradicated with further education (63).[14] Eventually the prohibition against bride capture became law across the entire RSFSR. As Gaguev notes for Kabardino-Balkaria in the 1970s, few were unaware of the threats posed to such actions by the Criminal Code, but when cases were shown to involve consent, they were less harshly prosecuted (1977, 78).[15] In the post-Soviet age, governments no less eager to be seen as modern and progressive nonetheless found themselves with more pressing battles on their hands, and cases of bride capture in circumstances of duress appear to have risen everywhere.

Detachable Men

Across the Caucasus there were long-standing ways to shift categories of identity—through slavery, child and adult adoptions, and the kidnapping of brides, to name just some examples. Aside from the kidnapped bride, no figure is more prominent in popular consciousness than that of the *abrek:* by competing definitions a disgraced village exile, a hostage never to return, a lone wolf in hiding to return in order to right historical wrongs, and a revolutionary looking to overturn oppressive established orders. Russian writers have devoted an extraordinary amount of attention to the abrek figure: in hostile terms when the oppressive order in the mid-nineteenth century was their own empire; in admiring terms simply because the free will exemplified by these "mountain pirates" seemed so refreshing in contrast to the close supervision of daily life under the tsars; in nervous but admiring terms when some of these same mountain pirates sided with Bolsheviks to change the political landscape in the 1920s; and in nervous terms again when the wars in Chechnya that began anew in the 1990s. Thus at least 150 years of an active abrek imaginary—to a large degree advanced by Russian popular culture—inspired legions of young Caucasian men to head to the hills once more. What these later abreks have in common with the better-known bandits of the landmark

---

14. Of the 155 crimes in question, 66 (or 42 percent) were for bride kidnapping, 44 were for marriage by bride-price, 6 were for marriages forced upon youth by their parents, 27 were for polygamy, and 12 were for sexual assault (Akopov 1930, 61).

15. The articles of the Criminal Code of the RSFSR discussed by Gaguev include Article 232, forbidding payment or acceptance of bride-price; Article 233, the forcing into marriage or restraint from free marriage decisions of a woman, including kidnapping; Article 234, against underage marriages; and Article 235, against bigamy or polygamy (1977, 78).

study by historian Eric Hobsbawm (1969) is an open criticism of established orders and a faith in their ability to transform them (see also
Barkey 1994).[16]

There are many genealogies for the abrek figure (*amanat* in Arabic,
qacaq in Turkish, and *aparaq* in Persian). What abreks share with brides
of arranged marriages is that they are commonly viewed as "detachable
kin"—not only as figures intended for temporary or permanent exile because of blood feuds but as limit-figures whose entry into new communities was often seen as consolidating those who received them. But the
degree of their detachability, as with women, has been nothing if not exaggerated in a figure whose very notoriety was central to the advancement of
the figure of the violent highlander.

In the 1860s, looking back on four decades of both lyrical encomiums
and harsh condemnation—both signs of the fascination that the lone autocrat of the mountains seemed to evoke—the Russian linguist Petr Uslar
remarked,

> In the age of romanticism [1820s–1840s] neither land nor people in the Cau-
> casus found much understanding....It was as if we were unable to see the
> hill peoples as other than a people possessed by some kind of frenzy [*besno-
> vanie*], as if they all suffered from inflammation of the brain, lashing out left
> and right before they created yet another generation of madmen [*besnuiu-
> shikhsia*]. And there was a time when these mad streams [*neistovye chada*] of
> our poetic fantasy brought half the Russian reading public to ecstasy! Other
> readers of the more judgmental sort also believed in the existence of these
> raging lunatics, but instead of expressing delight, recommended that they
> be ripped up from the roots. (1868, 4–5)[17]

Indeed it was from among the latter readers that the Russian etymologist
Vladimir Dal' issued his brief definition of the abrek in 1880 as

> m. *Cauc.* A desperate mountaineer, having given an urgent pledge or prom-
> ise not to spare his own head and to fight furiously; *also* fugitive, ready to
> join the first band of robbers he sees. (1882, 1:2)[18]

---

16. For a famous fictional example from neighboring Turkey, see Kemal ([1900] 1961).

17. Cited in Bobrovnikov (2000, 22).

18. Markelov (2002) and Matveev (2002) are two contemporary examples that diverge little
from Dal's definitive rendering.

A more ethnographic reading than Dal''s, however, suggests a far more complex and diverse set of practices by which a man from any number of societies across the North or South Caucasus could find himself leaving his own community in search of other callings.

The contemporary Russian scholar Vladimir Bobrovnikov traces the etymology of the word to the Persian *aparak,* or the more recent *avara,* meaning wanderer and robber, suggesting that the word became entrenched in a variety of Caucasus languages through both Persian and Turkic influences (2000, 24; see also Gould 2007).[19] Some scholars have suggested that the abrek must be considered from two vantage points: before Russian colonization, when he represented the sporadic figure who left his community as a result of vengeance, and after the Russians' arrival, when he braved the hardships of mountain exile to expel the infidel from his lands (Botiakov 2004, 8).[20] But this induces us to see Russia as the first and only colonizer in a region that was far from the savage *terra nullius* that more conservative imperial historians might prefer.

The Georgian anthropologist Marina Kandelaki prefers instead to begin with what she calls the institution of *amanatstvo,* referring to the Arabic word *amanat,* an object held for safekeeping. Kandelaki points to the use of the term as it has morphed across the Arabic, Persian, Crimean Tatar, Ukrainian, Azeri, Avar, Ingush, and Kabard, where the most important reference is the shift in meaning from objects to persons. Although the earliest uses of the term were invariably to designate objects held while men went off into battle or as collateral in complex treaty arrangements, eventually the word could designate all manner of persons.[21] In Daghestan,

---

19. Bobrovnikov (2002), referring to the Kabard forms *abredzh* and *abreg',* the Abkhaz *abrag',* the Ossetian *abyreg,* and the Megrelian and Svan *abragi,* notes that terms from these languages sometimes suggest less violent actors. Yalçın-Heckmann (personal communication) points out that in Turkish, *avare* has roots in religious orders, signaling dervishes, healers, and saintly characters, seekers who were themselves often sought out for their healing abilities. For more etymologies see Botiakov (2004, 5–8).

20. Bobrovnikov underscores that the term *abrek* came into wide circulation in the mid-nineteenth century at the height of resistance to Russian rule (2002, 26).

21. In early Persian society, Lambton writes that *aman,* "the custom of giving protection or safe conduct...to strangers or outsiders had prevailed among the Arab tribes before Islam. By it a stranger who was in principle outlawed outside his own group received for his life and property the protection of a member of a group to which he did not belong and the protection of that group as a whole" (1981, 202).

a bride could be referred to as an amanat, entrusted to the safekeeping of her new family; an orphan or even a guest could earn the same title (1987, 9). Yet surely the best-known example was the man cast out of his community for crimes and misdemeanors or a wounded counterpart who goes into hiding to plan a revenge assault.

> Slander, theft, insult, and transgressions of marriage rules—all this quali-
> fies as failure to submit to the internal order established by the community.
> Kidnapping, want of land, and unfavorable natural-climactic conditions
> for maintaining survival with limited resources also spurred mountain resi-
> dents to consider the status of an amanat. (20)

Likewise, this does not exclude the better-known forms of the exchange of firstborn sons as guarantors of treaty arrangements between rival leaders, a practice actively pursued across the Russian, Persian, and Ottoman empires (Khodarkovsky 2002).

In eastern Georgia, the most canonic form of amanat was sanctioned by the keeper of one of the village's religious shrines. Having gathered the community at the gates of the sanctuary, the keeper of the site would explain the circumstances that brought the seeker to their door. After testimony from the fugitive, senior male members of the community would alternately grill him on the theme of his vengeance predicament and remind him of errant amanats whom the community quickly regretted having admitted to their midst. If the man were allowed to stay, all would agree upon a day whereby the seeker would be expected to make an offering to the shrine or the community. A probationary period of anywhere from one to three years would be established to limit any premature considerations of marriage or other more formal absorptions of the man into the host community.[22] If well received, an amanat could be treated strictly as a guest and would be urged to do little labor in his first year of shelter. But risks were considerable for the sheltering community, as they were automatically joined to any retributive vengeance held against the fugitive by his opponents. For this reason, if the amanat had taken shelter not far

---

22. In his "Ballad of a Stolen Goat," Iskander (1993) ruminates in verse on the risks of housing the wayward bandit, who is expected to honor those who feed him no matter how criminal
his past.

from his home village, it would be expected that he make secretive visits by cover of night to make penance at his natal shrines in order to lessen the force of any retributions planned. In the most integrative circumstances, the rules of fictive kinship would direct the transformation of the amanat's identity in toto (Kandelaki 1987, chap. 2).

Kandelaki views the difference between the amanat and the abrek primarily as one of voluntarism. The amanat is most often the offending party in a blood feud, whose accidental killing or insult of another has set off a lifetime of organized counterassaults that leave him little choice but to surrender his labor and identity to any distant patron who will give him shelter. The abrek, by contrast, is more often the injured party who, rather than seeking the company of strangers, will tend to seek out the villages of nearby relatives to plan retribution. The abrek may also follow the rules of identity shifting by taking on new kin obligations in the time of his exile, but he is not cultivating a long-term transfer (1987, 106–110).

The significance of both amanat and abrek is less the liminal status of the figure cast between two worlds than the fact that they are still affirmed as a member in both, suturing the two together for better or worse. This was evident in the account of the fugitive lovers Khanifa and Khazgerii, who created new alliances under Prince Marshan but were never forgotten in the world of Prince Ozbek. For all the transformations wrought by fictive kinship, as many have observed, the amanat "still remains under the equal protection of his former community" (1987, 125). It is for these reasons that the languages of long-sought bride, honored guest, and nervously received fugitive so easily overlap. An 1846 article in the Tbilisi-based newspaper *Kavkaz* observed that such customs were observed "even among Armenians," reflecting the widespread sense that Christian peoples (implied as being more civilized) should be free of such customs.

> No attention is paid to whether protection is offered to someone in the right or in the wrong. For this reason, every bandit pursues his malefactions in the hope of finding such protection. Having offered respite, the host will not give up his guest until feuding parties have reconciled, or until blood has been paid with blood. If the matter cannot be resolved by either of these two means, then it will be referred to shar'ia law (a religious judge). When a judge decides to hand over a murderer to the leader of the wounded parties, the host is obliged to place the accused in the hands of his avengers, who

then proceed as they see fit—submitting him to strangulation, drowning, or
a life of slavery. (167)

Protection was everything, but no identity could shift entirely. Put most
simply, as the Azeri ethnographer Karakashly did in his study of South
Caucasus social structures, *arxalı k̇ȯpək qurd basar* [A dog with *arxa,* protection or backing, can crush a wolf] (1970, 312). But he will still be an animal of a different sort.

Moving across so many zones, the archetypal abrek poses as a central
liminal figure whose near shamanic ability to cross borders between material and even spiritual worlds suggests his role as a binding element across
alien lines. But this did not mean that mere mortals could not exercise
the finer points of social leveraging between the categories of amanat and
abrek. Consider the story of the legendary Shapsug warrior Beslan Abat.
During a famous conflict that he incited between himself and fellow clansmen, a conflict in which he quickly found himself on the losing side, Abat
took the unprecedented stance of seeking amanat status among neighboring Abazekhs, a stronger rival clan whose strength foreclosed the possibility of further attack by Abat's kinsmen.[23] The appeal for the Abazekhs was
manifold: their prestige was advanced by the absorption of a famous warrior from a rival clan into their own, and Abat himself brought with him
substantial wealth, which he shared in the form of sacrifices and tribute to
his Abazekh hosts. Technically, the advantages went still further.

> The client acquires a bulwark, while the protector earns the right to de-
> mand fines for any insult brought upon his client, as insults to the client are
> redirected to the noble protector himself and therefore merit compensation
> according to Cherkess law. (Khan-Girei 1847, 170)

Thus Abat's case was remembered not only for its audacity but also for his
willingness to sacrifice his status as leader of one of the most noble clans of
his people, recalling the idiom of social leveling in active use throughout
Caucasus folklore. His own diminished social status, however, did little to

---

23. For comparative purposes, Gilsenan (1996) again is an excellent source on the ways in
which these kinds of actions relied on complex balances of family, clan, and broader social group-
ings in intended balancings of perceived social structures.

take away from the more storied qualities of the detachable man who drew the lines of clan rivalry so clearly by crossing them.

With the more formal onset of the Caucasus wars in the mid-nineteenth century and with the capture in 1859 of the legendary Daghestani leader Imam Shamil—most famous for his armed opposition to tsarist rule—all agree that the figure of the abrek changed dramatically, making it increasingly difficult for observers to separate the mountain loner, whose exile was pitched against a clan-based community, from the bands of mountain militia whose common cause was the overthrow of a foreign imperial presence. From a limit-figure of exceptional status whose sporadic appearances in history and folklore underscored existing lines of division, the abrek became a more common and more violent figure whose presence around all mountain communities was increasingly the norm as Russian rule advanced across the North and South Caucasus. Some ethnographers, such as Bobrovnikov, see the abrek alongside other institutions as crucial binding elements that managed the fragile pluralisms in the region:

> Men's alliances, the cult of the dzhigit warrior, blood vengeance, and hospitality—all enabled small communities of mountaineers to survive under circumstances of near constant civil strife and armed struggles from north to south, saving them from descent into anarchy. (2000, 29)

The special salience here for those who see Pushkin and the many other Russian authors as having introduced Russian reading publics to a violent southern region is that the tales of Russian soldiers and aristocrats being held captive in the Caucasus Mountains entered a semantic landscape where plotlines and thus potential outcomes were far from predetermined. The detachable male could be transformed, reidentified, sold into slavery, or remade as kin. Moreover, his proxy status as collateral against more sweeping conflicts, in the case of the amanat, or his ability to seek shelter in neighboring communities so as to follow exact codes of social order, in the case of the abrek, was understood to serve the minimization rather than the increase of violence.

The reconstruction of such legacies naturally requires scrutiny of the provenance of all historical and ethnographic sources in such troubled contexts. The character of the unofficial Adyghe spokesperson, Khan-Girei, one of the Russian imperial army's more storied linguistic and cultural interpreters, recalls the role of mixed-allegiance civil servants in other parts of the globe, such as nineteenth-century Spanish South America, where local hired guides would intently exaggerate the savagery of their kinsmen in order to argue and extend their own indispensability as middlemen (Taussig 1986; see also Çelebi 1988). By the late nineteenth century, the image of the violent Caucasus seemed irrevocably fixed in popular Russian imaginations, but it may have equally served communities across the North and South Caucasus whose accessions to Russian sovereignty were as uneven as they were unsteady.

Limit-Figures in War and Peace

Historians and policymakers alike rightly contend that many societies of the Caucasus do have well-developed cultures of militarism. But where such patterns of violence come from is another matter. Recalling the earlier debates over the origins of Caucasus raiding practices in the last chapter, Shami (1999) has made the smart point that far too many scholars imagine the entire physiognomy of this region, in the form of "the violent Caucasus," to have somehow formed prior to and exclusive of colonization rather than in tandem with it. Instead, we should find little surprise in a Caucasus that has a highly developed language of militarism after near-constant foreign interventions since the onset of written record.

In historical and ethnographic terms, it seems clear that from at least Prometheus and Amirani onward, the Caucasus has been a site of social and cultural transformations—not only for persons held captive, moved, given, traded, ostracized, or reidentified but for entire sovereign systems. In the Russian imperial and later Soviet communist periods, the transformations and the violence clearly moved in all directions. The highly advanced Caucasus military systems made the Russian army fiercer, according to the decorated general, Grigorii Zass. *S volkami zhit', po-volchi vyt'*—to live with wolves is to howl like the wolves—is a proverb Zass relied upon to explain Russia's encounter with another symbol of Caucasus manhood, the "Chechen wolf" (Lunochkin and Mikhailov 1994). Others have shown that the popular perception of kidnapping as a "language" of force inclined early Bolsheviks to institute widespread hostage takings as part of their early Sovietizing Caucasus campaigns (Cherkasov 2004).

Whether or not the exchange of men and women across kin, alliance, or broader political lines contributed to a more balanced landscape of competing sovereignties in the Caucasus—as most accounts of practices of amanat and arranged marriage suggest—is something specific to each given exchange. In the spirit of relatively porous boundaries suggested earlier, the case of abreks and amanats suggests an open expression of enmity that is nonetheless mutually adjudicated through the proxy of a limit-figure toward peaceful ends. This is a far cry from the kinds of contemporary peace negotiations normally advocated by leaders who wait for the ceremonial smiling handshake or the mythical nonviolent surrender (Wagner-Pacifici 2005). The careful balance between enmity and the keeping of the peace seems a more prominent staple of the rough cohabitations achieved in the Caucasus of long ago than of those existing today. But what ethnographic records of the transformative traffic in sons, daughters, and lone wolves suggest is that any persons who entered the space of the Caucasus— Russian aristocrat, soldier, or Komsomol leader—would be defined as much by the terms of others as by their own.

5

CAPTIVE RUSSIANS

> In Europe we were hangers-on and slaves, whereas we shall go to Asia
> as masters. In Europe we were Tatars, whereas in Asia we, too, are
> Europeans. Our mission, our civilizing mission in Asia will bribe our spirit
> and drive us there.
>
> FYODOR DOSTOEVSKY, *Writer's Diary*

Did Russia need to "bribe [its] spirit" (*podkupit' nash dukh*) with missions across the Black Sea, the Caucasus, and central Asia? In these famous lines, Dostoyevsky captured one of the many paradoxes of the gift of empire. In his *Writer's Diary* of January 1881, Dostoyevsky celebrated the recent victories of Russian armies in Turkestan led by General Mikhail Skobelev, once of the Caucasus regiments and a decorated leader in the Russo-Turkish war (1877–1878), when Russia aimed to gain access to the Mediterranean and liberate Slavic peoples from Ottoman rule. Without question, Russia looked south and east for material reasons. But was that all? In his reflections on Russia's colonial ambitions, Dostoyevsky hardly mentions the peoples of the newly conquered lands. "Build only two railroads, start from that: one to Siberia, and another to central Asia—and at once you will see the results," he wrote with enigmatic confidence ([1881] 1999, 250). His famous epigraph about a Russian soul divided between Europe and Asia makes it clear that through colonial conquest, its civilizing mission, Russia would finally gain the respect of its European peers.

This is a gift, in effect, designed to impress other givers. Recipients are nowhere to be found; or to put it more precisely, one need not find the recipient because the empire was both giver and receiver in the most important respect. The gift of empire is foremost to oneself.

> We must banish the slavish fear that Europe will call us Asiatic barbarians, and that it will be said that we are more Asiatic than European. This shame, that Europe considers us Asiatics has been haunting us for almost two centuries.... They take us for thieves who stole from their enlightenment and who disguised themselves in their garb. (246, 248)

He continued, "The main thing is that our civilizing mission in Asia, from the very first steps (simply without doubt)... will lift our spirit; it will give us dignity and self-consciousness, which at present we either lack altogether or have very little of" (251). Thus, as we saw in earlier chapters, imperial giving is often less about the putative recipients—the Asiatics understood as even more backward than Russians themselves—than about the recognition afforded to the giver by the giver's peers. These pages in Dostoyevsky's diaries have everything and, at the same time virtually nothing to do with the Caucasus or central Asia. Instead, his ruminations take him from one European imperial seat to another, asking how Russia compares, how Russia can restore its rightful standing through new acquisitions. In conquest, Russia will find self-actualization and a place at the table. Dostoyevsky's reflections rest entirely on how Europe will receive the new giver rather than on how peoples of conquest will understand the gift.

The last three chapters suggested a setting for questions of sovereignty and boundary makings at all levels of Caucasus society. We now turn to some of the best-known Russian narratives of these themes, beginning in the age of Russia's efforts to enter the region as a leader. This is the entrance famously narrated by Pushkin in 1822 with the tale of the Russian aristocrat full of fear and admiration before a Circassian mountain society that would, at least in the figure of one young woman, gauge the valor of the Russian spirit and set the good prisoner free. It is a tale that, as this chapter will propose, sets the stage for a long tradition combining captivity and charisma in the southern territories. But it is also a tale studded with ambiguities, so many, in fact, that we can see how the language of the gift began to morph over time, from the closed-book conquests of Dostoyevsky, whose vision of Russian superiority in the south and east did not waver, to the less certain literary projects of writers whose own turns in the Caucasus suggest far more open-ended questions of exchange. The goal at hand is not to cover all of Russian literature's extensive commentaries on its engagements in the Caucasus, as this has been treated thoroughly elsewhere, but to focus on the ambiguities of Russian rule in the south (Layton 1994, 1999, 2001, 2004) in order to map the registers by which Russian gifts were seen to change over time.

At first glance, one could observe that this prisoner mythic cycle is fundamentally about the displacement of the Russian protagonist and the attendant anxieties of colonial power. As Linda Colley describes the British fascination with captivity narratives, which were winding down at the time of Pushkin's writing,

> For the British, overseas captivity crises in the seventeenth and eighteenth centuries, and even in the early 1800s, had often called forth more profound anxieties that winning and keeping territorial empire was too dangerous and might be beyond their capacity. Tales of captivity were not generated and scrutinized primarily because they deflected attention from Britons' own aggression, though this was sometimes part of their effect. They were scribbled and pored over as explorations of fear, risk, and deeply felt constraints. (2002, 264)

By contrast, some scholars of the captivity narrative industry—at its height in the United Kingdom and the Americas over the course of the eighteenth century—contend that the penny presses drove the content, regardless of historical accuracy or fealty to broader political significance (Pearce 1947; Slotkin 1973). But there are telling similarities among captivity narratives the world over, where kidnappings appear always to take place in a seeming vacuum of context; where colonization forms the broader setting; where the captors' fearsomeness is frequently exaggerated; and where captivity is, against all odds, often seen as a productive form of cultural encounter (Kolodny 1993). Fewer are the studies that have shown, in the Americas, for example, that the number of Indians taken prisoner, killed, or enslaved by the British (as well as by other Indians) was greater than the number of captive Euro-Americans. Indian societies across the Americas were far more prone to hostage exchange, similar to what in the Caucasus took the form of amanat, than they were to unilateral capture (Strong 1999, chaps. 2–3).[1] In this context, Layton rightly ventures that for Russian writers and their audiences,

> Russian belletrists orientalised the Caucasus so as to boost their claim to membership in the civilized part of the globe. In other words, the orientalisation of the Caucasus in Russian literature created a satisfying cultural mythology of Asiatic alterity. (1992a, 37)

Through captivity narratives, among many other genres and practices, Russia, too, would find its own civilizing mission, its own giving potential. At the pens of many of these writers, however, it was a mixed mission indeed.

From the publication of Pushkin's work in 1822, the Caucasus prisoner cycle has flexibly moved across genres to secure its place in the Russian cultural landscape from the classics of Pushkin, Lermontov, and Tolstoy to the commentaries of Eisenstein, the kinetic Soviet archetypes of Gaidai, and the story's cinematic reappearance in 1996, which was contemporaneous with the precarious ending to Boris Yeltsin's first Chechen war. In a wide variety of analytical approaches, we have seen the act of the captive's displacement as an end in itself, while at other times the Russian as prisoner is made into a symbol of the Russian love of suffering and the mysterious Russian soul. But stopping there, as most studies do, tells us little about the very canny means by which sovereign mythographies do their work—including communist mythographies that faced no less difficult a task in winning over widely disparate constituencies in 1917.

I argue instead that, across the changing political styles or sentiments of individual authors of the Russian captivity genre, the prisoner cycle enacts an art of emplacement by which Russian actors used negative plotlines to generate a symbolic economy of belonging in the Caucasus. They entered a physical place, found a mythic place, and generated a narrative place. By means of these narratives, the tale of the archetypal long-suffering Russian benefactor could be told and retold, possessed and repossessed, circulated

---

1. For similar vectors of captivity and the interdependencies generated between North African Muslims and European Christians in the Mediterranean, see Colley (2002, 69–71) and Laroui (1997, 243–245).

and recirculated. This modern myth was more productive than merely suggesting that the peoples of the Caucasus were misplaced or that the Russians were displaced. The highly charged characters were a means by which Russian publics (among others) could be *emplaced* in the chilly landscape of a long unwelcoming Caucasus region. While I root these stories in Russian cosmologies of persuasion, the goal is to examine the persuasive arts behind sovereign rule more broadly.

Here, rather than focusing on the nature of statehood as seen in conventional diplomatic or military histories, as chapter 2 investigated to some degree, I look to varied Russian traditions of expressive culture to identify subtler lines of identification with the country's presence in divided lands. Even when we find openly ambivalent portrayals of the blessings and the curses of the Russian presence in the region, as one can find from the mercurial writings of Pushkin through Tolstoy and beyond, we find a remarkably consistent set of thematics (Layton 1994; Ram 2003). Seemingly apolitical tracts of poetry, prose, ballet, opera, and musical comedy generate a remarkably consistent theme of innocence abroad and the noble burdens of giving.

Two arts of emplacement appear most actively. It is perhaps easiest to think of these as inversions, though it might be fairer to regard them as sleights of hand—in the spirit of a writer's pen or a cinematographer's mobile grip—dexterous and subtle craftings of plotlines that produce new social outcomes.[2] The first of these are sleights of power. In a savvy gesture of dissimulation, the prisoner tale is a chronicle not of activity but of passivity, not of aggression but of humility, not of gloried sovereignty but of storied submission. The Russian is not captor but captive.

These inversions rely heavily as well on gender. In the prisoner cycle, we find not the exchange of women—in the traditional sense of mountaineers kidnapping their brides from rival clans and villages—but the exchange of men. Gayle Rubin (1975) and later Luce Irigaray (1985) were among the first who suggested that the structuralist fascination with the exchange of women was ultimately about the homosocial—that is, men's relations with men—and Sandler has made this point most elegantly in her studies of

---

2. I prefer the term "sleight" to "arts," which can appear too mild, or to "strategy," which overstates conscious intent. By contrast, sleight suggests skill, adroitness, possible trickery, and best of all, habit. When an act by sleight is performed well it is hardly noticed.

Pushkin in exile (1989). Hence, although there is quite a powerful female agency at the heart of these stories (it is after all most often a Caucasian woman who sets the captive free), the themes of male harmlessness and impotence drive the plot.

In the second category, we find sleights of exchange. Each of the prisoner plotlines is about an exchange, or rather an intended exchange that never manages to take place. In Pushkin a young aristocrat is held for anticipated but unspecified trade, while in Lermontov unidentified young Russians are captive laborers in a Circassian village until one day when they may find usefulness as trade items. In Tolstoy and the 1996 film by Bodrov, Russian soldiers are intended for trade in exchange for Caucasian men taken as Russian prisoners-of-war. Already this plotline is a puzzle, for despite the fact that the Caucasus had been famous for its Silk Road trade routes since the ninth century, the ironic premise in these stories is that the mountain highlanders had little of their own to barter. In order to participate in the new social order, Caucasians had to acquire a new currency of exchange value—a Russian body.

Bearing this language of exchange in mind, we need to ask what was gained from the persistent circulation of these fictional tales of captured Russian bodies within the real-life context of Russian military intervention. What might the authors, playwrights, choreographers, and filmmakers have seen in telling and retelling this particular tale? Why did a long line of Russian greats take such interest in giving these suffering bodies to their respective publics? In being so given, are these Russian bodies and the stories made of them gifts in the classic anthropological sense?

To better understand how these stories were part of a broader colonial art of exchange, we can profitably defer to Georg Simmel, who reminds us that gifts make their entrance within embedded contexts. Hence, idioms of "first gift" and "second gift," as the calculus sometimes goes, are already somewhat misleading. "What is starting point, and what is consequence here, is something that can perhaps not be determined," Simmel wrote in his 1907 essay on "Exchange" ([1907] 1971, 47–48), a work that preceded Marcel Mauss's more famous *Essay on the Gift* published in 1925. According to Simmel,

> Many actions which at first glance appear to consist of mere unilateral process in fact involve reciprocal effects. The speaker before an audience, the

teacher before a class, the journalist writing to a public—each appears to be the sole source of influence in such situations, whereas each of them is really acting in response to demands and directions that emanate from apparently passive, ineffectual groups. The saying, "I am their leader, therefore I must follow them," holds good for politicians the world over. (43)

Once we move past the myths of isolated actors, as Simmel urges, most if not all renderings are not gifts but countergifts, actions that take place in settings already laden with values accrued from earlier interactions, earlier encounters, and earlier exchanges. And of course, exchanges do not always take place among equal actors or in equal coin.

If we pursue Simmel's language of exchange, we can bear in mind that these poems and ballets were not created in a political vacuum. From the sixteenth century onward, Russians were facing active, well-organized, armed resistance to their colonizing overtures. What was being exchanged in this physical space was often explosive volleys. What was being exchanged in the narrative place was the story of the prisoner from the Russians and cold shoulders (by the great majority in the early stages) from the Caucasians. In this narrative space of encounter, some Russians offered a remarkable kind of persuasive art. Or, to put it in the words of one Azeri historian I sought out when I asked her about local kidnappings, "These Russian fairy tales, they are worse than the bombs!" Yet does "exchange" quite fit this scenario, or are we not looking at something that Simmel directs us to, something closer to "sleights of exchange"? As chapter 3 emphasized, giving establishes the reputation of the giver as such, among her own cohort first and foremost. Focusing instead on sleights of exchange brings us much closer to the kind of agonistic social gambits Simmel mapped so well.[3]

The argument that the prisoner myth operates as an art of emplacement builds on these subtle inversions to reveal an imperial narrative of longing

---

3. Do these arts have to be seen as expressing intent? Simmel suggests not, for in an exchange the giver wants only one thing: "Giving up something else therefore does not have the effect of being a detraction from the satisfaction he seeks.... It does not count as a price" ([1907] 1971, 58). Hence, while it may seem curious to find a recurring Russian archetype of the Promethean long-suffering giver who gives his own body in the cause of civilizing and improving mankind, Simmel tells us that self-sacrifice is "by no means an external barrier to [one's] goals. It is rather the inner condition of the goal, and the way to it" (48). See also Beidelman (1989).

and belonging in the Caucasus—not just the mythification of Russian suffering. Despite violent plotlines in which Russians are ever the noble victims, they are also victims who give and whose generosity invites just respect. As the tales talk of war, they offer narratives of cohabitation and ultimately resigned consent. Understanding these everyday idioms by which the Russian Empire and its later communist successors worked to cement control over the Caucasus offers insight into the formulation of rule in a place not normally considered in broader debates about colonialism and sovereignty; yet it reaches out most broadly to the varied technologies of rule exercised by all states over diverse and uncertain subjects.

Fact and Fiction

While it is conventional to begin Russia's captivity cycles with Pushkin, it is clear that the poet had more than enough to work with from both the Byron of his admiration (Zhirmunskii 1923, 1924) and the real-life kidnappings that had been widely covered in the Russian press for several decades. Samuel Gottlieb Gmelin was a German botanist in the service of the Russian Imperial Academy of Sciences in 1774 when he was taken captive by a Daghestani khan and later killed. Gmelin's fate had no place in the agenda of the reigning empress Catherine, who some say was motivated to move further into the Caucasus to avenge and further prevent just such acts (Atkin 1988, 156; Barrett 1998, 79; Pollock 2006, 131).

Kidnappings of Russians, as of Caucasians themselves, were rife across the late eighteenth century. But it was the case of another foreign-born subject in the service of the empire, the Italian Ivan Petrovich Del Pozzo, who entered the Russian army as a volunteer in 1775, that made popular headlines next. On September 20, 1802, the then general Del Pozzo and his retinue of three Cossacks were overtaken in a raid by twenty-one Chechens. Evidently aware of whom they had captured, his Chechen holders demanded 20,000 silver rubles in ransom, a sum that would be diminished by intense negotiations over a year of the general's harsh detention (Potto [1885–1887] 1994, 1:658–661).

Perhaps the highest-profile case to reach Russian readers, however, came in the kidnapping of Major Pavel Shvetsov in February 1816. Shvetsov was slated for a furlough from his posting in the province of Shemakha (in contemporary Azerbaijan) and was planning to visit his brother, a police master in Kizliar, via Daghestan. Impatience reputedly got the best of him, dissuading him from traveling along the more established route and with the requisite party of guards. In two waves of fierce assault, Chechens overcame him and his retinue on horseback. He was held in Bol'shie Atagi and was initially ransomed for 10,000 rubles. But when his captors realized that neighboring Kabard princes considered Shvetsov within their circle of protection, they stowed him in a damp underground pit covered over by boards for a total of sixteen months. Russian newspapers took up the case and broadcast an appeal for donations toward his ransom. In light of the sensation surrounding his case, the ransom climbed to 25,000 rubles, leaving officials to fear that even were they to secure his release using the donated public funds, Chechens would hold the upper hand. Furious that he was being held to account by gortsy, the newly arrived Ermolov bargained the ransom back to 10,000 and then made a private deal with the khan of Avaria to publicly purchase Shvetsov's freedom in a gesture to communicate that not all mountain nobilities opposed the Petersburg court. Ermolov's plan, not secret for long, was to ensure that there would be no perception of Russian submission to any alien power (Potto [1885–1887] 1994, 2:52–58; see also Barrett 1998).[4]

Knowing that Pushkin spent time with the accomplished historian Semen Bronevskii during his visit through Feodosiia in 1820 (Pavlova 2004, 10), one might venture that the poet was apprised of these and other events taking place in the Caucasus, as much as or more than any other educated member of Russia's elite. Just as easily he might years earlier have found a copy of the 1816 publication of *Lettres sur le Caucase et la Géorgie,* the joint memoir of two years in the Caucasus by Wilhelm von Freygang, a German diplomat in the Russian imperial service, and his wife, Frederika, which recounted a number of captivities made famous at the time (1816).[5] All the same, much myth surrounds the origin of the idea for Pushkin's famous poem. While conceding that Pushkin was indeed aware of the fates

---

4. Following his release, Shvetsov resumed service at the post in Derbent but died of fever in 1822. In a final indignity, his remains were mistaken by grave robbers for those of a blood enemy, subsequently mutilated, and cast away (Potto [1885–1887] 1994, 2:58).

5. Although the book was published in Hamburg, it circulated in wide distribution for the time, with the 1816 edition on sale in Paris, London, and St. Petersburg.

of Del Pozzo, Shvetsov, and others, some have suggested that it was in fact an old Cossack who approached him one day in a shop in Kislovodsk and told him the tale of the mountain captivity of an elite Russian traveler and the mountain girl who set him free (Egorova 1997, 101). Pushkin himself, on the other hand, remarked to Zhukovskii that it was a distant relative of a famed captive who offered the specifics (Bartenev 1866, 1139; Zhirmun-skii 1923, 113).

But to suggest that a well-known plot is all that was needed would be to mistake literature—the artful arrangement of matter and its ornamentation—for the matter of history itself. Pushkin, in any case, had more than enough examples of captivities factual and fictional from his correspondent, Byron, and many others to suggest the material by which to render his own poetic verse. Catherine II herself some decades earlier had even entered the captivity field when she penned two children's stories of her own, "The Tale of Prince Fevei" (written in 1783) and "The Tale of Prince Khlor" (written in 1791). In the first, Fevei is the son of a Siberian leader of Chinese descent whose strength, beauty, and character are of such proportions that neighboring Kalmyk princes are eager for him to visit so that they may better understand their new imperial foe. They make an attempt to kidnap the prince—a token of imperial futures at large—but fail (1849, 261–278). It is with Khlor, son of the Prince of Kiev, that Catherine makes a more direct statement on her own empire's practices. This prince, again, is of such uncommon strength, beauty, and character that yet another Turkic people, this time the Kirghiz, strain to assess their newly minted rival. The Kirghiz khan himself dresses as an old beggar woman to play on the prince's generosities and ensnare him. After running the prince through a complicated task—to find "the rose without thorns that does not prick"—the khan concedes the boy's talents and releases him to his parents (281–296). In both cases, the future of an empire located on Russian soil is envied by deceitful Muslim Turks. But it is more than envy, as Harsha Ram has pointed out in discussing the "Tale of Prince Khlor."

> The Russian autocratic state, the fairy tale suggests, never exists as a prior given. Rather, it is endlessly produced and reaffirmed in the violent encoun-ter with an alien and eastern force—a war, a skirmish, a theft—an encounter from which the very principle of Russian statehood is derived. Khlor is not fully a prince until he is kidnapped and restored: he must go to the East to

return, enlightened but already quasi-oriental. The Russian state is thus figured primordially…in this identification with empire that transforms the
tsar into the very despot he opposes. What is despotic is not the east as such,
it seems, but rather the theft, concretely territorial and symbolically imaged,
that transforms nation into empire. (1998, 45)[6]

It is thus the very theft of the Russian body that, by the pen of Catherine II,
ratifies the centrality of Russia abroad.

Finally, by way of antecedents, while Pushkin may have been the first
to suggest the prisoner theme in verse, he may not entirely lay claim to the
title, whether he was aware of it or not. That distinction goes to the French
writer Xavier de Maistre, best known for his short story *Voyage autour de
ma chambre* but also once a traveler in the Caucasus in 1811, a journey that
inspired *Les Prisonniers du Caucase,* first published in 1816. De Maistre followed the convention of the many British writers before him with a tale
that begins with capture and ends with release, sparing hardly a moment
for a context that might explain either. An impatient Russian major and
his young aide-de-camp are held captive by raiding Chechens who fume
over the major's inability to write letters persuasive enough to marshal ransom monies but who nonetheless willingly enjoy the duo's musical talents
as a form of entertainment. In a scene of identity switching endemic to the
genre, the young aide takes on the Muslim faith, trading the name Ivan
for Hussein in order to turn events in their favor. As in later tales, a young
mountain child plays the role of consoling agent, and the Russian captive
is called upon to render his opinion in matters of justice when the elders
of the mountain society that hosts him are unable to control their fiercer
passions in decision making. The two men escape after more than a year of
considerable hardship, taking the lives of young and old to meet their task.
The story ends in the wedding of the major and the reaffirmation of social
distance as the implacable servant, now restored to Christianity, watches
the major's wedding ball from outside through a window. Estrangement
is a theme that underscores DeMaistre's understanding of the raids raining

---

6. Or, according to a later interpretation by Ram of the same short story, "It is not difficult to
discern here the makings of a historical allegory: temporarily subjugated by the eastern nomads
yet learning from them, Russia frees itself only after absorbing elements of the very culture it
opposes" (2003, 106).

down on the Russian men. "The Caucasus mountains have long been embedded in the Russian empire," he wrote, "but have not belonged to it" (1884, 5).

Negative Pleasures

"Prisoner of the Caucasus" was among a cycle of narrative poems produced during Pushkin's early romantic period. As a rule, critic Stephanie Sandler writes, "These are not love stories with happy endings.... For all the lightness of tone and whimsy of foreign landscapes," she writes, these are stories filled with "a vocabulary of domination and defeat" alongside "passions for violence and subjugation" (1989, 141). Sandler calls these themes Pushkin's "negative pleasures," highlighting the poet's famous ability to elevate the theme of inner torment to high art. While this kind of generative discourse of the negative might for some evoke Kant or Hegel, it draws on long-standing themes in Russian anthropological writing that reflect on the suffering of the Russian soul: Dostoyevsky's capacity for finding depths in the darkness, the microphysics of *khandra* (cultivated melancholy), as well as popular discursive practices of litany and lament (Pesmen 2000; Ries 1997).[7] Not in spite of but very much because of the open-endedness of Pushkin's Russian and Circassian characters, a long line of imitators have taken satisfaction in the retelling and remaking of perilous encounters.

Pushkin expressed more than considerable reluctance about his poem when he first published it in 1822, not least because he had never actually met a Circassian; however, Circassian names and places seemed to stand in collectively for all of Russia's newly acquired southern possessions. To one correspondent, he admitted, "The blankness of the plot approximates the poverty of its invention; the description of Circassian custom...is not connected with the least reality, and has little bearing on [even] the likes of a geographic article or traveler's account." To another, Pushkin remarked that his Circassian passages were "a mere hors d'oeuvre" in the service of

---

7. The term *khandra* and its corresponding imperfective verb *khandrit'* are taken from the Latin *hypochondria* (Fasmer 1971, 221). The term is so closely associated with Pushkin that it is common to refer to the art of melancholic swooning as *pushkinskaia khandra* (Vinogradov 1929, 799–800).

a simple story (1958, 50).[8] For all of Pushkin's magisterial poetry, this love story is indeed a simple one: young woman falls for wounded man; man breaks woman's heart; woman liberates man from suffering; woman has no reason left to live.

By all accounts, it was a curious choice of setting for a romance. While Pushkin had never met any of the Circassians he describes so confidently in the poem, he knew enough of the mayhem set in motion by ongoing Russian assaults and the mass dislocations of Caucasus life to observe elsewhere, "The Circassians hate us! ... We have edged them out of their free pasturelands, their villages have been destroyed, and entire tribes annihilated. With every passing day they move deeper into the mountains and make attacks from there" (1938, 449).[9] Yet in many respects this Circassian willfulness was entirely part of the appeal for the wandering young Russian aristocrat of the poem, who was clear in his dissatisfaction with high-society Russian life and his newfound admiration for the free will of mountain peoples. In Pushkin's rendering,

> The world and people he had weighed,
> The worth of fickle life he knew,
> For he had found friends' hearts untrue
> And dreams of love from folly made.
> Quite sickened, victimised for ever
> By vain ways he had long despised,
> By enmity two-tongued and clever
> As well as slanders undisguised,
> As Nature's friend, this world denying,
> He left behind his native bounds
> And sped away to distant grounds
> With freedom's joyful spirit flying.

> ([1822] 1997, 59)

Indeed, Pushkin's deft handling of bruises left by Russian society and those incurred at the hands of captors were later amplified in Griboedov's famous

---

8. The quote appears in an 1822 Pushkin letter to V. P. Gorchakov.

9. The citation is from Pushkin's essay "Journey to Arzrum." While traveling to the Turkish border in 1835, Pushkin finds a copy of his own "Prisoner of the Caucasus." He "reads it with great satisfaction. It was all weak, youthful, incomplete; but a great deal was discerned and expressed correctly" (Greenleaf 1991, 943).

phrase in the more expressly political "Bandits of Chegem" written in 1826. "Chains at home," he wrote, "captivity abroad!" (in Ram 2003, 141).[10]

Pushkin's long poem offered a tangled projection of love, politics, and geography, but lest it be read solely as a romance of Caucasus freedoms, as some chose to see it, a lengthy epilogue praises the Russian military intervention and blames the Circassian defeats on their having abandoned their own traditions (Ram 2003, 194; Layton 1994, chaps. 2–3; Proskurin 2006, 109; Svirin 1935, 205).[11]

Although Pushkin wrote his romantic tale in the full flush of the Russian military campaign in the early 1800s, the families of soldiers who sent their sons to battle, as well as Russian reading publics more generally, received heavily edited information on events in the South. Nothing appeared in the imperial press about the Russian assault on Chechnya in the 1780s, for example. So it would appear to be fate that his contemporaries acclaimed Pushkin as the leading source on Caucasian history and ethnography for the empire or, as Belinskii once referred to him, the "discoverer" of the Caucasus" (in Layton 1994, 16).[12]

As we saw earlier, the Russian mission in the Caucasus was volatile from the outset, but by dint of quick study and mutual appropriation, codes of encounter shifted to terms that Russians felt Caucasians would recognize. Thus one finds that Russian forces were quick to adopt the very practices of kidnapping and hostage taking they perceived as distinctive to mountain life (Pollock 2006, 82). One eventual plan set out by Russian imperial administrators was to turn their limited numbers into a positional strength,

---

10. Svirin, echoing the newly minted Stalinist interpretation that the nineteenth-century Russian presence in the Caucasus was exploitive, asserts, "In the fate of the captive, Pushkin has marvelously managed to demonstrate the contradictory position of the liberal nobility under oppressive colonial monarchy" (1935, 200). Some of the broadly synthetic discussions of Pushkin's prisoner work include Austin (1997); Layton (1994); Ram (2003); Sandler (1989); and Zorkaia (1994). For article-length reviews of the prisoner theme across genres, see Austin (1984); Barrett (1998); Goscilo (2003); Michaels (2004); and Potapova and Tsyganova (1998).

11. The poem's architecture and many afterlives are thoroughly cataloged in Egorova (1997); Kravtsova and Rosenfel'd (1999, 39–47); Stefanovich (1927); and Zhirmunskii (1924). Gamzatov (1999) reviews the full range of Pushkin's poems set in or in some way invoking the Caucasus.

12. Layton builds on the portrait of Pushkin offered in Belinskii ([1844] 1955). The same point is echoed in the opening lines of Hokanson (1994). As Belinskii wrote, "The grandiose image of the Caucasus, with its warlike inhabitants, for the first time was reproduced by Russian poetry— and only in Pushkin's narrative poem for the first time was Russian society acquainted with the Caucasus, already known in Russia by arms" (([1884] 1955) in Hokanson 1994, 341).

pursuing an explicit policy of social destabilization to disrupt internal clan and political alliances so that, as the new overseers, they might stand out as the only stable actor (Bournoutian 1994; Swietochowski 1995).[13] Kidnappings were among the tools to this end, ones that came with long genealogies in Caucasus rules of engagement and that would become increasingly familiar over time to Russian reading audiences.

Myth and Gift in Russian Retellings

Following the logic suggested in earlier chapters, that captives, for Caucasians, were part of a broader cosmological framing that made them both boundary markers and status makers—"good to think," in the Lévi-Straussian sense (1963)—Russian audiences soon seemed to agree. But the story proved in need of some fixing. Many readers objected to Pushkin's conclusion that allowed the Circassian woman to drown while praising Russian military glory—this kind of patriotism suggested stark limits to the empire's benevolence toward its new constituents. As a result, within only six months of the poem's printing, a more politically agreeable version was produced at the Petersburg Imperial Ballet, choreographed by the French artist Didelot with music by Cavos. The ballet was a remarkable first step in the transformation of Pushkin's tale for new audiences. This time Circassians are the aggressors, and Russian troops take up arms only in their efforts to free their compatriot. The Circassian woman ably swims to shore with her beloved, the two are joined in holy matrimony, and her Circassian khans take pains to pledge allegiance to the Russian crown publicly.[14] It was a story of Russian might, in one sense, but one that hinged on an early example of kinship through conquest so common across Russian alliances, recalling the military aphorism, *stat' bratom zavoevannomu*, in becoming a brother to the conquered.

---

13. In the postsocialist context, see Nazpary for a similar argument about "chaotic modes of domination" (2002).

14. Some have suggested that Didelot's work was a success precisely because the choreographer did not know Russian and therefore felt freer to interpret the work to earn the favor of imperial patrons. For his part, Pushkin continued to express his amazement at the mass interest in what he considered one of his least thoughtful works (Tarasenko 1938, 51). For more on the 1823 Petersburg production, see Asaf'ev (1949); Bogdanov-Berezovskii (1949); and Slonimskii (1938). For later 1827 performances in Moscow, see Anonymous (1827) and Grosheva and Il'in (1949).

Not all later renditions of the prisoner cycle adopted this happy ending (uncommon for late nineteenth-century Russia),[15] yet the new ballet
story captured public consciousness in a way that soon had nearly everyone trying his hand at the genre.[16] Throughout the 1830s and 1840s, well-
documented kidnappings continued in full force.[17] In a handful of equally
well-publicized instances, Russian readers took note of bodies—almost
always those of children found in the wake of Russian assaults—taken to
Moscow or Petersburg for transformation. Their experiences directly recall what historian Rustem Shukurov described as one of the fundamental
principles of imperial rule, the *nauchenie,* or raising of subordinate peoples
to civilized heights through instruction (" 'Kavkazskii nerv' " 2000, 19). For
all the urgency of religious conversion and Russian rules of order, what
constituted Russian publics themselves was being challenged by these new
kin alliances across borders.

A number of Petersburg memoirs from the first half of the nineteenth
century recount such stories, which followed a remarkably consistent se-
quence of thematic elements: capture, baptism, popular attention, exceptional promise, and early death. Perhaps the most extraordinary of this
genre is the story of a young Turkish boy taken by a Russian general from
a rubbish heap and given to his friend Durnov for raising. The boy leads
an exemplary life and is ready for baptism at age fifteen. Eager himself for
the rite of entry into the Russian Orthodox faith, the boy requests that he
be granted a month of strict privacy in his room, a ladder, and some paints.
At the end of the month, his room reveals a stunning mural of gilt angels.
The community sees the young Durnov's artwork as a sign of deep Christian
divinity and entertains him as a future church leader. But the morning
following his baptism, he is found dead in his room, hands folded over his

---

15. Tsivian (1991) explores the tensions early Russian film directors had to face in generating at least two endings to feature films: one for domestic Russian audiences, in which the main
characters all died, and a second for European export, in which everyone lived happily ever after.

16. Kudriashev wrote "Kirgizskii plennik" in 1826; Murav'ev produced his own poem of the
same title two years later, and Stankevich and Mel'gunov offered "Kalmytskii plennik" in 1832,
to suggest only three examples. One reviewer said of Murav'ev's "Kirgizskii plennik" (1828), "We
have a Caucasus Prisoner, so naturally a Kirghiz one was needed next.... What a passion for imi-
tation!" (Anonymous 1828, 170). For a full list of the over two hundred poems that were produced
on the prisoner theme after Pushkin, see Trubitsyn (1912, 483, 502–504) and Zhirmunskii (1924,
213–228). Brooks (1985) and Zorkaia (1994) offer a sense of the wide range along the theme.

17. See, for example, Ekel'n (1841); Karpeev (2000); Klinger (1860); Tsvizhba (2000); and
Zagorskii (1898).

chest (Leibov 2000). By this account, a young Turk from the Second Rome (rescued from rubbish) is given refuge in the realm of the Third Rome and is given the gift of civilization in the form of Christianity. The boy leads an uneventful life until the moment when he can most fully actualize that Christian devotion. Once he has demonstrated this complete transformation to his Russian patron, most fully recognizing the gift itself, he dies.

However much such memoirs took liberties, they found resonance in the more widely known literary works with which they were in conversation. But like any fictional account that has the power to render in print that which would not be otherwise as easily entertained, poetry and prose offered elegant ways to express some of the ambivalence that Russian elites felt about the blood being sacrificed for the pacification of the south. Lermontov's youthful Caucasus works are often compared to Pushkin's, most often for their subject matter if not for the almost direct reproduction of many of Pushkin's lines. In Lermontov's "Prisoner of the Caucasus," a young Russian appears on the threshold of a Circassian village in a near death state, bloodied and bound. He awakes to find himself in shackles, surrounded by Russian comrades who share his new fate, watching their chains rust as they tend the livestock of their captors. The unnamed youth has his own Promethean moment.

> There it is my captive watches:
> How sometimes the eagle flies,
> Stretching his wings across the wind,
> Spotting victims amidst the brush,
> Claws are enough for the feathered friend—and suddenly
> The victims are borne aloft with a cry...
> ...So! He thought, I am that sacrifice
> held captive as its food.
>
> (1948, 186)

As in Pushkin, a besotted maiden appears one night in the darkness.

> He sees before him suddenly:
> The young Circassian girl!
> And with a caring hand extending him
> Her own bread and cool drink.
>
> (189)

Night after night the two meet, until finally she admits her love for the young man who she knows is committed to another and proclaims her willingness to leave with him forever. Despite knowing she is spurned, she uses a saw to release his chains, and the lovers flee along a path. Before they make it to the river, a bullet from the gun of her father fells the Russian prisoner. The Circassian maiden, having fainted, awakes to find her lover dead and soon surrenders herself to the consuming waves of the Terek. As some scholars of the captivity narrative observe, the genre facilitates captivity as a form of exchange, but as we find so often in the Caucasus oeuvre, love is troubled, exchange is remarkably utilitarian, and the vectors of power are rarely challenged. Tales come to an end, and the Caucasus hero almost always expires once his or her central function—the recognition of Russian goodness—is accomplished.

As Propp (1968) and many others long ago showed, archetypes can be reinforced even when (and often because) they are expressly challenged. Consider Lermontov's later poem "Mtsyri," written in 1839. Here Lermontov renders his ambivalence to heavily sleighted exchange clearly in the tale of a young Georgian boy, like the real-life Turk above, who is retrieved after an assault.

> A Russian general one day
> Through mountains slowly made his way.
> He had a captive boy with him;
> The child fell ill; too small and slim
> He was to travel, ride, or drive;
> The boy was six or even five,
> Shy as the mountain chamois's breed.

> (1983, 313)

The boy grows up to be a man in the company of the Russians who saved him and goes on to become a monk ("Baptized, he lived like a recluse, / Life was for him of little use" (313)), but he never ceases his eastward glances. On his early deathbed, he concedes to his Russian elder that he never ceased to yearn for his life of freedom, excitement, and the lushness of the hills.

> Two lives like mine I'd give with joy
> For one and even shorter life,
> If it were only filled with strife.

I knew one passion's might surge,
A single but consuming urge…
To seek the world of rock and cloud,
The world of men, like eagles, proud.
This urge would torture me and rend,
But I have fed it to the end.

(315)

In the alien land that gave much to reform him, the young man dies a "wretched, orphaned slave" (317).[18] Ultimately, with the young man offering only the partial recognition incumbent upon him for having received the gift of patronage, Lermontov pronounces his an unhappy death. The limits of Russian giving have emerged again.

Pushkin and Lermontov continue to garner the lion's share of attention for Russia's literary romance of the Caucasus, but it might be noted again that their works circulated alongside the dozens of other authors who were read for the same stories of rapture and grief. In the 1830s, for example, a young Aleksandr Bestuzhev, once the editor of Petersburg's refined literary journal *Poliarnaia zvezda* (The Polar Star) and later exiled to Siberia and the Caucasus for his participation in the Decembrist revolt of 1825, assumed the pseudonym Marlinskii when he began publishing tales of mountain adventure. He soon found himself competing with Pushkin and Lermontov in readerships.[19] It is no surprise that Marlinskii's oeuvre included "The Story of an Officer Held Captive," the tale of a Russian officer shuttled from village to village among Avars. This soldier, like Marlinskii himself, gets by with limited knowledge of eastern Caucasus languages. Once captured, he is admired knowingly by Avar women and held by rough Avar men who seek glory in his banditry as much as good business in the captive trade. "In general we Europeans never understand these primitive tribes," Marlinskii's soldier reasons in lands where banditry rules not for the pursuit of sheer violence but because "bread isn't found easily among the rocks" (1892, 20–21). In logics of sovereignty where the privilege of individual persons has always been the standard

---

18. Lotman (1985) elaborates this theme when he remarks that in the later Lermontov, the East is not capable of change.

19. Bagby (1995b, 271) judges him "the most popular writer of prose fiction in the 1830s."

by which freedom or captivity is measured, Marlinskii tellingly speaks of Caucasus rules of "the body as citadel" (*krepost' tela*) (21). As an educated interloper, the young soldier's advice is sought on multiple fronts, and he is even invited to help resolve disputes along with village leaders. But Avar admiration for all things Russian had its limits. "When I told them that our [Russian] land was rich and fertile, they objected, 'Then why do you covet our bare rocks and poverty?'" (33). Some Russian readers asked the same question along with them.

Marlinskii's success was such that young men signed up by the hundreds to serve in the war that had been unfolding for decades; many spoke in "Marlinisms," the elaborate, purple rhetorics that the author favored in his works. Marlinskii himself died at the age of forty at Cape Adler on the Crimea, in a skirmish with Circassians who left him cut to pieces on a hillside (Sheliga-Pototskii 1848). Yet in death as in life, his capacity to inspire legend was undiminished: many speculated that he continued to live in the hills, had finally gone over to the other side and was advising Imam Shamil, and had found love with the Circassian maiden of Russian dreams (Sakharov 1994).

As this brief discussion of some of the better-known works of this era shows, for all the ambivalence wrought by authors, the invitation to critical reflection over the empire's role in the south, as refracted through Petersburg censors, was a complex one.[20] The political and social allegiances held by Marlinskii may have been among the more sensationally divided of the authors under study so far, but a recent elegy to his life and work leaves little doubt as to his capacities for sacrifice. In the eyes of Vsevolod Sakharov (1994), Marlinskii was "The Guardsmen's Prometheus."[21] That is to say, he descended from the heights of Russian society, became one with Russian soldier and Daghestani trader alike, and gave to the people.

While romantic authors cast the Caucasus as a place where men of passion forged character, the intractability and sheer duration of the Caucasus war wore thin on a telling number of critics of the tsarist policy. As the

---

20. While I focus here on a limited number of well-known standards, it should be noted that Layton's work on Polezhaev (1999) and Druzhinin (2001), as well as Ram's (2003) analysis of both Derzhavin and Griboedov, goes a good way toward advancing this point.

21. For more on the life and work of Bestuzhev-Marlinskii, see Bagby (1995a, 1995b); Kosven (1961, 158–158); Layton (1992b, 1994, chap. 7); Leighton (1975); and Zamotin (1913, chap. 3).

early socialist thinker Alexander Herzen wrote of the reign of Nicholas I (r. 1825–1855), "His dismal rule has continued for twenty-seven years. A typical example of his deeds is the Caucasus War, which engulfed entire armies" (Bondarevskii and Kolbaia 2002, 13).

As the Russian intelligentsia gained a more nuanced understanding of the multiple registers of human cost, yet another talented young writer, Lev Tolstoy, entered the Caucasus forces in 1851 at the age of twenty-three.[22] Like Pushkin, Lermontov, Griboedov, Marlinskii, Derzhavin, and Polezhaev before him, Tolstoy saw the Caucasus as a formative ground for both his art and his political views. His most critically acclaimed Caucasus work, *Hadji Murat* (2003), published only following his death, is often cited for the deep disapproval he felt for the Russian presence in the region (Friedrich 2003; Layton 1994, 1997b). Fictionalizing the real-life story of an Avar noble who began to cooperate with the Russian army in 1851, Tolstoy captured the vanities of a detached Russian command alongside a deeply divided Caucasus populace, tired of war but by no means in favor of Russian rule. The work deservedly stands out for a stark portrait of how indifferent even those who cooperated with the Russian army proved to the empire.[23]

Tolstoy's is ethnographically a more earnest work than much of what Russian readers had seen before. Though he lacked the more extensive personal experience in the Caucasus of Marlinskii, he had served in the military regiments in the Caucasus and had spent much time with the extant historical and anthropological literatures on the region as he worked on the novel (Sergeenko 1983). In the work, Hadji Murat himself leaves little doubt as to the nature of cultural exchange on the Caucasus frontier:

> "We have a proverb," said Hadji Murat to the interpreter. "The dog gave meat to the ass, and the ass gave hay to the dog, and both went hungry," and he smiled. "Its own customs seem good to each nation." (2003, 117)

That is to say, exchange might take place, but exchange does not guarantee mutual understanding or solidarity. In the opening and closing sequences of the novel, the character of Hadji Murat is tellingly symbolized

---

22. He became a commissioned officer in 1854.
23. See also Zhemukhov's study of Khan-Girei in this context (1997).

by a thistle, to be plucked or mowed down, underscoring that he is never quite a full acting partner. At the outset, the narrator pauses over how much energy is spent on the plucking of the crimson shoot, "which in our neighborhood they call 'Tartar,'" a term used in Russian as in other languages to broadly describe a person of east Asian descent but more commonly in Russia of the eighteenth and nineteenth centuries to suggest anyone from the Caucasus. The narrator reflects on how, once plucked, the flower will die, even though it has defended itself with its thorns. "But what energy and tenacity! With what determination it defended itself, and how dearly it sold its life!" He adds, "Man has conquered everything, and destroyed millions of plants, but this one won't submit" (4, 5). At the close of the novel, punished by Shamil for his cooperation with the Russians, Hadji Murat flees from Russian house arrest near the palace of the khan in Sheki, is felled by the bullet of a Russian guard, and falls dead, "like a thistle that had been mown down." (149). Like my Sheki host in 1999 who demanded to know just who had been civilizing whom in the encounters between Russia and the Caucasus, Tolstoy's novel posed a similar question. It was likely for this very reason that the work was initially banned, not appearing until 1912, two years after Tolstoy's death.[24]

Yet while *Hadji Murat* entered Russian popular circles some years after the formal end to the Caucasus war, on the eve of World War I and in the twilight of tsarist rule, Tolstoy's own "Prisoner of the Caucasus," perhaps the best-known prose rendition of the cycle, penned decades earlier over a two-week period in 1872, had a much broader impact precisely because it was intended for and found a successful home in children's schoolbooks. In this iteration, Tolstoy gives the captive a name, Zhilin, and offers a few short paragraphs at the outset to establish a frame for captivity: Zhilin's elderly mother beckons him home to visit her in her final days and pledges that she has found a girl for him to marry. Tolstoy borrows the cause for capture from the dozens of fictional and real-life kidnappings that preceded him: the impatience of Zhilin and his fellow traveler, Kostylin, to get on their way, free of the cumbersome pace of their sizable Cossack contingent. Here the men's captors—Chechens? Azeris? Avars?—are again

24. A wide variety sources written by Caucasians pursue the ambiguities in Hadji-Murat's cooperation with Russian officials much further. See Alikhanov (2005, chap. 11); Gadzhiev (2005); Khaibulaev (2002); and Takho-Godi (1927). I thank Rebecca Gould for sharing these texts.

simply "Tatars," the loose umbrella designation that allowed for more humanity than *gortsy* but effectively placed all of Russia's (then) 5 million Muslim residents under one identity. The two prisoners are traded as part of a debt negotiation to Abdul-Murat, father of the thirteen-year-old Dina. Abdul-Murat instructs both men to write letters to procure their ransom and agrees to treat them well while the letters find their destinations. He does so until Zhilin leads an escape attempt, and their fates worsen. Outside the fray of these pivotal struggles, the young Dina is enchanted with a series of dolls that Zhilin crafts to knowingly win her favor, and soon she is bringing him food under cover of night. Prior to his first escape, in fact, Zhilin wins over an impressive number of villagers with his craftsmanship and canny ability to curry favor for the purposes of his release.

To each their own customs, as Tolstoy would later suggest in the tale of the ass and the dog. Zhilin is loyal to Kostylin long enough to support him during their first attempt at escape, loyal enough to allow himself to be captured again rather than desert a comrade. For his part, Abdul-Murat keeps his word in this desperate encounter, releasing the more retiring Kostylin when his sizable ransom arrives because he gave his word. Zhilin, who wanted no part of the bargain to begin with, had sent his letter to a false address and has escaped by this time on his own with Kostylin's blessing, as well as with the help of the young Dina, who brings him a pole to vault out of the deep pit and weeps at his departure (1977).

Tolstoy's "Prisoner of the Caucasus" was first published in the journal *Zaria* in 1872 but soon began to reach its widest audience in generations of children's readers after its release as part of the fourth volume of Tolstoy's *Azbuka* (Primer) that same year. In just under four decades between the story's release and Tolstoy's death, the primer had sold over 2 million copies and was distributed across the empire (Moores 1992, 29). Soviet critics would later read the story's ambiguities as proof of the failed colonizing mission in the South, thus guaranteeing an enduring readership across the twentieth century.

These ambiguities are very much at the heart of a passage from gift of empire in Dostoyevsky to the kinds of binding offerings suggested in Tolstoy, presenting quandaries for both Russian givers and Caucasian receivers. Yet this distinction between gifts of empire and the more ambiguous gifts of later narrative offerings does not mean that the two could not exist side by side. As one schoolteacher remarked in an assessment of the relevance of Tolstoy's "Prisoner of the Caucasus" to Russian schoolchildren after the fall of the USSR, "It is very Russian and indeed, very Christian, that the captive finds love and pure hearts around him" (Kurbatov 1999, 38). In her view, the captive finds recognition of his innate goodness—a Russian goodness and a Christian goodness—even in a time of war.

What labor might the idea of the prisoner or captive perform across these examples and among their many readers? Although some consider the Russian *plennik* to be taken from the Latin word *pellis* (fur or skin), the word is more commonly traced to the Old Church Slavonic *plen,* a term with a wide range of meanings: plunder, spoils, trade good, harvest, or profit (Fasmer 1971, 314–315).[25] Of course not all captives are held for ransom: they might be killed, sold, absorbed into their new communities, or lost in escape. But this etymology is suggestive in its invocation of an exchange of bodies both real and imagined.

This leads back to the notion of negative pleasures and their negative capabilities. What is perhaps most striking about the use of the term *plennik* is that in story after story, captivity is willingly given. Although certain tales such as "Prisoner of the Caucasus" simply assume circumstances of captivity (eschewing any explanation of how the prisoner came to be captured or why), the many references to captivity throughout Pushkin would seem to have occurred by romantic volition (Vinogradov 1929). As Vladimir Propp (1968) might have it, such circumstances are necessary to get any myth off the ground; the transgression of the protagonist casts him from home and leaves him to wander in alien lands. Yet we might ask all the same, why this particular mythopoeisis? Rather than looking at this narrative in terms of displacement, we should ask, what kinds of emplacements are effected?

The prisoner stories are about encounters—deeply unequal exchanges of cosmology, arms, bodies, and emotions in which Chechens, Circassians, Azeris, and other Caucasian peoples are always spoken for but, quite literally, rarely speaking. Some Caucasian peoples managed these encounters more smoothly than others: ample historical records suggest that the

---

25. The noun and adjective forms *plennik* and *plennyi* used almost exclusively in this cycle from Pushkin onward are closer to "captive" than "prisoner." I alternate between the two to avoid repetition. The Russian *zakliuchennyi,* denoting someone who is assigned to a fixed term of confinement for an offense under the law, is the conventional term for "prisoner."

perceived commonality of Christianity made it easier for Armenians and Georgians to navigate the new corridors of Russian administration. Responses in the predominantly Muslim regions, by contrast, ranged from the resigned consent of Azeris to the more active resistance of most Chechens. But the collective Caucasian *froideur* to Russian governance was perhaps the coldest of any Petersburg had encountered. In this context, the aestheticized giving over of the archetypal Russian prisoner into Caucasian hands was surely one of the more popular and influential ways of narrating the benevolent goodwill of the Russian crown.

Pushkin's impact, particularly on elites of his day, was considerable given the high degree of print censorship that controlled popular perception of the Russian presence in the South. Layton observed, "Russian readers knew vaguely of warfare occurring in the Caucasus, but for most of them young Pushkin provided the first specific evocation of tsarist armies in combat against the tribes" (1994, 32). Likewise one cannot underestimate his impact on the less educated publics across Russia who were the driving market for *listy* and *lubki,* the penny press sheets of poetry that circulated widely. As Mel'ts (2000) has shown, these brief but enormously popular extracts from the works of Pushkin and many others sold by the thousands, beginning with wood prints and later in lithograph form. It is striking, however, that Mel'ts found no evidence that a single *lubok* carried Pushkin's name until the 1880s. In the same loose context, there were a number of evidently intentional misprints in order to simplify language for the widest readership. As we saw with the 1823 ballet, such freedom known long before the days of copyright could take the very plastic prisoner into a wide variety of arenas.

The Art of Self-Giving

Prometheus most likely would not have chosen to spend thirty thousand years chained to a rock at the top of a mountain, but he was not only a selfless giver but also a foreteller of the future. When we recall that his name translates as "he who knows beforehand," we can establish that Prometheus knew that his punishment for giving fire to mankind would be a long and painful one, but he gave of himself for this greater cause. In this spirit, the well-known Russian semiotician Iurii Lotman suggests that self-surrender, or what he calls "self-giving," has long-standing roots in the Russian political arts. In the expressly unequal relations between profane supplicants and divine sovereigns, seemingly one-sided rhetorical gifts are offered upwards, as if unconditionally. In this way, the seemingly unconditional gift *places* the giver in a fresh state of social relations. Taking the example of one thirteenth-century Russian work, "Daniel the Prisoner," Lotman recalls how one early Russian captive curries favor with his more powerful warden and talks his way out of captivity through self-abnegation. Daniel was said to have told his captor: "You may say [to me], oh Prince [that I] have lied like a dog. But princes and noblemen love a good dog" (1984, 130). Seeing these early wiles transformed in the eighteenth and nineteenth centuries, Lotman notes that even the tsars themselves were known to engage in their own sleights of power—playing the underdog, as it were. He writes,

> It is typical that although everyone knew that Russia was an autocracy, and that to [understand] this was...[both] official ideology...[and] practical government, it was considered a breach of taste to acknowledge it as fact....Alexander I [who had exiled Pushkin to the Caucasus] would repeatedly stress that autocracy was an unfortunate necessity that he personally did not favor. (1984, 136)

The phenomenon of willingly rendering oneself captive perhaps reaches its apogee in Andrei Bitov's 1969 *Captive of the Caucasus,* one of the handfuls of instances where little more than the title and captive symbol are borrowed. In his series of short travel stories in Armenia, Bitov finds ready ground for romantic projection, describing the republic as a

> land where everything was what it was: a stone was a stone, a tree was a tree, water was water, light was light, an animal was an animal, and a person was a person....Where all the stones, herbs, and creatures had their own corresponding purposes and essences [and] where primordial meanings would be restored to all concepts....I found the word *authentic* and settled on it. I talked with a man who was a man and talked like a man. He and I ate food that was food and drank wine that was wine. ([1969] 1992, 63, original emphasis)

In this travel memoir, Bitov falls in love with a non-Russian-speaking Armenian woman, so alien to him in her beauty that he names her Aelita after the interplanetary goddess of the famous science fiction novel and cinema classic *Aelita Queen of Mars*.[26] As a houseguest, he begins to put himself in her possession.

> I was a kind of furniture. The children didn't see me because they were absorbed in Aelita; Aelita didn't see me because of her nature; my friend's wife tried to keep out of sight as much as possible, perhaps because she had absolutely no idea how to occupy me. So I sat, and suddenly discovered that, like the children, I was already used to Aelita, the way furniture is used to its owner. (78)

Finally he rhapsodizes,

> I'm locked up. I'm in a cage. Every day they transfer me from cell to cell. The diet is good; they don't beat me. I don't know how long I've been here. The sentence should come soon. I don't know if I'll see you, my darling... I'm in a cage—everybody's looking at me. No. They're the ones looking at me from inside a cage! I'm the one on the outside! I've tricked them all!... I'm... a captive of the Caucasus. (90)

In this most extreme example of self-giving, Bitov, casting himself as yet another prisoner-trickster, makes a place for himself in a primordial world.[27] He is in love with Aelita, yet he never openly tries to seduce her. He is the epitome of the good Russian prisoner—at home while abroad.

These sleights of power were lampooned in the 1966 motion picture *Kavkazskaia plennitsa* (*Girl Prisoner of the Caucasus*) directed by Leonid Gaidai, a musical comedy of near-cult status and the source for dozens of lines committed to heart by millions of viewers.[28] In this version, the male

---

26. The story by Aleksei Tolstoy ([1923] 1985) was made into a film in 1924 by the early Soviet director Iakov Protazanov.

27. Bitov's final reflection—"What would I have understood, what would I have seen, if I hadn't been in the cage with the parakeets and grasped the fact that in addition to my time there was a *different* time—theirs?" ([1969] 1992, 91, original emphasis)—evinces the familiar distancing mechanism of allochronism, "the time of the other," analyzed so thoroughly by Fabian (1983). In this rendition, the mythically charged Armenians, for all their collective virtues, manly men, and seductive women, do not occupy the same time/space coordinates as the historically driven Russians. They are cast as "cold societies," to borrow the terms of Lévi-Strauss (1976, 29–30), in contrast to the pell-mell of faster-moving Russian society (Grant 1993).

28. Goscilo cites 76 million cinema tickets sold (2003, 197).

Figure 6. Natal'ia Varlei as Nina and Aleksandr Demianenko as Shurik in Leonid Gaidai's 1966 blockbuster, *Girl Prisoner of the Caucasus*. Courtesy of Mosfil'm.

Russian hero is the hapless bottle-blond anthropologist Shurik, who tells the story of one of his expeditions to study toasting rituals in "a mountainous region." Shurik is so cheerfully inept that he attempts to start his donkey as he would a car and is so easy to intoxicate, despite fervent protest that he does not drink, that he is eventually held against his will at the local detox center after breaking up a ceremony at the Palace of Weddings by drunkenly demanding that everyone speak more slowly so that he can get it all down in his field notes. He is soon in love with the comely Nina: student, Communist Youth League member, and sportswoman. In a plot so cartoonish that one recalls the cycle of Donald Duck films made by the U.S. State Department in the 1940s to improve trade relations with Latin America (Burton 1992; Dorfman and Mattelart 1975), three Caucasian stooge gangsters see their opportunity to kidnap Nina for marriage to a local official.[29]

Playing on Shurik's ethnographic obsessions, they persuade him that bride kidnapping is a vital, time-honored tradition and that Nina herself

---

29. See Prokhorov (2003) for an excellent discussion of the cult status of Gaidai's "Three Stooges"—Vitsin, Nikulin, and Morgunov, known collectively among fans as the troika ViNi-Mor. Volkov (2003) takes up the same theme. The literary scenario for the film can be found in Kostiukovskii et al. (1998).

will only symbolically protest as they carry her away. Heartbroken that Nina has seemingly chosen someone else, Shurik wistfully waves her good-bye as she is bundled off in her sleeping bag on an overnight camping trip. In a telling inversion of just who has the agency in the entire prisoner cycle, upon realizing what has happened, Shurik vows, "I'm the one who stole her, I'll get her back!" Meanwhile, Nina the sportswoman, a far cry from the archetype of backward women of the Caucasus and central Asia whom Soviet planners labored so intensively to emancipate in the 1920s and 1930s, is well able to liberate herself, despite Shurik's own valiant (albeit less effective) male attempts.[30] Before the couple ride their donkey off into the sunset, the three gangsters are brought before a Soviet tribunal to shame them for their backward patriarchal behavior.

In *Girl Prisoner of the Caucasus,* as elsewhere, the specifics of who the Caucasian protagonists really are or where the story takes place is left to the imagination. The film's opening voiceover pledges an ecumenical approach: "Shurik insists that this story really happened in one of the mountain regions. He didn't say *which* region, so as not to be unfair to all the other regions where just such a story might also have happened." Evidently not all viewers succumbed to Gaidai's efforts, as Georgian officials refused for months to release the film to audiences on grounds of national insult (Mamedov 1999, 108).[31] Nonetheless, the film's flexibility with well-entrenched Soviet archetypes worked to significant advantage. As Vladimir Etush, who played the character of Comrade Saakhov, noted in an interview, the Armenians liked to think he was playing a Georgian, and the Georgians liked to think he was playing an Azerbaijani. "Everyone liked it when they thought I was making fun of their neighbor."[32] In the

---

30. For Caucasus plotlines, Nina's prowess—despite the fact that her character was played by a Russian actress—was a remarkable step up from the dozens of other characters who had peopled Russian language cinema of the Caucasus, where Caucasians could frequently act as heroes but heroes ensnared by a frequent inability to control their passions (Mamedov 1999).

31. By stark contrast, Vakhitov (2004) suggests that the figure of Saakhov, the regional bureaucrat and would-be groom who is punished in a Soviet court of law at the close of the film, reflected the rise of provincial nationalist movements across the USSR under Khrushchev, movements that ultimately brought down the Soviet Union and that should be forbidden in an imagined, future, re-Sovietized Russian Republic. Michaels (2004) offers particular attention to the film in the context of Soviet nationality relations.

32. Etush's commentary from the 2001 DVD release of *Kavkazskaia plennitsa,* released in English as *Kidnapping Caucasian Style* (Moscow: Russian Cinema Council). Likewise, the character

tradition established by Pushkin, who glossed all the Caucasus as Circassian, and the more liberal Tolstoy, who called everyone a Tatar, the by then massive and scrupulous Soviet ethnographic corpus is sidestepped to striking advantage. By the late twentieth century, the more popular rendering becomes Chechen.[33]

In the more recent film rendition of the prisoner cycle, director Sergei Bodrov eschewed satire for a return to a grittier, if somewhat muffled, political critique of Tolstoy. The film is yet another example of how gifts extended in the later years of Russia's struggles in the Caucasus have been viewed in such a variety of competing ways. Filmed in Daghestan and set in another unnamed North Caucasus locale that unmistakably evokes the Chechen war of the early 1990s, a Russian soldier named Zhilin is now the only son of a single working mother schoolteacher in the Ural Mountains. Despite the often-brutal military setting, the theme of harmlessness and seemingly harmless sexuality begins from the very first scene, as dozens of nude Russian army recruits parade before their indifferent female medical examiners. Once in Caucasian captivity, Zhilin shows his quiet charms by fixing clocks for his captor's companions and making toy puppets for his (in this version) very young female warden. In a fitting turn for the subject at hand, the production's hired bodyguards took one of the French cameramen hostage to provoke salary renegotiations after learning that the film's twelve-year-old lead actress was receiving a greater pay packet than all of them together (Specter 1996).

One sign that the film is squarely intended for Russian audiences is the curious contradiction between the consistent flow of subtitles and the "mountain of tongues" shared by the actors playing Caucasian characters— the captor's daughter speaks to her father in Azeri, her father answers in Georgian, their kinsmen address them in Avar, and so forth.[34] Exchanges

---

of Nina's uncle, played by the Armenian actor Frunzik Mkrtchian, was given the traditionally Muslim name Dzhebrail. Moscow's Kavkazskaia Plennitsa Restaurant, as of 2002 when I had occasion to visit, sheared away this generality by billing itself as Georgian. Gaidai shot the film on location in the Russian Republic town of Adler, outside Sochi on the Crimean Peninsula. It is the same location where Bestuzhev-Marlinskii was felled by Circassian forces in 1837.

33. The film's themes are later echoed in the song of the same title by Tamara Gverdtiteli, "Kavkazskaia plennitsa," from the 1980s (Goscilo 2003, 198, 203–205). The song can be heard online at http://lyrics.mp3s.ru. I thank Serguei Oushakine for pointing me to Gverdtiteli's work.

34. Drawing an implicit line between the Russian/Christian and Caucasian/Muslim themes in the film, Bodrov, the director, eschewed certain parts of the final product in remarking,

Figure 7. Sergei Bodrov, Jr., as Zhilin in the 1996 Oscar-nominated *Prisoner of the Mountains.* Courtesy of Boris Giller Productions and MGM CLIPSTILL.

either fail or take place in rough coin. Early on Abdul Murat believes he has reached an agreement with the local Russian commander but is deceived. Later he and Zhilin's mother come to an understanding, but it is too late: Abdul Murat's son flees his Russian cell, while Zhilin and his fellow captive, Larin, kill their guard, Hasan, and make off into the night. The one Russian-Caucasian exchange in the film that does succeed is more telling: inside the Russian base, a soldier enters a store and asks for two bottles of vodka. As though burdening the soldier, the shopkeeper asks for money and receives a revolver in return. "Keep the change," the soldier says. The same gun will later be sold to Abdul Murat.[35]

Vectors of gender and power in the film are flipped at key junctures. After a mountain elder takes the Russian soldier captive in order to bargain for the return of his son from a Russian military prison, the male Russian commander "lacks the nerve to make the exchange."[36] Both men decide to summon the soldier's mother. The Russian commander admits

---

"[Co-screenwriter] Arif Aliev is a Muslim. He had good ideas, and he's responsible for the magical-realist scenes that are personally not my cup of tea" (Von Busack 1997).

35. The flow of ammunition between sides is a central theme of the later film *Blokpost* (dir. Alexander Rogozhkin, 1998), explicitly set in Chechnya.

36. For the liner notes from the film, see "Plot Summary for Kavkazskij plennik (1996)," International Movie Data Base, online at http://us.imdb.com/Plot?0116754. It is not the first time

to her that the pathos (and anger) of a mother's physical presence is needed to accomplish such illicit trade in wartime.[37] And once again it is a young girl—the captor's now twelve-year-old daughter with whom Zhilin has platonic but affectionate ties—who finally sets the strapping soldier free.[38]

For all the gracious humility of the Russian soldier in this variant, again the nameless Caucasians meet their by now expected end. As the unshackled Zhilin meets freedom while crossing onto an open plain, helicopters (making a nod to the Ride of the Valkyries in *Apocalypse Now*) fly overhead to bomb the village where the soldier was being held. Almost wistful about the corpses left in his wake, the soldier remarks in a voiceover, "I always wish for them to come to me in my dreams—these people that I loved, these people I [know I] will never see again. But they just don't come." Still another exchange fails to take place. Despite the film's ominous conclusion—and the real-life war going on as it was filmed—the director has often explained his work as a peace film, preferring to look at love rather than helicopters (Gillespie 1999). The film has nothing to say about Russian policy in Chechnya as good or bad.[39]

Although the chilly reception found by Russians in the Caucasus from the early 1800s to the present day suggests that the Russian civilizing mission has yet to win over all its disparate non-Russian publics, we might also recall Eisenstein's insight that Pushkin's characters were flat, not rounded, more like signs that could take on new signifiers and signifieds in each retelling (Stewart 1991). Even in the few instances when the prisoner myth is used to actively question Russian interventions in the Caucasus, the arts

---

that Zhilin's mother will have saved him, as the screen version, in an addition to Tolstoy, suggests in a scene where he recounts how his mother retrieved him from a fall into a well.

37. For an excellent analysis of the role of the mothers of Chechen soldiers and the broader resonances of this movement across Russian society, see Oushakine (2009).

38. In both Tolstoy (with ransom negotiations) and Bodrov (with boxing), Zhilin's efforts to appear as manly as possible are met with laughter by his Caucasian holders. Whereas Tolstoy portrayed Zhilin as the more active of the two captives, the Bodrov version has Zhilin taking the female role as both men dance to the Louis Armstrong classic "Go Down Moses" ("Let My People Go").

39. Burdens of responsibility shift when comparing Tolstoy and Bodrov. Tolstoy's short story suggests that although war is bad, soldiers themselves are inherently good. Thus Abdul Murat insists to Zhilin that neither of them is fundamentally at fault, "You Ivan—good! Me Abdul—good!" (1977, 126, 129). Bodrov inverted this formula when he commented in an interview, "Nationalists have said I was blaming Russia for the conflict in Chechnya. I said, no, I'm Russian. I don't blame Russia; I blame soldiers" (Von Busack 1997).

of emplacement are strikingly consistent—relying on sleights of history, sleights of power, and sleights of exchange. The resounding silence of the Caucasian highlanders, for example, persists even in the openly antiwar prisoner short story by Vladimir Makanin (1995), published in the same year that Bodrov's film was made. On this battlefield, gender and its capacity for plot reversals are again at issue. The Russian army takes a handsome Caucasian soldier, and the Russian protagonist Rubakhin has to wrestle with his uncomfortable erotic longings for his silent captive.[40] Again the action comes to a close in water: carrying the Caucasian on his back in a routine river crossing, Rubakhin and his company become targets for distant sniper fire. Fearing for his life at the height of his own homosexual panic (set off by what is later revealed to be friendly fire), Rubakhin strangles and drowns the object of his affections. Unable to stop dreaming of the Caucasian whose life he has taken, the Russian soldier asks himself with annoyance, "What's so interesting about these mountains?" The story's narrator Makanin concludes, "[The soldier] wanted to add, 'How many years now!' But instead he said, 'How many centuries now!' " (1995, 19). This is a savvy ending for Makanin and perhaps the most openly restless of all works in the prisoner cycle. But once again the myth is loosest on the range of appeal of its own arts of emplacement: while the Russian foregrounds his own inner torment, it is the Caucasian who almost always dies in the end.

---

40. In a key comment on Makanin's story, Goscilo observes, "Homoeroticism, while fully acknowledged, serves as a device of estrangement to destabilize timeworn perspectives on the Caucasian theme and recast them, rendering them more intricate. An 'X' rating is not Makanin's goal. Rather, he conceives of the Caucasus from a Russian viewpoint as a mystery tagged by an 'x' from a different semiotic system" (2003, 199).

6

Caucasian Reflections

I saw the Eagle descending from the sky, and prepared myself for the
unpleasant sensation of having a meal made of my entrails. I was getting
used to it, but even at the millionth time, it is not particularly nice. But that
morning, instead of attacking me at once, it was ashamed of its job, I think,
and never stopped to say Good-morning—it fluttered down beside me and
perched on a ledge, a few feet away to the left.
"Well," I said, "Won't you get it over?"
"Get what over?" it replied nonchalantly, scratching some sign in the snow
with its claws which looked to me rather like a five-pointed star.
"Why, your unpleasant custom, of course," I answered, thoroughly puzzled.
"Oh, that's off," it said dryly, "Jove's hooked it."
"Why, what do you mean?" I cried. I was getting excited by then,
I can assure you.
"Gone to Belgrade, they say, or it may be Paris. Who cares? There's
a new government."
"A new government! At last!"
"Call themselves Bolsheviks. They're sending a delegation to you in a few
days. I've got orders to bring you food until they come." It shook out its
wings and prepared to fly away again. "So long," it said as it took off. "And
call me comrade next time."

John Lehmann, *Prometheus and the Bolsheviks*

Struggles over sovereignty have long focused on the language of
bodies—real and imagined—because so much of the supremacy inherent
in sovereign forms comes in the exercise of power over human life itself,
between taking and protecting it (Agamben 1998; Foucault 1997; Hansen

and Stepputat 2006). Perhaps one of the reasons that the figure of Prometheus, one of the most famous captive bodies ever held in the Caucasus,
has served so many changing scenes of political rule in the Caucasus for
at least twenty-eight centuries is that firm stewardship in the Caucasus
region by would-be overseers was never entirely a done deal.

In honor of Prometheus's reputation as an enemy of autocratic rule,
a noble trickster who wrested from tyrants the means of production—
fire—in order to put it into the hands of the people, Karl Marx hailed the
mythical taker qua giver in his 1841 doctoral dissertation as "the noblest
saint and martyr in the philosophical calendar" (Ziolkowski 2000, 115).
And, as we see in the fantastical epigraph from British literary editor John
Lehmann above, based on his travels in Soviet Georgia, the USSR's new
beginning meant that this Prometheus, at last, might no longer need to suffer for his generosities. That symbol of Russian autocracy, the eagle, once
a tormentor, had turned into a comrade. By way of ancient mythology, the
Soviet Union, no longer extracting surplus value off the backs of its labor-
ing classes for the profit of the few had, via quite a different route from
that of its imperial predecessors, joined the fraternity of givers.

In his book *Thank You, Comrade Stalin!* (2000) Jeffrey Brooks tracks
how from the 1920s onward, Soviet officials established an economy of the
gift to assert that goods and services provided by the Soviet state operated
above and beyond the normal flow of economic activity. They were, in
effect, gifts for which the general population should be grateful. In what
Brooks describes as the "theft of agency" of average citizens, journalists
quickly set about expressing that gratitude in print with impressive regu-
larity (27). In this case, the taker acted instead as both giver and receiver.
Thus, for example, victory in World War II, in which 22 million Soviet citizens perished, extended an economy of the gift where such immense debts
owed by the people to their leader could effectively never be repaid.[1]

Brooks makes clear that the logic of the Stalinist gift was by no means
confined to exchange among Russians alone:

> In no area was the official discourse as rigid as in portrayals of Russian
> and non-Russian identities. In the evolution of Stalin's treatment of the

---

1. Ditchev (2002) offers a rougher version of the same argument. For an excellent study of
object-gifts presented to Stalin, see Ssorin-Chaikov (2006).

nationalities, the state's gift to non-Russian republics on the periphery became increasingly Russia's gift. To make other nationalities passive bene-
ficiaries of Russian achievement was to reverse the pre-1917 image of the
empire as a treasure trove from which Russia drew riches. This reversal
intensified in the late 1920s, when maps associated with the five-year plan
showed the periphery as the recipient of fruitful Soviet investment. (242)[2]

Where the nineteenth-century empire found few expressions of fulsome
gratitude among its adopted peoples, their socialist successors made sure
that such testimonials would be generated everywhere in print. Yet the Soviet Union did generate very real allegiances among many of its citizens,
who took pride in the enormous federation's values of fraternity, equality,
and collectivism.

Over the course of the Soviet period, peoples of the Caucasus met
widely different fates. In the most favorable light, republics such as Armenia found relative security from earlier hostile neighbors after centuries of
Ottoman and Persian domination. Across the Caucasus, agriculture continued to be a central economic force given the particularly rich cultiva-
tion of fruits, nuts, cotton, tobacco, and wine. Significant industrial centers
emerged, led by machine production, metallurgy, and oil and natural gas
industries, as well as chemical engineering, particularly in the areas of fer-
tilizers and plastics. Across the North Caucasus and Georgia, especially
along the Black Sea coast, tourism boomed. Nonetheless, although planners sought to reverse the imperial pattern of drawing on the Caucasus
solely as a supplier of raw materials, the region's consistently low economic
performance relative to the USSR's more northerly regions exacerbated
long-standing fault lines. Across the Caucasus many were uneasy about
their relationship to yet another set of distant governors. Each of the three
republics of the South Caucasus knew short periods of independence after
1917, while a Transcaucasian Federation briefly consolidated the diversely
configured peoples of the North Caucasus before being folded again into
the renovated political structures of the former empire.

---

2. Speaking more broadly of both the non-Russian republics and the satellite states of eastern
Europe, Brooks adds, "In stressing the Soviet Union's role as benefactor, journalists unwittingly
communicated the one-sidedness of this relationship. Convincing Russians that the foreign and
domestic empire was a drain on their resources, the press prepared the way for their lack of protest at its collapse, as well as psychological regret for lost glory" (2000, 243).

In the spirit of Shamil, armed rebellions against Soviet power were active throughout the 1920s and 1930s (Derluguian 2005; Grant 2004; Statiev 2005). In the most extreme cases, entire populations of Chechens, Ingush, and Crimean Tatars were deported overnight to the nether regions of central Asia and Siberia for their perceived support of invading German forces in World War II (Conquest 1960; Gammer 2006; Uehling 2004). By the early 1970s, with the Soviet Union reaping the benefits of rising oil prices, peoples of the Caucasus knew fewer of the privations in basic foodstuffs that had characterized the initial postwar years and enjoyed a general increase in standards of living. Urban centers such as Erevan, Baku, Tbilisi, Nal'chik, Maikop, and Krasnodar, among others, were demographically distinguished for their highly cultivated intelligentsias, however constrained they might have been in certain political arenas. Beyond politics, what remained to them, writes sociologist Georgi Derluguian,

> was jazz, yoga, the guitar ballads of Vysotsky and Okudjava, the films of Tarkovsky, Wajda, Bergman, and Fellini, the prose of Hemingway, Remarque, and Saint-Exupery, or perhaps the faded lithographs, copper jars, old daggers, and other such artifacts from the rapidly disappearing traditional life of their ancestors. (2005, 299)

Once in the hills of northwest Azerbaijan I offered a version of this portrait of Brezhnevite relief to a schoolteacher when we were talking about the post–World War II period across the region. "Had not the 1970s offered some respite from the privations and tumult of previous decades?" I asked. "Sure, we lived better then, better than now," he remarked. "But do you want me to say that, somehow, come 1970, we were grateful for being able to buy fish again in a seaside republic? For being able to know that I could go to a state store and find eggs?" He grimaced as if to ask whether I had any idea of how long that really meant. "It took fifty years!" And, of course, twenty years after that, upon the close of the USSR, restructuring began anew.[3]

This brief excursion through the Caucasus in the Soviet period is one significant way to narrate a modernizing if uneven advance of civilizational forms over the twentieth century. But there were also other, rather more

---

3. Interview, Sheki, July 2002.

hegemonic narratives about Caucasus life that circulated widely. These imaginary but powerful facts of Caucasus life were built by the inheritors of Pushkin's *Kavkazskii plennik* legacy—the poems, novels, ballets, operas, television dramas, and perhaps above all, the films that featured swaggering mountaineers, armed cavalries, burkas, and daggers. It was a world of fearsome warriors, calculating knaves, and just as often hapless innocents whose inability to conform to Soviet life good-naturedly taught millions of others how they could do better. It was a package that enabled urban Caucasians in turn to elevate themselves above their (often imagined) country neighbors (Manning 2007). The result was a dense, intertextual net flung over the region, one that remained essentially unrevised over the Soviet period, with Caucasians themselves most often in the role of silent partners.

What, then, have prominent Caucasus cultural actors written or said to respond to years of this very active Russian imagination? When it comes to written sources, the answers are, of course, not simple. While early Soviet historiography, as seen in earlier chapters, rushed to condemn tsarist rule, after World War II it became impolitic to suggest anything not openly supportive of Russian sovereignty in the Caucasus over the previous two hundred years. This means that in the dominant language of publication, we have comparatively little extant writing on how Caucasians came to reflect on Russian rule that is not either deeply Aesopian or, for example, in the case of the exiled leaders of the briefly independent Caucasus republics, highly polemic.[4]

Beyond Russian-language texts, the question of exactly what Armenian, Azeri, and Georgian leaders may have felt at the outset of concerted rule in the early 1800s is most often left to paleographers of Arabic, Persian, and

---

4. From 1925 to 1939, assorted anti-communist Caucasus leaders, including former diplomats, nationalist activists, and scholars operated shadow consulates and organized protest events across Paris, Warsaw, Prague, Istanbul, Bucharest, Rome, and Berlin. Suggesting no sign of abatement in Promethean-themed images of struggle against iron rule, the full name of the organization was the Promethean League of the Nations Subjugated by Moscow. It claimed responsibility for as many as 80 million citizens of the Soviet Union, speaking in the name of Karelians, Komi, Udmurts, Mordva, Mari, Ingrians, Ukrainians, Don Cossacks, Kuban' Cossacks, Georgians, assorted mountaineers of the North Caucasus, Azerbaijanis, Tatars, Turkmen, Tajiks, Kazakhs, Kirghiz, and Buryats. Administratively, it was dominated by Ukrainians, Georgians, and Azerbaijanis. Armenia was not part of the league given the organization's pro-Turkish orientation (Smal-Stocky 1947, 332). From 1926 to 1938, the league published its own monthly review out of Paris, *Prométhée*. It continued from 1938 to 1940 as *La Revue de Prométhée*.

Ottoman Turkish (in the case of earlier languages of rule in all three contemporary South Caucasus republics), as well as to scholars of early Armenian and Georgian and the relatively more recent (post-thirteenth-century) Azeri, as archives struggle to preserve long unattended non-Russian-language manuscripts. Some publications, such as the satirical journal *Molla Nesreddin,* published in Baku at the outset of the twentieth century, illustrate the episodic commentaries that could be communicated through the humor of Aesopian language. Only in recent years have a number of important new works exploring pivotal events in Caucasus history from the points of view of Caucasian actors begun to emerge (Duve and Tagliavini 2000; Eschment and Harder 2004; Karagezov 2005; Sanders, Tucker, and Hamburg 2004; Shnirel'man 2001, 2006). Meanwhile, anthropologists and historians at work on captivity narratives in the Americas and south Asia have offered, as have the previous chapters in this book, the parameters by which local knowledges about kidnapped bodies were alternatively established and circulated (Chatterjee 2008; Lepselter 2005; Strong 1999).

How then can we best learn of Caucasians' own perceptions of kinships created through conquest, through communism, and wrought anew after the fall of the USSR? This question is made more compelling if we appreciate the degree to which, at the level of the literate classes, the lives of those once regarded as sovereigns and subjects had long overlapped in regimes of education, privilege, and taste, as any number of postcolonial theorists have been demonstrating over the last twenty-five years. Thus, while many Caucasians may never have appreciated the structural condescension built into Russian images of their lives, most, of course, joined Russian reading publics in considering the works of Pushkin, Lermontov, Marlinskii, and Tolstoy as masterpieces in their own right. Save for Pushkin, each of those writers spent significant time fighting in the Caucasus, earning him the respect accorded to the braver men of letters, even from those on the proverbial other side. Whereas the nineteenth-century poetic corpus was an essential component of the lives of Caucasus intelligentsias at the dawn of the Soviet period, likewise, the films of Pyr'ev and Gaidai for any Caucasians over the age of thirty today were all an essential part of childhoods now lost to another era, spent in a country that no longer exists. Moscow, after all, was their capital too.

In order to map these shared histories, I conducted interviews in Moscow and Baku over the last several years with persons who might be broadly referred in this context as "knowledge producers"—Caucasus scholars, journalists, and pollsters, as well as screenwriters and directors whose works have very directly reached out to broad audiences. By placing these alongside memoirs, and with a comparative look at some classics of Soviet and post-Soviet Caucasus cinema, I aim to explore a canonic history through the lens of lives led in close cohabitation. In interviews, I asked about the myths, archetypes, and real-life moments that brought the Caucasus into focus for broader Soviet and more recent Russian publics. The choice of subjects I present here was made more on the basis of their specific provocations than for their intended typicality, though it would be fair to suggest that they cover a range of positions around the question of Caucasians' varied routes to integration with broader Russian and Soviet worlds. Given how much has circulated about the prisoner myth and about the Caucasus more broadly in the USSR since World War II, I pay particular attention to films produced not only in the central Moscow studios but in the capitals of the Caucasus itself. Throughout all these iconic moments from the Soviet period and after, what emerges is a picture of collective social relations that are distinguished by kinship metaphors rarely found in most market economies, metaphors that speak through a language of family relations encouraged by socialist political leaders. They mark the full flush of ties that bind and, of a piece with long-standing, older Caucasian codes, of families that sometimes become unbound.

Kinship metaphors and family ties in these broader historical and political contexts bring us back to earlier observations that so much narration of sovereign struggles hinges on talk of individual bodies and limit-figures, especially at times when those sovereignties are most openly challenged (Aretxaga 1991; Feldman 1991; Hansen and Stepputat 2005; Mbembe 2003). In eastern Europe after the fall of the Iron Curtain, for example, at a time when political leadership was so much in question, talk of reburying dead leaders was everywhere on people's lips. To recall Katherine Verdery's phrasing (1999), dead bodies themselves were everywhere "on the march," summoned by newly reconfigured nationalist publics (see also the excellent study by Todorova 2009). History itself can take different shapes, as Verdery observes, when political movements rely on competing kinship idioms and genealogies (1999, 117). As we will see here, when the Caucasus was joined to the USSR after the October Revolution, the union set in place an entirely fresh set of social relations cast largely in kinship terms.

Closed Societies, Open Theft?

Sergei Arutiunov is a leading Caucasus scholar in Moscow who has been among the few to probe how the Caucasus has come to be variously described as open or closed by a succession of political observers (2003). I asked him about why the societies of the Caucasus, an area so long famed for its pluralisms and histories of trade, would be thought of as closed, in the way that so many twentieth-century novels and films focus on mountain redoubts and the armed resistance shown to early Soviet administration. "This was a land of continual invasion," he remarked.

> This doesn't mean that societies were closed. Historically we can point to the degree to which all societies of the Caucasus absorbed the customs of their neighbors quite openly, looking north to Muscovy, west to Rome, Byzantium, very likely to Mycenae (though that is more speculative), and east to Tehran, Isfahan. Just not south. Baghdad was never a dream, since most writers considered Arabs a vulgar people and, despite actively taking on Islam, tried to shed the mantle of Arab culture as soon as it was imposed upon them.

What did this mean, then, for the Caucasus' own cultural and political arenas?

> Our best records date from the nineteenth century, but by that time it had to be clear to any local leader in the Caucasus that they were at everyone's periphery and at no one's center. So they made their own tiny centers, and constantly tried to best each other.

Does this mean that the focus on theft and brigandage in the Caucasus was merited?

> Certainly, if we allow that the question of Russian propriety in administration is never questioned, then these things—theft by Caucasians—of course took place. It was not a paradise. But the actual question of theft is not so distinctive. If we consider that the theft of livestock was the principal transgression over time, far more so than the theft of persons, then there is very little difference with, say, Scotland of just a few centuries back. Next you add in competition for prestige. The Abkhaz, for example, were in tributary

relations with Kabards for many decades in the late eighteenth and early nineteenth centuries. They constantly faced the dilemma of how to provide for Kabard princes when they came to stay for as long as a month, and had to be fed every day, and not just mutton. It was a great honor to have them as guests. Hence, they robbed the neighboring Mingrelians of their cows. There is no record of anyone robbing just for the sake of it, however much respect might have been accorded to men of bravery. These were questions of status and hospitality not entirely unlike what one might have once seen at the potlatches of the Kwakiutl in the Canadian northwest, though taking place in a world area that has far fewer natural forms of wealth.

In Baku, I put the same set of questions to Maya Iskenderova, a historian working on comparative imperial and Soviet histories of the Caucasus. She had a somewhat different response:

> Closure, openness—these are your terms of debate, they are questions of privilege. We have earned the title of "closed societies" [*zakrytye obshchestva*] among those scholars, mainly European scholars, who could not under-stand why anyone would not surrender their sovereignty gladly. Take the case of the Lezgins—what does it mean to call them a closed society? From the very beginning, they simply refused to recognize Russian sovereignty. That's all. They saw themselves as having nothing to do with places like Georgia, or the khanate of Sheki that signed formal treaties. This was not their empire. And they paid for this.... Russian sovereignty in the Cauca-sus wasn't like under the Ottomans with the [politically freer but economi-cally demanding] *millet* system, or even under the Persians, who at least by the end of the eighteenth century were so weak that they were not in a po-sition to regularly control daily life outside their own centers. Russian con-trol meant a total surrender of one's boundaries. And this was ultimately a transgression of all the social codes of the Caucasus that had developed over centuries. I would look upon all Caucasus societies as having seen far more mechanisms of open exchange in the past. But when you have been invaded so many times, what are you supposed to do? Closure was a way of life; it was a means of survival.

Did idioms of closure apply then between societies of the Caucasus, as well as toward foreign sovereigns? She responded with an example not far from Herzfeld's earlier remarks about the status of raiding livestock (1987):

Take the case of cattle. It's only today under a different sense of individualized property that we consider this a case of theft. If someone steals between one valley and the next, naturally, it's a crime. But people knew each other's lives and fates, it was clear how one group stole to survive or prosper. When someone stole cattle, the point is that he showed himself brave enough to cross boundaries that were very real and at the same time, quite metaphorical. [By stealing] he was able to suggest a strength that could fend off potential threats, and he produced something of value for the interior life of his own society. At the same time, obviously, it's hardly something you want to advertise. There's no question that societies develop a higher sense of morality when they expand their worldviews, when they are in more productive contact with their neighbors. But let's be honest: those ideas are a luxury for some. Not everyone has neighbors they want to get to know better.

But it was not always a question of cattle. Persons were taken too.

Certainly, but kidnapping people is another matter. That has its own story too. Of course brides were not like cattle, and plain out-and-out kidnapping was kidnapping. You didn't take someone against his or her will unless you really meant war (or it was during war)....Let's remember the context in which these things take place. There's a village near Qazax [in northwest Azerbaijan] where I grew up, it's called Yuxari Salaxli. Then there is Dash Salaxli. From Dash Salaxli, no one takes wives, why? Because there's a long record of families in Dash Salaxli being stingy [*xæsis*], they ask for too much in dowries, and they never stop bargaining with you your whole life. So parents never like it when their sons start seeing girls from that village. Here kidnapping enters the equation as a way for a young man to convince his parents that they can get around this tradition. If he says he'll kidnap a girl from Dash Salaxli, which is to say, if he gets the girl to agree to it secretly in advance, then his parents will be less worried, because there will less brideprice at stake.

I pointed out to her that, at least in the post-Soviet age, there was more than enough evidence of bride kidnapping with women being captured by strangers very much against their will (Amsler and Kleinbach 1999; Werner 2004). Iskenderova, like most, saw this as a modern aberration, acts wrought by impoverished families reaching in the wrong directions for perceived enhancement of lowered reputation and the rewards of additional household labor.

Her answer relegates bride kidnapping to the lesser privileged, in a way that allows urbanized elites to mark their own gradations of social distinction. But kidnapping was never just a dream of the poor. At least a dozen evenings I spent in Azerbaijan in city and countryside ended over tea where men of relative means would recount kidnappings that they wished they had pursued. "I love my wife and I am very happy," a farmer outside of Sheki once told me. "But I think my mother is still a little disappointed, quite honestly. When I was growing up, she'd always say to me, 'If you're really *my* son, you'll steal a wife.'"[5]

Parallel Civilizations

In a city such as Baku—as across so much of the Caucasus, where anti-Russian sentiment has slowly grown since the fall of the USSR, particularly against the backdrop of crimes against Caucasians across Moscow—the effect of that fall on the late Soviet elites who made their careers in a fully bilingual atmosphere is often bruising. "Everyone casts aspersions on Russia today," a senior female imperial historian remarked to me, "but they were the ones who came to save us from more assaults by the Ottomans and the Persians. It was hardly as if we were the Garden of Eden and suddenly someone interrupted our peace and happiness." All the same, much historical evidence does support a rather well-recorded ambivalence toward early Russian protections, an ambivalence that she was seeking to diminish. Extant Russian sources suggest a language of "invitation" that was by turns welcomed and spurned, often at the same time in the same documents being directed to St. Petersburg (Berzhe 1866; Pollock 2006). Early nineteenth-century correspondence between Russian generals and the khan of Sheki, for example, is bedeviled with the ambiguities of a Caucasian leader looking to seek temporary Russian protection while implying that the door might be open for longer term agreements, and of Russian officials looking to assert permanent sovereign control while implying that they are doing so only by terms of mutual consent.[6]

---

5. Interview, Bash Shabalid, 2002.

6. For examples from Sheki see "Vypiski iz raporta chlena Soveta namestnika Kavkazskogo o lichnykh i imushchenstvennykh pravakh, privilegiiakh musul'manskogo sosloviia," ARDTA, f. 998, s, 1, i. 13, and Mostashari (2006).

One rare complete memoir from the start of the 1900s comes from Prince Dimitri Shalikashvili, whose life story rapidly undoes many of the stereotypes of Caucasus primitivism (1956). In this account of elite circles in the Caucasus only a hundred years after the Russians had assumed control, the same ambivalence can still be felt. Born into a noble family of considerable wealth in Tbilisi in 1896, he spent the first years of his childhood moving between Tbilisi and a seaside resort in the north of France, accompanied by the family's German doctor and British governess. His family brought the first automobile to Tbilisi from Paris, and they shuttled across the Georgian countryside supervising multiple estates. Paris was, of course, "another world," as the prince described it in one early visit when he paused to recall that it had been only weeks before "that we were sitting in our forest oasis [at the family estate] in Gurjani, where our very safety depended on the Lezgin *ovcharki,*" dogs so fierce that they were prone to attacking the Shalikashvilis themselves, and none but their keepers could come near them (35). The family fell on hard times following the early death of his father in 1904 and the 1905 unrest in Baku that put many of the oil wells inherited by his mother out of commission. Yet the young Dimitri's life continued to turn on a series of well-to-do military schools at home in Georgia and abroad. He was fluent in English and French from a young age, knowing only a smattering of Georgian, and his family considered themselves patriots of their homeland, with a twist. They lived through Russian language and culture yet they were never entirely a part of it.

Despite [our Georgian allegiances] we spoke Russian at home. Such families like us in Tbilisi were once a great number, though to somehow explain it would by necessity chalk it up to a kind of unhealthy sloth.... There was no special antagonism toward Russians, unlike the Poles, and most did not realize their own gradual Russification. (19)

In the spring of 1918, following the October Revolution, the Regiment of the Horse Guard dismissed an excited Shalikashvili where he had served in Petersburg to celebrate what he called "the end of a detested empire" (n.d., 20). He returned to Tbilisi, where he soon joined the Department of Defense of the independent Georgian Republic (1918–1921), negotiating with the British and Turks for the continued security of the fledgling state. He was in Ankara lobbying for Turkish protection when the

Bolsheviks took control of Tbilisi, and his life after that would never be the same. Properly anticipating persecution at home, he never returned to Georgia and eventually lost contact with his mother and sister, the princesses Shalikashvili. He later learned that they had turned to selling cigarettes on the street in order to survive. He went on to make a modest living in Istanbul running a beach club and a restaurant; he served in the Polish army in Warsaw; he served in the Waffen SS when Germany declared war on the Soviet Union, pledging to liberate the Caucasus from communist hands; and eventually he made a home in the United States, where his son would go on to serve as chairman of the Joint Chiefs of Staff in the Clinton administration.

Looking back at Georgian history, like most twentieth-century Georgians, Shalikashvili reflected sorely on the fall of the Georgian kingdom in 1801. Recalling the treaty that sealed the first Russian protectorate, he remarks how the difference between "seeking protection" and "pledging sovereignty" was, as elsewhere, a fraught balance, one attested to by almost continual rebellions against Russian power across the nineteenth century. "Conquest of the land hardly meant accession," he made clear (1956, 39). Shalikashvili joins with those who see an imperial balance sheet where Georgians may come out losing, but likely less so than if they remained vassals of the invading Turkish and Persian armies. He found himself grateful for an education spent in part in St. Petersburg and took pride in the fact that the Russian viceroys had perhaps the best relations with Georgians over all other Caucasian peoples. Yet while Russians and Georgians may have found a certain modus vivendi—particularly after imperial legislation began to incorporate Georgian nobility into the Russian system of privileges and recognitions in the 1820s—even the most elite Georgians of Shalikashvili's day, many decades later, knew their place on mornings when Georgian bodies were piled in the streets, explained away as "Cossack excesses" in efforts to control rebel elements (1956, 69). Even the most privileged families such as his, largely Russophone, knew their standing.

In his youth as in later exile, Shalikashvili strained to disprove the widely held official policy that there was no distinction between Russians and non-Russians in the eyes of the tsarist government. In the United States, he railed against the diaspora of White Russians, who saw the restoration of the entire empire, including the Caucasus, as their natural inheritance.

A certain number of Russian émigrés err in considering themselves inheritors of the late Russian empire, as if they will exercise rights over other peoples once under its banner [in the event of the fall of the Soviet Union].... We would simply note here that the Russian empire ceased to exist in 1917 and the non-Russian peoples exercised their independence. (1954, 2)

Yet, in the anthropomorphizing of nations, Shalikashvili insisted, who was the older and who was the younger, in world-historical terms? This was a familiar question. Georgia, after all, he insisted, is "one of the oldest states in the world with over two thousand years of recorded history, a state that adopted Christianity six hundred years before Russia" (1954, 3). Who, then, was to civilize whom?

Misspent Youth, or the Caucasus as Child

In the evolutionist languages of the nineteenth century, gortsy, the seemingly intractable Caucasus highlanders, occupied the lion's share attention of poets and historians alike. Gortsy were mountain men of unrestrained libidinal profile, quick to violence and motivated by glory. As such, they found a regular place in the cinematic mythographies of the Soviet period, in historical dramas that cast the future of the Caucasus in starkly Manichaean terms.[7] Yet if gortsy most broadly spoke to a less developed, hence "earlier" form of social organization, it was their youthful exuberance or lack of worldliness—a certain want of mature civilization—that often defined the Caucasus' most popular mass culture figures in the Soviet period (Fabian 1983). In the figure of this otherwise fully grown mountain man, we find instead man-child, in need of education, refinement, and most of all, the right guidance.

Consider three films from across the mid- and later Soviet eras. The popular 1941 film *Svinarka i pastukh* (released in English alternately as *Swineherder and Shepherd* and *They Met in Moscow*), directed by Ivan Pyr'ev

---

7. Consider, for example, among the work of Azerfilm Studios: *Axırıncı aşırım* (d. Kamil Rüstəmbəyov, 1971), *Böyük dayaq* (d. Həbib İsmayılov, 1962), *Dəli Kür* (d. Hüseyn Seyidzadə, 1969), and *Yeddi oğul istərəm* (d. Tofiq Tağızadə, 1970). These were Azeri-language films of a certain Caucasian thaw generation, intended for local audiences only, and their reception was knowingly circumscribed.

and produced by Sergei Eisenstein, presented a polished love story of star-crossed lovers for wartime audiences in trying times. On a collective farm in northwestern Russia, the accordion-playing Kuzma loves Glasha, the energetic swineherder. Glasha pays little attention to Kuzma, however, apparently loving her work more. When her achievements in the workplace earn her a prize trip to Moscow's Exhibition of Agricultural Achievements, she falls in love with Musaib, a tall, dashing Caucasian shepherd of no particular origin, played by the distinctly non-Caucasian Vladimir Zel'din, of Douglas Fairbanks hue.

Having met in Moscow, the couple pledges to reunite in a year's time to renew their affections and their shared commitment to animal husbandry. At home in the hills, Musaib, bursting with joy and standing tall in his trademark burka and lamb's-wool hat (the ubiquitous *papag*), yet unable to read or write, showers Glasha with letters by dictating them to a young shepherd apprentice. But upon receiving Musaib's letters, Glasha is unable to understand the boy's prose. She takes them to the local Armenian café proprietor, who professes, "I know all the languages of the Caucasus. But sadly, not this one." That is to say, he knows the languages of men of letters but not the letters of men of the mountains. In other words, Musaib's letter is not as lettered as it should be.

A jealous Kuzma takes advantage and plays havoc with the lovers' correspondence, volunteering a "friend's" translation to Glasha and insisting that Musaib has already married. Musaib himself, when not pining for Glasha, is shown bravely fending off packs of marauding wolves to save sheep on dark, stormy nights atop mountain peaks. Truth conquers in the end. When Musaib arrives alone at their Moscow assignation, he learns that a despondent Glasha has agreed to marry the scheming Kuzma. He flies to the kolkhoz on horseback and rescues her from an unhappy wedding day. At the sight of the Caucasus brigand, Kuzma speaks to archetype when he tries to fend off his rival. He sounds a familiar alarm—"He's kidnapping my bride!"—while another onlooker betrays the timeless ambiguity of mixed marriage: "We build up our cadres, only to have another republic come take them away."

On-screen Soviet internationalism seems to triumph. But does it entirely? Kuzma leaves cuckolded in a cloud of pillow feathers, unable to match the sturdy Caucasian in bravery or strength. But, however fated, the marriage between Russian and Caucasian is ambiguously sealed. Glasha has chosen the manlier Musaib, but Musaib himself is as much child as man, still a work in progress. Coming from a society rooted in another time and more advanced social structures, Glasha's task ahead appears to be taming the energies of her new spouse.

Some twenty years later, in 1964, the far more sober Georgian-Russian film *Otets soldata* (directed by Rezo Chkheidze, released in Georgia as *Jariskatsis mama* and later in English as *Father of a Soldier*) took on the participation of Caucasians in the Great Patriotic (Second World) War more directly. In this film, a loving father, played to nuanced effect by Sergo Zakariadze, overcomes significant hardship to travel great distance upon learning that his son has been taken to a faraway hospital after being wounded on the western front in 1944. Finding the hospital bed empty— his son has recovered and returned to the front—the father is possessed by the son's example and becomes a fighter himself, enlisting over the reluctance of commanding officers who consider him too old. Father and son are reunited in a Berlin under Soviet siege on April 14, 1945. Together they defend the Soviet cause, and as the father loses the son to enemy gunfire, his pride is no less dimmed.

In the film, Zakariadze's character is a simple man with a heart of gold, unsophisticated in the ways of the world. But his popularity with audiences across the former Soviet Union, especially those in the seats of government in Moscow, might be best summed up in the father's acts of giving. In this context, the father does not give so much as give back. He has given his son to the army and is proud of him. Under most circumstances, that would be more than enough. But the father cannot stop there. En route to the distant hospital, he practically heaps his gifts of high-grade tobacco onto the cart driver who takes him along the final leg of his trip; it is as if he cannot give enough. Later in the hospital, in the absence of his son, he bestows heavy parcels of homemade food and wine upon soldiers he has never met, friends of his son. When he tries to enlist, officers of experience look down upon him for what they consider a foolish effort by an old man to join the Soviet cause; but his lack of worldliness is what also enables this giving. Among cinemagoers, Georgians and other Caucasians of all backgrounds who fought in the war had equal cause in turn to share in this character as their own. But the message all the same was, Georgians may be famed for their generosity, but they have not yet fully learned how to give appropriately. They are unschooled givers.

To suggest that the role of the Caucasian naïf was purely a Russian invention would be, of course, to miss the point of durable, polyvalent characters honed over long periods of time. In the 1994 Azeri-language film *Həm ziyarət, həm ticarət* (A Little Pilgrimage, A Little Trade), begun in the late perestroika era and released after the fall of the Soviet Union, director Rasim Ocaqov offers his countrymen a familiar sight. Set against the backdrop of Soviet citizens heading abroad for the very first time, Ocaqov follows the trail of Mustafa, who leaves the provincial Azerbaijani city of Sheki for Istanbul at the call of distant relatives who beckon him to a family event. Mustafa, a retiring tour guide of great shyness, is soon showered with commercial requests from neighbors and is sent off with much fanfare. In Istanbul, he and his wife are bewildered by the choice before them in markets. They live modestly by taking meals of bread and jam in their hotel room and are soon beset by all manner of tricksters who take advantage of their provincial inexperience. They barely make it home through the kindness of the one real relative who graciously shows them a kinder Turkic diaspora; their message to audiences is that home is best after all. But their travails are also a heuristic exercise for the thousands, then the tens of thousands, and later the millions of Caucasians who would soon leave their homelands to seek a living abroad. The affectionate naïf, one of the quintessential Caucasus personae, is also a guide for rehabilitation.

When Caucasus directors tried to move away from tales of archetypal naïfs, they ran into problems. At the 1972 Tbilisi film festival, Moscow officials balked when jurors wanted to award the best-actor award to Adil Iskenderov, who played Kerbalai Bey in the Azerbaijani-language film *Axırıncı aşırım* (The Last Mountain Pass). Iskenderov's predicament was not only that he had delivered a fine performance. The problem was that his character, Kerbalai Bey, a mountain rebel who resists early Soviet power, proved to be all too sensitive and supportive of the finer points of Caucasus codes of ethics to be sufficiently distinguished from the Soviets who would wrest his lands from him. As the film critic Aydin Kezimov told me,

> There is a scene when the revolutionary cell sends Abbas Guli [a Soviet official] to confront Kerbalai-Ismail. They debate whether Soviet administration can deliver on its promises and are obviously antagonists. But remember that in the Caucasus, a guest is a guest, and even when your worst

enemy comes to visit you, it is your responsibility to honor them as a guest and see that they get home safely. So when Kerbalai realizes that [his Soviet opponent] has been killed in his own home, he goes and kills his own deputy for having besmirched his honor.

You can imagine, when all this reached Moscow, they were beside themselves. "What is going on?" they said. "We're giving you money, we're financing your film, and you're praising...a bey?!"...Moscow wouldn't let it be shown. Why? Because a representative of the Soviet ideal, Abbas Guli, and his opponent, Kerbalai, are presented as equals. Who is the enemy here? There is no enemy! "But what's going on, you have to have a villain!" Indeed, they were right. How can you have a villain, like Kerbalai, who invites his enemies to his home, sits down and talks with them, feeds them, and ensures their safe passage home? In effect, Kerbalai was even more cultured than the Soviets he was opposing. The Soviets were there to do what? To expropriate Kerbalai's land holdings—in effect, his family name, the places where his family are buried, and the private pilgrimage sites. So it would not be hard for audiences to understand him. [In the film] he says, "I kept silent when they took my cows. I kept silent when they took my sheep." But when they came to take his land, he couldn't stand it any more and he wouldn't surrender.

Moscow saw the ending and said, "Take the part out where Kerbalai kills his own staff for breach of honor. Just let him be a villain." What did they do instead? The film was reedited beyond reason and the result is confusing. Everyone starts shooting at everyone at the end, and you can no longer figure it out. That's how the film [now] ends.[8]

At best, most Caucasus film productions on topics of any gravity trafficked in the ambiguous. Few captured this spirit better than the 1969 Baku production of *V odnom iuzhnom gorode* (In a Southern City, directed by Eldar Quliyev, and released in Azerbaijani as *Bir cənub şəhərində*), the work of first-time screenwriter Rustem Ibrahimbekov. In a classic portrait of troubled youth, writer and director tell the story of a young man named Murad, living at the end of a quiet residential, multifamily courtyard sequestered from one of Baku's busy downtown streets. The southern city in question is the setting for a paradigmatic morality play of honor, shame, and pluralism. Murad's friends include Tofiq, who is pledged in marriage

---

8. Interview, Baku, April 2005.

Figure 8. Baku street scene from *In a Southern City,* 1969. Courtesy of the Filmfond of Azerbaijan.

to Murad's sister. Tofiq has earlier served in prison and is the subject of the constant efforts of his friends to enable him to satisfy his job as an agricultural inspector and report regularly to his parole officer. Life would appear to be, on the surface, guided by this network of persons who support one another in times of need. They rally when the hapless Tofiq has a rare opportunity to go to Moscow to attend a ceremony honoring his war-hero father. Things come apart for Murad, however, when Tofiq returns from Moscow newly married—to a blonde Russian journalist, at that—thus dishonoring Murad's sister and family. In a final scene where Tofiq attempts to normalize relations by appearing in the courtyard with his new wife, the anguished Murad—torn between his internationalist beliefs and the family obligation to defend his sister's honor—sets upon Tofiq with a knife.

The film managed to upset censors in all directions—in Baku, where Azeri producers worried that their depiction of street crime would only strain Russian-Caucasus relations, and in Moscow, where studio heads were taken aback by a lead character who would not automatically have known the right thing to do under the circumstances. Yet it proved enormously popular with audiences in Baku, Erevan, and Tbilisi for allowing

Figure 9. Eldeniz Zeynalov as Tofiq and Hesen Memmedov as Murad in the 1969 film *In a Southern City.* Courtesy of the Filmfond of Azerbaijan.

the possibility that Soviet internationalism had its limits after all, in a world on-screen that suggested it could be entirely and organically of the USSR and somehow still apart from it.

Kinships Bound and Unbound

Given his early success with the screenplay for *In a Southern City,* I sought out the well-known writer and director Rustem Ibrahimbekov to learn how he viewed this question of history and Caucasian archetype. How did he see the transformation of the Caucasian in Russian culture over time? He began,

> If we are going to talk about the image of Caucasians, then among the most important will be from Tolstoy—*Hadji Murad*—earlier than that, Pushkin's poetry. We can point to the usual characteristics—the very brave, the masculine, the vibrant Caucasian who belongs to a civilized world, a highly organized world driven by honor and distinction that is, nonetheless, not very clear [to the Russian reader] beyond these key loyalties: to freedom, independence, honor, and so forth.

If we take the same image today, then in Russian cinema and literature, the Caucasian is a street trader, a bandit, dishonorable, cruel. We all know the picture.

That is to say, over the course of approximately 150 years, this image has been transformed monstrously [*chudovishchno*]. To a certain extent, it corresponds to reality. To a certain extent it is fair, and in other respects it is invented....

It is difficult to track these kinds of changes over such a long period, when it is obvious that the shifts are, from one generation to the next, hardly noticeable.... But we can point to some crucial moments. In the prerevolutionary period, even in the full flush of the Caucasus wars, we don't see such an active, attendant war of propaganda. That is, Russia battled the Caucasus to conquer it but didn't besmirch [*ne oblivala griaz'iu*] its opponents. In subsequent conflicts, when we saw repeated armed revolts in the North and South Caucasus against early Soviet power—for example, in the 1920s and beyond—this same anti-Caucasus moment was stemmed by the official Soviet policy of the equality of nations. To trumpet your own nation or denigrate another was nationalism, plain and simple, and it was not permitted anywhere, not in literature, the newspapers, or the movies.

Take, for example, the earlier film by Pyr'ev, *Svinarka i pastukh*. Here you get a projection of the same image—the hero of the film lives by honor, pride [*dostoinstvo*] and so forth, a likable naïf put forth in a humorous light. This tradition was common across the Soviet period. This was its own mythopoeisis [*mifotvorchestvo*], not malevolent but not very realistic either. Even when films such as *Kavkazskaia plennitsa* took up darker themes such as blood vengeance in the Caucasus, paradoxically you find the good-humor element even more.

Ever since Russia found itself again in conflict with Chechnya, with the first Caucasus war of the 1990s, during the fever of independence movements—everyone reacts to these movements differently, but my own conviction is that they were inspired primarily by the speed of events around them, and it is the very speed by which they have taken place, rather than the motives for their taking place, that has created the problems.

In explaining these problems, Ibrahimbekov turned to a language of parents and children that echoed the very same images of patron and naïf about which he spoke. It was a language mirrored in Soviet nationality politics of an older Russian brother and younger non-Russian siblings (Tillet 1969), and one found across the USSR. Yuri Slezkine traced this theme

across the entire Soviet gamut when he commented on the indigenous "defiant warrior girls" of early Soviet-era Siberian fiction, whose antecedents
could be found in the romantic literature of the Caucasus. "Only now instead of being a captive and an admiring lover the Russian was a father-
figure and the self-assured master of the situation, while his ally the girl
did not have to choose between him and her freedom-loving people: her
role was to bring the rest of the tribe under Russian protection (given the
new filial nature of the relationship, this role was sometimes played by a
child)" (1994a, 295). The vast family of Soviet nationalities, in another of
Slezkine's felicitous phrasings, cohabited much like residents of a communal apartment (1994b). But such cohabitations did not please all. Ibrahimbekov continued:

> It makes sense when you picture grown children leaving the home. They
> kiss their parents good-bye, and their parents offer them what they can.
> That's well and good. But picture the children getting up and marching
> out—one takes the sink, the other takes the beds, the other takes the tables.
> And the parents are left in an empty apartment. That's more or less what
> took place. Of course Russians are not happy about this.
>
> To the outside world this looked like the happy collapse of the evil em-
> pire. To us—we also wanted freedom, but no one anticipated that it would
> come about in such a barbaric fashion, or that power would be taken over by
> criminals. An explosion, it was a real explosion, and no surprise when you
> picture such a powerful system in such a small cage.[9]

Parents, children, apartments, families—was the bond of Russian to non-
Russian in the USSR really that of parent to child? The phrasing was one I
was more accustomed to hearing during years of my own research among
indigenous peoples of the Russian Far East. I asked Ibrahimbekov if this
was the best metaphor. He chose new phrasing, moving to "fraternal" over
"parental," falling back on the better-worn metaphor about the brother-
hood of nations in the former socialist system.

None of these themes came up by accident, as Ibrahimbekov had explored the struggle among putative equals in great detail in his 1998 bilingual Russian-Azeri film *Ailə* (The Family, released in Russian as *Sem'ia*).

---

9. Interview, Baku, April 2005.

The opening scene is set in a downtown Baku communal apartment, home to some dozen adults, headed by the patriarch Isaak Sadykovich, whom we find in quiet tension with his long-standing Armenian roommate Qarik. The apartment is a web of tangled alliances. When two college-age Azeri and Russian lovers want to marry, Isaak Sadykovich insists that the Azeri girl finish her studies first, while the boy's mother accuses Isaak Sadykovich of anti-Russian sentiment. A gallant Azeri artist carries on an affair with his married Russian lover, who is involved in an elaborate art scam at the young man's expense. The putative matriarch Sofia Mikhailovna, former sister-in-law to Isaak Sadykovich, cares for the orphaned Elmira, now a young woman. The apartment is by all measure filled to overflowing with residents of all peoples of the Caucasus, grumbling but living ably side by side.

All members of the apartment are, however, by no means in agreement when Isaak Sadykovich announces the impending arrival of his childhood friend Qezenfer, who seeks refuge from increasing ethnic tensions between Armenians and Azeris in not-so-distant Armenia. It is with the prospect of adding yet another member to the full house that Qarik and Sofia Mikhailovna propose plans for elaborate housing exchanges that would see all parties dispersed to their own smaller flats and rooms across the city, some more comfortably than others. In the film, the complicated standoff among those who want the multinational family to remain in place and those who would rend it asunder is less one of position than one of voice. For Isaak Sadykovich's benevolent but firm hand strictly refuses to allow naming ethnic affiliation in the home.

As tension builds, the future of the apartment is waylaid by greater events. Not long after Qarik, a third-generation resident of Baku, is seen being taunted by ethnic Azeris as he attempts a new living selling art books on the street, large-scale pogroms against Armenians ensue across the city, as they did in late 1989 and early 1990, as Armenian demands for the reappropriation of western Azerbaijan's Nagorno-Karabagh region mounted. Confronted by thugs entering the communal apartment as a frightened Qarik perches on an outside ledge, a horrified Isaak Sadykovich has a heart attack and dies. In the days that follow, the traumatized Azeri college girl leaves for Moscow, and the dashing artist is killed at the hands of Russian art dealers whose plan he foiled.

Isaak Sadykovich's death and the sudden dissolution of the collective suggest the end to an internationalism held close by so many. But as events unfold, that internationalism is revealed to have carried its own secrets. The hounded Armenian Qarik, on the eve of his exile to Moscow and later to Los Angeles, confesses to a shocked Elmira, Isaak Sadykovich's adopted niece, that he is her real father. Worried that Elmira might suffer as the illegitimate child of a mixed union, even in the quieter days of a Brezhnevite Baku in the 1970s when Elmira was born, Isaak Sadykovich, the apartment's leader and resident humanist, had urged Qarik never to disclose his paternity.

The theme of family relations drives this film, with an evident interest in the rise and fall of cohabitations and cooperations that speak directly to a USSR then unraveling. Beyond the melodrama itself, capturing the death of a patriarch and the splintering of collective allegiances, the film most provocatively takes up the status of naming in earlier Soviet codes of internationalism. While it is apparent in retrospect that most though by no means all characters knew the respective ethnic backgrounds of their companions, Isaak Sadykovich's strict supervision makes it clear that it was inappropriate to name difference as such. This was a theme not far from Ibrahimbekov's work of almost thirty years earlier, *In a Southern City*, where the silent Murad struggles with a knife for reasons never named but understood by all, in a struggle between the individual and himself, between the individual and the collective, between family honor and internationalist values.

In *The Family*, the initial comfort of the communal apartment setting calls to mind, almost in a punning way, Freud's famous discussion of *heimlichkeit*, literally meaning a state of familiarity suggested by home but a term more broadly signaling the appropriate or the normal. The events that marked *The Family*, such as the unraveling of the Soviet Union and the strictures of convention along with it, open up characters to what Freud called *unheimlichkeit*, or the uncanny ([1919] 1959), where scenes of distinctly strange and uncomfortable discovery, such as Elmira's learning that she is not an orphan after all (nor wholly Azerbaijani), are elements of life long suppressed by strictures past. Chronicling this seemingly inexorable, post-Soviet drive to reveal and to name—Gorbachev's policy of glasnost', after all, was more about revelation than mere openness—the film astutely captures a brand of now painfully familiar nationalist fever driven by increasingly narrowed political communities that look to remake history in their own image.

Yet in the struggles over naming, old habits seem to die hard. For at the very moment that Qarik is "named" as Armenian, he is also "unnamed" by way of his forced disappearance from Baku. What were his options? In the film, his fate is imminent exile. Yet as his real-life counterparts have discovered across the South Caucasus today—such as the approximately hundred thousand Armenians who remain in Baku or the Azeris living still in Erevan—had he remained behind under such uncertain circumstances he would soon have had to become accustomed to an environment where his background and nationality would best remain discreetly unspoken.[10]

Ibrahimbekov's are not the only works that present the Caucasus as a scene of fraught family values. Among the most famous Caucasus writers is the legendary Soviet satirist Fazil' Iskander, the author of a number of masterworks of prose and poetry. In his brilliant novel *Sandro of Chegem* (1979), he presents prolix tricksters and wise men of all stripes from a distant Abkhazia of childhood memory, men whose likeability, it might be noted, hinges on the same man-child ambiguities seen in so many other Soviet-era Caucasus works. In these characters, some have seen an invitation to Russian readers to discover "a gentler Caucasus" (Maslova 2001), while Iskander himself once said of his most famous character, "Sandro is the childhood of all mankind" (Kucherskaia 2004, 8).[11] I visited Iskander to ask him about the logic of casting a character such as Sandro, whose quick-witted uses of homespun irony could show up the tyranny of Stalin, as a man-child. Iskander replied,

> Sandro, to me, was not so much about childhood or adulthood but a different way of life. In *Sandro of Chegem,* I represented Abkhaz, to the extent that I know them, as far more patriarchal than Russians—that was the point. It was this very patriarchy that I had in mind as "the childhood of mankind."...In this sense we are talking about a fundamentally different way of the life than the technocratic path of so many contemporary socialist

---

10. This plot twist was later echoed in the decision by increasing numbers of Caucasians living in Moscow after the fall of the USSR to change their names in order to "de-Caucasize" them (Konovalova 2006).

11. When Elena Maslova (2001) wrote that Iskander "made a gift to readers of...Caucasians with kind faces," the implicit contrast was, naturally, to the Caucasians most Moscow or Petersburg residents meet in marketplaces or on subways, a subject of fear and uncertainty.

or capitalist societies. In this sense, patriarchy is the childhood of humanity, an earlier stage. In my opinion it is also a more human way of life, especially when we think of social codes, of proprieties. Civilization may or may not survive, it may come to an end, and it may end well or may end badly. Patriarchy is the nucleus [*iadro*], and patriarchy is immortal. Patriarchy is what will remain long after civilizations rise or fall.[12]

Did that mean there was something about Abkhaz society that was also up for criticism? Iskander's reply again raised the question of just who was civilizing whom in Soviet-era cultural missions:

It's hard to say in simple terms what I was doing. Without a doubt I wanted to share with people a sense of the advantages of a patriarchal society. Yet, of course, it was also the case that I wanted to be a thorn in the side of the So-viet, socialist, so-called civilization by demonstrating the ways in which that system was more lowly, more crude, and more primitive than [the Abkhaz]. Perhaps my own society appears more primitive to the untrained eye, but I saw it as, internally, far richer in humanity. Naturally I was interested in raising the social level of our people, but it was also with the goal of looking critically at Soviet life. . . . I saw advantage, of course, in our Abkhaz way of life. But I unequivocally looked to deliver a blow to Soviet life by exposing its injustices and absurdities.

By Iskander's pen, a kin-based society not only was superior to a Soviet one but was also what enabled the Abkhaz to weather the Soviet period.[13] Nonetheless, his assertion that the Abkhaz were of an earlier time is a re-minder of evolutionisms long mapped onto Russian-Caucasian relations overall.

The Russian Question Today

While Iskander generated his fictional Abkhazia in part to suggest a strug-gle over preeminence between Caucasian peripheries and federalist cen-ters, the more recent postsocialist era provides ample illustration for how

---

12. Interview, Moscow, October 2006.
13. For a similar point see Lipovetsky (2000, 286).

tables can turn over time. Yet for all the structural newness of postsocialist life, the question of social ostracism once discussed by Abkhaz scholar Iurii Anchabadze (1979), tracking the many ways by which bodies crossing recognized social lines of clan, kin, religion, or nationality could be accepted or rejected in widely circulated Caucasus social codes, still has relevance today. I had cause to recall Anchabadze sitting at a wedding once in Baku when I asked a businesswoman if her perception of Russians as having been diminished in importance in Baku life came from specific experiences. "It's not a question of events or action," she responded.

> It's a form of behavior. It's about the absence of reaction, neither positive nor negative. As if someone has already died, and there's no point in dwelling on it. And death, for all its tragedies, is nonetheless a fact of life [she switched from Azeri to Russian and repeated, "death is *zakonomerno*," a natural event governed by law]. In the end it is not sad or tragic because it's a fact. That's what we're talking about.

Most were less categorical. Ayaz Salayev, one of the most accomplished film directors of the post-Soviet period in Azerbaijan, grew up in the Soviet era and is the product of Moscow's finest film academies. I asked him how he perceived the state of Russian-Caucasus relations after the close of the USSR. He remarked,

> I had the chance to spend many years in Moscow and I am incredibly grateful for that time. It would have been entirely different if I had studied here, or even gone abroad. It was a first-class education with real masters. But [Russia] is also a country today [2005] where xenophobia is on the rise....I remember being at an international film festival a few years ago and a Russian woman said to me, "You seem so nice—what a relief to meet an Azerbaijani who I don't have to worry about robbing me." I didn't even know how to respond. What do you say?

I asked him if this meant that fear was one of the driving forces behind the intense distancing of relations.

> I don't know about fear, I can't really say. Certainly it's not as if most Russians ever considered Caucasians as possessing their own actual civilizations or anything like that that would make the Caucasus a competitor in any

sense. Maybe you could say that it's comparable to the situation with blacks in the U.S. a few decades back. You know, people would say, "They really know their jazz." Everyone knows it's not a compliment. It's the same thing every time I am in Russia at a wedding. Forget that I'm from Azerbaijan and might be a Muslim. People will say, "You have to give the first toast, you're so good at it," as if we're all happy Georgians, as if everyone is a tamada [chairman, but more commonly "toastmaster"], and so on.

Was there a noticeable difference, then, after the Soviet period?

Of course, once perestroika began, people had a chance to say what was on their mind. The Caucasus suddenly produces nothing but villains. That alone tells us all was not calm in the minds of even the creative intelligentsia, certainly.

But at the same time, I can't tell you that there has been a direct response on the part of Azeris, at least not that I have seen. There was always a careful correctness, in the first place, to leave Russia to the Russians where questions of culture and discrimination were concerned. Even if the Soviet Union was your own country, you could certainly be made to feel like a guest, and it wasn't a rare experience. In the second place, my own generation [born in the early 1960s] grew up with the self-censorship that Russia, in particular, was simply not open to criticism.

But truly, I simply think that people have not gone in that direction because they aren't thinking about it. Russia simply isn't on people's minds. Politically, it is more than clear that in the event of a problem, Russia isn't going to protect us. Maybe America, maybe Europe, that's not the point. The point is that it won't be Russia. So it's almost as if Russia has dropped out of people's consciousness. It's just not on people's minds.[14]

Had Russia simply dropped out of people's minds, or was there something fundamentally errant in Russia's policy toward the Caucasus, not least when the results of Chechnya's independence drive after the fall of the Soviet Union was so evident to all? So too, as Anchabadze (1979) demonstrated in communities across the Caucasus through at least the nineteenth century, errant bodies best remained unspoken.

Throughout all these commentaries, Russia and the Caucasus are writ large in ways that efface any number of internal differences across

14. Interview, Baku, March 2005.

enormously complex communities. But that is the very stuff of archetype
that historian Fekhruddin Maniev looked to address when I asked him if
there was a meaningful unity to the Caucasus in Russian media circles:

> The paradox is that the Caucasus has never been a united place and may
> never be. Even in Azerbaijan alone, I assure you that you'll find at least
> a third of the city of Baku enormously in favor of the return of the Soviet
> Union and all things Russian with it, another third who exclusively blame
> Russians for their problems, and a remaining third who never give it a mo-
> ment's thought. But the perception of the Caucasus in Russia, on the other
> hand, however strange it might have been over time, has perhaps never been
> clearer. Not even when entire populations of Crimean Tatars and Chechens
> were being deported to Kazakhstan in the 1940s was so much calumny di-
> rected at us.
>
> I was in Moscow just this last November [2004]....I was heading out to
> the edge of the city on the subway to take a commuter train. There were
> five of us in the car—me with my briefcase, in a suit and tie, quite official-
> looking, two young Russians, an older Armenian man, and a younger guy,
> who I figured was Azeri like me. Nothing special. The only strange thing is
> that there were only five of us on a subway car in the middle of the day. We
> reached the last station and everyone stood up to head out the door. The Ar-
> menian man was first, then the Russians, then the Azeri, then me. Out on
> the platform, I stopped to rearrange my papers when I noticed how the Ar-
> menian man seemed to be looking in his pockets for something. The two
> Russian guys had spat all over the back of his coat before getting off the
> train. The younger Azeri and I fished in our pockets for some kleenex and
> helped him get cleaned up. There was this kind of lament we all shared—
> we know that we probably wouldn't meet at home because we can't sort
> out [the Armenia-Azerbaijan conflict over] Nagorno-Karabagh in our own
> lands. But in Russia, we'll always be Caucasians. It's as if it's the discrimina-
> tion that keeps us together. Isn't that strange?

Russian civilizers had once maneuvered around the question of ancient
Caucasus primacies suggested by Blumenbach ([1775] 1969) by making a
distinction between *kavkazoid* ("Caucasian" as Caucasoid, the racial category, or the more commonly used *evropoid,* Europoid), and *kavkazets* ("Caucasian" as resident of the Caucasus). A further euphemism became popular
in the late Soviet period, *litso kavkazskoi natsional'nosti,* literally meaning
"subject of Caucasus nationality" and most often used indiscriminately to

identify the semilegal guest workers who came to Russian urban centers to sell fruits and vegetables or work on construction sites. In more fraught postsocialist contexts such as here, when Russia's immigration question became more controversial, the euphemism gave way more paradoxically to *chernye,* or "blacks" (Mamedov 1999). Did Maniev now see Azeris responding likewise to Russians in ways that shut them out of daily life in Baku? Maniev shrugged.

> You can't say that anyone is being mean to them. It's more that, outside government, and for all the social mixing, most Russians never really made a niche for themselves here. And they haven't made any new ones.[15]

Unsure that Russians ever were quite the marginals that Maniev suggested, I visited the offices of a professional opinion pollster I had once met through friends. How much had Russia been disappearing from people's minds? I asked.

> Russia is an enormous country, of course. It exists. Everyone can point to it, and perhaps most important, millions of dollars come from Russia every week from sons and fathers and brothers who have left to go work there. But in a social sense Russia has lost the place that it occupied for so long. For many it is completely alien, even if they were once born into a country where Moscow was their capital city. There's no contact, no connection for most. That is, chances are that a million Azeris [the number most often cited for work-related emigration to Russia circa 2005] would travel to Africa too if that's where they could earn a living. . . . It's just a space people go to occupy to make a living.[16]

I asked him whether, somehow free from Russia, one did not have to be a "Caucasian" any longer.

> A few years ago I went down to Iran, to Tebriz, and I was so surprised to see how similar so many things there were [between Azerbaijan and Iran]. When I think of "the Caucasus," I think of [the Azeri mountain towns of] Sheki or Quba. But the rest of Azerbaijan, to me, it's more Persian than

---

15. Interview, Baku, March 2005.
16. Interview, Baku, March 2005.

Turk. Personally speaking, I'd say, we're all tired of being *Kavkaztsy*. But that's the rub. The moment that you enter Russia, the whole idea is mobilized again. *Kavkaztsy* reborn.... And it works across the contemporary Russian political spectrum, whether "democrat" or "conservative." It's as if the same imperial thinking has been buried deep in social consciousness and hasn't changed a whit in two hundred years. We're *inorodtsy* [aliens of a different birth], and that's it. You know, like when they say, "We've done so much for you." It's supposed to put us in our place.

Inorodsty was a term frequently once used to describe all manner of non-Russian peoples in the late tsarist and early Soviet periods (Shternberg 1910). It lost frequency as socialist ideology, which hinged on the premise that the working man has no country, insisted on shared biological ties across all communities. But as the Soviet family of peoples began to come apart, so too did its driving logics.

"We've done so much for you." I thought of the pollster's familiar phrasing and remembered when it had come up in Moscow a month earlier with Arutiunov. He had spoken with a practiced style about how the Caucasus figured in the Russian imagination.

> You have to remember that there were four cultural hearths in Soviet society. The first was Moscow-Leningrad. (At a certain point it became clear that Novosibirsk was intended to join them but it never really made it.) The second consisted of the Baltic high cultures. Everyone in Russia understood that these people were really European, not *nashi* [ours], and really more advanced. The third was central Asia, everyone looked down upon them. Many read the works of Chingiz Aitmatov or Olzhas Suleimenov, but one would have to debate just how much their work was thought of as central Asian. The fourth was the Caucasus, foremost represented by Tbilisi, which had once been a defeated city on the verge of attack in 1800 and yet went on to host a parade of accomplishments that the USSR took pride in as its own—the Shakespeare Festival that took place there in 1976, festivals to showcase Brecht...masterpieces of cinema, and so on.

I was fascinated by a commentary that set over seventy years of the Soviet cultural mission into a single frame. But I had a final question. If the Caucasus could be distinguished from central Asia by its perceived success story—its retreat from the precipice by dint of Russian aid—what then caused such tension today? "The problem," Arutiunov remarked, "is that there is the sense that peoples of the Caucasus are not grateful for all that was done for them." Were they ungrateful children? Ungrateful younger siblings? He went on to give examples of leading Caucasus nationalist figures who publicly and firmly rebuffed the Soviet legacy, too quickly for the Russian center. In short, Arutiunov was saying, it was a question of failed reciprocities and of gifts gone unanswered.

7

From Prometheus to the Present

Rings and other jewels are not gifts but apologies for gifts.
The only gift is a portion of thyself.

Ralph Waldo Emerson, "Gifts"

Empires, like the more abstract category of sovereignty that they look to exercise, are not concrete structures but flexible organizations based on ever-moving, contested relationships. The stability of empire, as in all forms of political rule, comes as often from the arts of persuasion—the logics by which sovereignty can be naturalized—as from the power of the sword. In both Russian and Caucasus histories of encounter, the gift became an increasingly shared natural logic of sovereign rule, perhaps among the oldest in anyone's political playbook. We are all told to beware of strangers bearing gifts.

The language of the gift often conjures related notions of exchange or reciprocity. Reciprocity can, of course, under certain conditions, play a role in the art of the gift, but this colloquial sense invites frequently too-quick perceptions of balanced parity, equal trades among equal partners. Such a notion not only is often inaccurate but misses the agonisms inherent in the public nature of the gift. Gift giving, as I have sought to demonstrate here, can be effectively unilateral. Gifts may be simply pronounced and delivered, establishing the generosity (though not immediately the acumen) of the giver. Whether they are received, how they are received, and whether they are successful are secondary questions. When gifts are recognized as such, they foremost invite not immediate reciprocity but time, as Bourdieu suggested (1977, 6), the interval of time before a potential return gift can be levied. That time creates a field of social relations, ongoing interactions that may be positive or negative but exist all the same, foremost in the eyes of the giver. Captivity has always been a metaphor of the gift; Bourdieu observed that gifts and debts are ways "of getting and keeping a lasting hold over someone" (1990, 126).

The magic of the gift is that it suggests a generosity that is seemingly among the most natural of human drives, the innocent desire to help. Yet as Bourdieu also recalls, that naturalness comes in the form of a "censured, euphemized...violence" (1990, 126). At its most fundamental symbolic levels, gift giving is deeply ambiguous, exerting a violence that binds, keeping both loved ones and enemies close at hand.

The gift of empire, with which this book began, is all of these things. It builds on a logic that to better the lives of others is a godly practice; it encompasses those to whom gifts are intended; and it can ratify many forms of sovereign rule. In the case of Russia and the Caucasus over the last two hundred years, where political relations were as varied as any can be, the ambiguous language of the gift well captured the regular pulls of peace and conflict between North and South.

The artful use of the idea of the gift in political fields was hardly developed by the Russian Empire. The tale of Prometheus from the age of the rise of the Greeks is but one place to start in considering the confusion between giving and taking among peoples soon to be conquered. Remarkably plastic, the language of giving has morphed across time and space with telling resonance. Like Stalin, Chechen leader Dzhokar Dudayev had a league of journalists who penned panegyrics of gratitude for his rule. Prior to his death near the close of the first Chechen war (1994–1996), newspapers in Grozny filled with epigraphic praises, making clear that Dudayev, too, was a giver. "You called yourself 'a sacrifice of history,' and, like Prometheus, you stole fire to give it to the people—Dzhokar" (Tishkov 2004, 86). Like all idioms of power, the language of the gift has been open to loose interpretation and wide appropriation.

Russian captivity narratives set in the Caucasus offered likely satisfaction for a wide variety of Russian, Soviet, and Caucasian publics alike. But they were not constant over time: leaning to increasing ambiguities of both form and content, they very much mapped a history of mutual appropriation between specific governing actors and the peoples of the Caucasus with whom they widely interacted. These multiplex and varied narratives suggested that for all the fraught dimensions of the Russian engagement in the lands to its south, those engagements could be perceived by the spirit of altruism and the honor of sacrifice as much as by the moral ambivalence through which Russian critics saw the massive undertakings in the South. Early in the nineteenth century, this message was carried foremost in poetry and prose by some of Russia's most famous writers, soon to be followed by scores of imitators.

The political landscape, clearly, was challenging. Pushkin and Tolstoy, for their part, gave more than enough evidence of support for the newly adopted Caucasus peoples to suggest that they did not see imperial rule as an unalloyed good. It is another question how such finely tuned works were received, beyond the voices of metropolitan critics, when the widest circulations of the classic statements on the Caucasus by writers such as Pushkin and Tolstoy came in legions of adaptations and imitations, creating a popular language of imperial rule that often spoke for itself. Manifold tales of young men and women held by rough but admiring captors offered Russian publics the chance to see the goodness in themselves through the sacrifices of captivity or even death.

In public spheres of both tsarist Russia and the USSR where the circuitous languages of patriotism and dissent were raised to high art, these numerous gestures of poetry, ballet, motion picture musical comedy, and restaurant interiors were politically significant indeed. The subtle power of aesthetic production in these sublimated contexts is precisely what enabled such wide-ranging and deeply rooted effects. The very discretion of these colonial and communist arts lent them fantastic productivity, enabling Russian poets and statesmen alike to craft new places in unwelcome spaces, to generate new realities, new cognitions, and new forms of political legitimacy.

Politics aside, it is clear that some writers, at least, were aware of the powers of their fictions. In 1837, Aleksandr Bestuzhev-Marlinskii lamented in the preface to "Tale of an Officer Held Captive among the Gortsy" that contemporary Russian readers had shamefully little at hand to properly learn about the Caucasus. But scholarship of the kind penned by early greats such as the historian Bronevskii, he contended, was not the answer. Where might one get the best information? Not from Caucasians themselves, who were too close to the scene to properly explain, nor from the Russian officer, who learned to dance the lezginka (the dance widely attributed to the North Caucasus that became a sensation in Petersburg at the outset of Russian rule) but nothing beyond that. If you looked for answers about the customs, morals, and attitudes of Caucasus peoples from the native, soldier, or merchant, Marlinskii wrote, "You will wait in vain, as if waiting for apples from a birch tree.... Only one source remains: Conversations with officers returning from captivity in the mountains, and in turn, Russians who sought refuge there" (1837, 175).

Such conversations were Bestuzhev's to extend. "Learning to write with a ruler bored us even in school," he added.

> So if you put together a notebook with tricolor silk ties, as is custom, and very neatly write in headings like "On highlander rule, on religion, on language, their history, morals, customs," and so forth...then roll that notebook into a cylinder, tie it up with string, and throw it hard onto the fire.... We learned far more about Scotland from the novels of Walter Scott than we did from such Histories." (177)

The kinds of stories by Marlinskii and many others, based on events real and imagined, offered very specific kinds of negative reading pleasures (or pleasures taken from negative plotlines), with powerful capabilities built on long traditions of self-giving in which some actors can, if only in narrative form, place themselves alongside powerless brothers-in-arms (or well-armed brothers) who are, just like them, only human. This is, in effect, an art of emplacement.

Dissimulations of power and selfhood may have taken from Pushkin a certain lead in the Russian colonial arts, but they were no less active in the communist era. The Bolshevik "victory of the proletariat" was one of the most rhetorically skillful renditions of the power of the underdog in the twentieth century (although it is more likely Shurik whom Soviet-era audiences remember most warmly). Whether Russian writers and publics continue to find satisfaction in the sufferings of noble givers in far pavilions remains to be seen. In August of 1990 while speaking to regional leaders in Kazan', Boris Yeltsin stirred surprise with his famous invitation,

"Take as much sovereignty as you can handle" (Merzabekov 1990, 1).[1] It was as if, out of exhaustion from giving, sovereignty was, if only briefly, for the taking. That same year Russian writer Aleksandr Solzhenitsyn (1990) urged his countrymen more directly to give up the secessionist Caucasus territories. Russians, he suggested, had been giving too much of themselves for too long. For Solzhenitsyn this was one sovereign struggle on which the book might be closed for good.

By moving beyond exclusively Russian frames, in the consideration of ethnological accounts of the exchange of bodies on Caucasian terms, we should see a key generative dimension in putatively negative acts such as kidnapping or stealing. This enables us to see the long-standing and relatively more porous statuses of sovereign rule negotiated through a variety of practices across the region. The theft of cattle does not always signal hunger; it can be a challenge to the neighbor one considers a subordinate or even a route to closer ties with that same neighbor. Young men and women marry for all manner of reasons, but kidnapping and elopement need not necessarily be seen as transgressive ones, particularly when on many occasions, just such marriages upended orthodox hierarchies, creating fresh alliances with the unlikeliest of parties. What the abrek who seeks refuge in a neighboring province, the captive in wartime, and the bride or groom who trades one home for another all have in common is that they are subject to considerable personal transformation. Wrought anew, they still carry the markers of the lives they left behind, offering the possibility of binding together, discursively if not by blood, worlds that might otherwise remain separate. Consequently, as real-life examples and real-life archetypes, they oblige us to consider fields that remain open, not only those we perceive as closed in times of strife—to recall one of the most powerful paradigms of knowledge about the Caucasus of all, the Caucasus as closed space, as a set of warring societies closed to outsiders and to one another.

Since the fall of the USSR, a number of armed conflicts in the Caucasus have begun or begun anew. Although Russia has formally acted as a mediator in some, there have been calls to purposely destabilize the region once again—as advocated by a respected Russian newspaper in 1997—on

---

1. During his visits across the USSR in August of 1990, Yeltsin made repeated versions of the same invitation. See "Berite stol'ko suvereniteta" at *Krylatye slova i vyrazheniia*, http://slova. ndo.ru/.

the theory that unity among the political trading partners of the Caucasus would shut out Russian economic and security interests (Anonymous 1997).[2] In the course of what have been two Chechen wars since 1994, as well as armed conflicts in the various breakaway republics—bringing upheaval to the region and over a million internally displaced persons—thousands of soldiers and civilians, Russian, Chechen, Georgian, and Daghestani alike, have been kidnapped across the North and South Caucasus (Dixon 2000; Filipov 2000; Gordon 2000; Koval'skaia 1998; LeVine 1997; Musaeva 2001).[3] In this context, the "good prisoner" symbol has lost little of its salience, serving as the basis for countless news headlines and, perhaps most notably, in varied Defense Ministry press releases, where, in Russia, the term *Kavkazets* (Caucasian) or *litso kavkazskoi natsional'nosti* (subject of Caucasian nationality) is most commonly conflated with Chechen (Ram 1999, 15).[4]

In a survey of Russian central newspapers over a ten-year period, from 1997 to 2006, one can find over five thousand headlines that include the phrase *kavkazskii plennik* (prisoner of the Caucasus), and over twenty-two thousand that included its female variant, *kavkazskaia plennitsa*.[5] A vast number recall the films of both titles and the careers of the beloved stars of the older film especially. A significant number, however, track the ongoing spate of kidnappings across Russia and the Caucasus as the area continues to know this particularly targeted and strangely suturing kind of violence. The suggestion is that ancient metaphors of prisoners of the mountains continue to find a wide circulation.

If one seeks to destroy a neighbor, one can presumably send a bomb and be done with it. If one is after money, more anonymous forms of theft

---

2. This position resonates with the earlier findings of Bournoutian (1994) and Swietochowski (1995) on Russian interest in keeping the Caucasus destabilized in the early nineteenth century.

3. In the most widely reported cases, foreign businessmen and aid workers have been among the kidnapped in the wave of seizures of the last decade (Lomsadze 2002). Among the non-Russians, the most widespread disappearances are of Chechen civilians taken by Russian forces (Dudayev 2003).

4. Non-Russian media have largely followed suit, with one example perhaps most plainly suggestive of the political uses of captivity: see Gordon (2000). For more on the *litso kavkazskoi natsional'nosti,* see Mamedov (1999).

5. A survey in June 2007 of the Universal Database of Russian Newspapers, http://www.russianlibrary.ru/newsearch/basic.jsp, yielded 5,486 articles including *kavkazskii plennik* and 22,447 with *kavkazskaia plennitsa.*

might be the most direct routes. Kidnapping sometimes takes as its premise that ransoming can also produce funds or other persons worthy of exchange. But the act of holding a person captive also creates relations or
spaces of encounter that begin to narrate and sometimes negotiate broader
claims. I thought of this strange kind of suturing one day in Baku in the
autumn of 2002, when I completed an interview with the director of *In a
Southern City,* the 1969 film that tracked Soviet canons of internationalism, another gift from another time to peoples in the workers' paradise.
His assistant was walking me off the near-empty studio lot, a shadow of
its former grandeur that was only slowly being reclaimed after the fall of
the Soviet Union. He told me that he, too, was working on a film, set in
Nagorno-Karabagh, since 1992 the site of the protracted, seemingly intractable war between Armenia and Azerbaijan. "It's a feature film, a really good story, but also a political story," he told me. "What it's called?" I
asked. *"The Hostage,"* he replied.

GLOSSARY

abrek (multiple origins): Male figure in the Caucasus who leaves his community, conventionally for a period no longer than several months, to plan vengeance or seek respite; a seeker of refuge without the usual requisites of kin protection, subject to transformation by the host community.

adat (Arabic): Custom, conventionally understood in contrast but by no means exclusive to formal state or orthodox religious laws.

amanat (Arabic): Literally, an object or person held for safekeeping, entrusted by covenant. In Qur'anic translations, "trust." In the Caucasus, variously, a diplomatic hostage, guest, or daughter-in-law; sometimes close in meaning to *abrek*.

ARDTA: Azərbaycan Respublikası Dövlət Tarixi Arxiv (State Historical Archive of the Republic of Azerbaijan).

bey (Turkic) (in Russian, *bek*): Originally, "chieftain" or "leader." Variously, an honorific term of respect, akin to "Mr." or "Sir."

Circassian (Russian, Cherkess; Turkish, Çerkez): A term once used loosely to refer to all peoples of the northwest Caucasus, it more properly refers to the Adyghe-speaking peoples of that region and their diasporic descendants.

gortsy (Russian, s. *gorets*): Literally, "residents of the highlands," often glossed in English as "mountaineers." Formally designating the relatively decentralized, highlander peoples of the North Caucasus, it could embrace all peoples of the North and South Caucasus when used pejoratively.

Kavkaz (Russian): Caucasus. Normally divided into North (also "Ciscaucasia") and South ("Transcaucasia").

kula (Kilivila/Trobriand): Ceremonial trade taking place across the archipelagoes of Papua New Guinea, where reputations could be forged through the arts of exchange.

RSFSR: Russian Soviet Federated Socialist Republic, the largest of the fifteen republics of the former Soviet Union.

shamkhal (Kumyk): Honorific that designates a range of hereditary rulers across the Caucasus.

Tatar (Russian, multiple origins): An umbrella term commonly used during the Russian Empire to designate, variously, all the peoples of the East ("Asiatics"), peoples of the Caucasus and central Asia, and the empire's Muslim constituents. Normally (but not always) distinct in designation from the locally identified Crimean Tatars, or the residents of the Republic of Tatarstan (s. m. Tatarin) of the contemporary Russian Federation.

REFERENCES

Abrahamian, Levon. 2007. "The Chained Hero: The Cave and the Labyrinth." *Iran and the Caucasus* 11 (1): 89–99.

Aeschylus. 1932. *Prometheus Bound.* Edited by George Thomson. Cambridge: Cambridge University Press.

Agamben, Giorgio. 1998. *Homo Sacer: Sovereign Power and Bare Life.* Stanford: Stanford University Press.

Ajami, Fouad. 2006. *The Foreigner's Gift: The Americans, the Arabs, and the Iraqis in Iraq.* New York: Free Press.

Akaev, V. A. 2000. "Kavkazskaia voina: Starye kontseptsii i novye podkhody." In *Kavkazskaia voina: Spornye voprosy i novye podkhody,* edited by A. I. Osmanov, 17–22. Makhachkala, Russ.: Akademiia nauk.

Akopov, S. 1930. "Bor'ba s bytovymi prestupleniiami." *Revoliutsiia i natsional'nosti,* nos. 4–5:58–69.

Alikhanov, Maksud. 2005. *V gorakh Dagestana.* Makhachkala, Russ.: Epokha.

Alimova, Bariat M. 1986. "Brak i svadebnye obriady u tabasarantsev." In *Brak i svadebnye obychai u narodov Dagestana v XIX–nachale XX v.,* edited by B. M. Alimova, 29–46. Makhachkala, Russ.: Akademiia nauk.

———. 1989. *Brak i svadebnye obriady v proshlom i nastoiashchem (Ravninnyi Dagestan).* Makhachkala, Russ.: Dagestanskoe knizhnoe izdatel'stvo.

166   *References*

Allen, Nick. 2000. "Marriage by Capture." *Journal of the Royal Anthropological Institute* 6 (1): 135.

Amsler, Sarah, and Russell Kleinbach. 1999. "Bride Kidnapping in the Kyrgyz Republic." *International Journal of Central Asian Studies* 4:186–216.

Anchabadze, Iurii D. 1979. "'Ostrakizm' na Kavkaze." *Sovetskaia etnografiia,* no. 5:137–144.

Anonymous. 1827. Review of "Kavkazskii plennik." *Damskii Zhurnal* 20 (October): 61–63.

———. 1898. "Materialy dlia istorii severnago Kavkaza, 1787–1792 gg." *Kavkazskii sbornik* 19:218–281.

———. 1997. "SNG: Nachalo ili konets istorii?" *Nezavisimaia gazeta,* March 26, 5.

Arans, Olga R., and Christine R. Shea. 1994. "The Fall of Elpenor: Homeric Kirke and the Folklore of the Caucasus." *Journal of Indo-European Studies* 22 (3–4): 371–398.

Aretxaga, Begona. 1991. *Shattering Silence: Women, Nationalism, and Political Subjectivity in Northern Ireland.* Princeton: Princeton University Press.

Arutiunov, Sergei Aleksandrovich. 2003. "'Zakrytoe obshchestvo'—al'ternativa megapolisnomu potrebitel'stvu?" In *Adat. Kavkazskii kul'turnyi krug: Traditsii i sovremennost',* edited by V. A. Dmitriev, 11–17. Moscow: Mezhdunarodnyi nauchno-issledovatel'skii institut narodov Kavkaza.

Asaf'ev, V. 1949. "Pushkin o russkoi muzyke." *Sovetskaia muzyka* 6:7–13.

Ascherson, Neal. 1995. *Black Sea.* New York: Hill and Wang.

Atkin, Muriel. 1988. "Russian Expansion in the Caucasus to 1813." In *Russian Colonial Expansion to 1917,* edited by Michael Rywkin, 139–187. London: Mansell.

Austin, Paul. 1984. "The Exotic Prisoner in Russian Romanticism." *Russian Literature* 16:217–274.

———. 1997. *The Exotic Prisoner in Russian Romanticism.* New York: Peter Lang.

Avramenko A. M., O. V. Matveev, P. P. Matiushenko, and V. N. Ratushniak. 1995. "Ob otsenke kavkazskoi voiny s nauchnykh pozitsii istorizma." In *Kavkazskaia voina: Uroki istorii i sovremennost',* edited by V. N. Ratushniak, 24–43. Krasnodar: Kubanskii gosudarstvennyi universitet.

Ayres, Barbara. 1974. "Bride Theft and Raiding for Wives in Cross-Cultural Perspective." *Anthropological Quarterly* 47 (3): 238–252.

Babaeva, R. 1964. "Materials for the Study of Marriage Ceremonies on the Apsheron Peninsula in the Past." *Soviet Anthropology and Archeology* 6 (2): 3–11. (First published, in Russian, in *Azerbaidzhanskii etnograficheskii sbornik* 1 (1964): 177–190.)

Baberowski, Jörg. 2004. "Tsivilizatorskaia missiia i natsionalizm v Zakavkaz'e: 1828–1914 gg." In *Novaia imperskaia istoriia postsovetskogo prostranstva,* edited by I. Gerasimov, S. Glebov, A. Kaplunskii, M. Mogil'ner, and A. Semenov, 307–352. Kazan': Tsentr issledovanii natsionalizma i imperii.

Babich, Irina L. 1999. *Evoliutsiia pravovoi kul'tury adygov, 1860–1990-e gody.* Moscow: Akademiia nauk.

———. 2000. *Pravovoi monizm v Severnoi Osetii: Istoriia i sovremennost'.* Moscow: Akademiia nauk.

Baddeley, John. [1908] 1969. *The Russian Conquest of the Caucasus.* New York: Russell and Russell.

Bagby, Lewis. 1995a. *Alexander Bestuzhev-Marlinsky and Russian Byronism.* University Park: Pennsylvia State University Press.

——. 1995b. "Bestuzhev's Byron: Cross-Cultural Transformation." *Canadian-American Slavic Studies* 29 (3–4): 271–284.

Barkey, Karen. 1994. *Bandits and Bureaucrats: The Ottoman Route to State Centralization.* Ithaca: Cornell University Press.

Barnes, R. H. 1999. "Marriage by Capture." *Journal of the Royal Anthropological Institute* 5:57–73.

Barrett, Thomas. 1995. "Lines of Uncertainty: The Frontiers of the North Caucasus." *Slavic Review* 54 (3): 578–601.

——. 1998. "Southern Living (in Captivity): The Caucasus in Russian Popular Culture." *Journal of Popular Culture* 31 (4): 75–93.

——. 1999. *At the Edge of Empire: The Terek Cossacks and the North Caucasus Frontier, 1700–1860.* Boulder: Westview.

Bartelson, Jens. 1995. *A Genealogy of Sovereignty.* Cambridge: Cambridge University Press.

Bartenev, P. 1866. "Pushkin v Iuzhnoi Rossii. Materialy dlia podrobnoi biografii." *Russkii arkhiv* 8–9:1090–1214.

Bataille, Georges. 1985. "The Notion of Expenditure." In *Visions of Excess: Selected Writings, 1927–1939,* 116–129. Minneapolis: University of Minnesota Press.

——. 1988. *The Accursed Share: An Essay on General Economy. Vol. 1.* New York: Zone.

Bates, Daniel. 1981. "Marriage by Kidnapping among the Yörük of Southeastern Turkey." In *Contemporary Anthropology: An Anthology,* edited by Daniel G. Bates and Susan H. Lees, 212–223. New York: Knopf.

Baum, Bruce. 2006. *The Rise and Fall of the Caucasian Race: A Political History of Racial Identity.* New York: NYU Press.

Beidelman, Thomas O. 1989. "Agonistic Exchange: Homeric Reciprocity and the Heritage of Simmel and Mauss." *Cultural Anthropology* 4 (3): 227–259.

Beissinger, Mark. 2005. "Rethinking Empire in the Wake of Soviet Collapse." In *Ethnic Politics after Communism,* edited by Zoltan Barany and Robert G. Moser, 14–45. Ithaca: Cornell University Press.

——. 2006. "Soviet Empire as 'Family Resemblance.'" *Slavic Review* 65 (2): 294–303.

Belinskii, V. G. [1844] 1955. "Stat'ia shestaia. Poemy." In *Polnoe sobranie sochinenii,* 7:358–384. Moscow: Akademiia nauk.

Berzhe, Adolf, ed. 1866. *Akty sobrannye kavkazskoiu arkheograficheskoiu komissieiu.* Vol. 1. Tiflis: Glavnoe upravlenie namestnika Kavkazskago.

——. 1866–1904. *Akty sobrannye kavkazskoiu arkheograficheskoiu komissieiu.* 12 vols. Tiflis: Glavnoe upravlenie namestnika Kavkazskago.

Bethea, David M. 1998. "Slavic Gift-Giving, the Poet in History, and Pushkin's *The Captain's Daughter.*" In *Russian Subjects: Empire, Nation, and the Culture of the Golden Age,* edited by Monika Greenleaf and Stephen Moeller-Sally, 259–273. Evanston, IL: Northwestern University Press.

Bitov, Andrei. [1969] 1992. *A Captive of the Caucasus.* Translated by Susan Brownsberger. New York: Farrar, Straus and Giroux.

Bliev, Mark Maksimovich. 1983. "Kavkazskaia voina: Sotsial'nye istoki, sushchnost'." *Istoriia SSSR* 2:54–75.

———. 2004. *Rossiia i gortsy Bol'shogo Kavkaza na puti k tsivilizatsii.* Moscow: Mysl'.

Bliev, Mark M., and Vladimir V. Degoev. 1994. *Kavkazskaia voina.* Moscow: Roset.

Blumenbach, Johann Friedrich. [1775] 1969. *On the Natural Varieties of Mankind.* New York: Bergman.

Boas, Franz. [1897] 1966. *Kwakiutl Ethnography.* Chicago: University of Chicago Press.

Bobrovnikov, Vladimir. 2000. "Abreki i gosudarstvo: Kul'tura nasiliia na Kavkaze." *Vestnik Evrazii/Acta Eurasica* 1 (8): 19–46.

———. 2002. *Musul'mane Severnogo Kavkaza: Obychai, pravo, nasilie.* Moscow: Vostochnaia literatura.

Bogdanov-Berezovskii, V. 1949. Pushkinskaia tema v balete. *Sovetskaia muzyka* 8: 42–50.

Bondar', V. V. 1995. "Rol' naezdnichestva v rossiisko-kavkazskikh otnosheniiakh v kontse XVII–pervoi treti XIX v." In *Kavkazskaia voina: Uroki istorii i sovremennost',* edited by V. N. Ratushniak, 127–132. Krasnodar: Kubanskii gosudarstvennyi universitet.

Bondarevskii, G. L., and G. N. Kolbaia. 2002. "The Caucasus and Russian Culture." *Russian Studies in History* 41 (2): 10–15.

Botiakov, Iu. M. 2004. *Abreki na Kavkaze: Sotsiokul'turnyi aspekt iavleniia.* St. Petersburg: Petersburgskoe vostokovedenie.

Bourdieu, Pierre. 1977. *Outline of a Theory of Practice.* Translated by Richard Nice. Cambridge: Cambridge University Press.

———. 1990. *The Logic of Practice.* Translated by Richard Nice. Stanford: Stanford University Press.

Bournoutian, George A. 1994. *A History of Qarabagh: An Annotated Translation of Mirza Jamal Javanshir Qarabaghi's Tarikh-e Qarabagh.* Costa Mesa, CA: Mazda.

Bracken, Christopher. 1997. *The Potlatch Papers: A Colonial Case History.* Chicago: University of Chicago Press.

Breyfogle, Nicholas. 2005. *Heretics and Colonizers: Forging Russia's Empire in the South Caucasus.* Ithaca: Cornell University Press, 2005.

Bronevskii, Semen Mikhailovich. [1823, 1996] 2004. *Noveishiia izvestiia o Kavkaze, sobrannyia i popolnennyia Semenom Bronevskim,* edited with commentary by I. K. Pavlova. St. Petersburg: Petersburgskoe vostokovedenie.

Brooks, Jeffrey. 1985. *When Russia Learned to Read: Literacy and Popular Literature, 1861–1917.* Princeton: Princeton University Press.

———. 2000. *Thank You, Comrade Stalin! Soviet Public Culture from Revolution to Cold War.* Princeton: Princeton University Press.

Brower, Daniel, and Susan Layton. 2005. "Liberation through Captivity: Nikolai Shipov's Adventures in the Imperial Borderlands." *Kritika* 6 (2): 259–279.

Broxup, Marie. 1992. "Introduction: Russia and the North Caucasus." In *The North Caucasus Barrier: The Russian Advance Towards the Muslim World,* edited by Marie Broxup, 1–17. New York: St. Martin's.

Brubaker, Rogers, and Frederick Cooper. 2000. "Beyond Identity." *Theory and Society* 29 (1): 1–47.

Bryan, Fanny. 1992. "Internationalism, Nationalism, and Islam." In *The North Caucasus Barrier,* edited by Marie Broxup, 195–218. New York: St. Martin's.

Buck-Morss, Susan. 2000. "Hegel and Haiti." *Critical Inquiry* 26 (4): 821–865.

Burbank, Jane, and David Ransel. 1998. *Imperial Russia: New Histories for the Empire.* Bloomington: Indiana University Press.

Burton, Julianne. 1992. "Don (Juanito) Duck and the Imperial-Patriarchal Unconscious: Disney Studios, the Good Neighbor Policy, and the Packaging of Latin America." In *Nationalisms and Sexualities,* edited by Andrew Parker, Mary Russo, Doris Summer, and Patricia Yaeger, 21–41. New York: Routledge.

Calhoun, Craig, Frederick Cooper, and Kevin W. Moore, eds. 2006. *Lessons of Empire: Imperial Histories and American Power.* New York: New Press.

Catherine II. 1849. *Sochineniia Imperatritsy Ekateriny II.* Vol. 1. St. Petersburg: Smirdin.

Çelebi, E. 1988. *Evliya Çelebi in Diyarbekir: The Relevant Section of the Seyahatname.* Leiden: Brill.

Charachidze, Georges. 1986. *Promethée ou le Caucase: Essai de mythologie contrastive.* Paris: Flammarion.

Chatterjee, Indrani. 2008. "Captives of Enchantment? Gender, Genre, and Transmemoration." In *History in the Vernacular,* edited by Raziuddin Aquil and Partha Chatterjee, 250–287. New Delhi: Permanent Black.

Cherkasov, A. A. 2004. "Institut zalozhnichestva na Kubani i Chernomor'e v 1920–1922 gg." *Voprosy istorii* 10:106–113.

Cohn, Bernard. 1996. *Colonialism and Its Forms of Knowledge: The British in India.* Princeton: Princeton University Press.

Colarusso, John. 2002. *Nart Sagas from the Caucasus: Myths and Legends from the Circassians, Abazas, Abkhaz, and Ubykhs.* Princeton: Princeton University Press.

Colley, Linda. 2002. *Captives.* New York: Pantheon.

Conklin, Alice. 1997. *A Mission to Civilize: The Republican Idea of Empire in France and West Africa, 1895–1930.* Stanford: Stanford University Press.

Conquest, Robert. 1960. *The Soviet Deportation of Nationalities.* New York: St. Martin's.

Conrad, Joseph. [1902] 1990. *Heart of Darkness.* New York: Dover.

Cowie, Elizabeth. 1990. "Woman as Sign." In *The Woman in Question,* edited by Parveen Adams and Elizabeth Cowie, 117–133. Cambridge: MIT Press.

Cutler, Anthony. 2000. "The Empire of Things: Gift Exchange between Byzantium and the Islamic World." In *Center 20: Record of Activities and Research Reports, June 1999–May 2000,* 67–70. Washington, DC: National Gallery of Art, Center for Advanced Study in the Visual Arts.

———. 2001. "Gifts and Gift Exchange as Aspects of the Byzantine, Arab, and Related Economies." *Dumbarton Oaks Papers,* no. 55:247–278.

Dal', Vladimir. 1880. *Tol'kovyi slovar' russkogo iazyka.* Vol. 1. St. Petersburg: M.O. Vol'f.

Datsiuk, B. D. 1955. *Rabovladel'cheskii stroi i rabovladel'cheskie gosudarstva.* Moscow: Vysshaia partiinaia shkola.

Davis, Natalie Zemon. 2000. *The Gift in Sixteenth-Century France.* Madison: University of Wisconsin Press.

Degoev, Vladimir. 2004. "The Diplomacy of the Caucasus Wars as a History Lesson." *Russian Politics and Law* 42 (2): 68–76.

De Maistre, Xavier. 1884. *Les Prisonniers du Caucase.* Paris: Librairie de la Bibliothèque Nationale.

Demos, John. 1994. *The Unredeemed Captive: A Family Story from Early America.* New York: Knopf.

Derluguian, Georgi. 2005. *Bourdieu's Secret Admirer in the Caucasus: A World-System Biography.* Chicago: University of Chicago Press.

Derluguian, Liubov'. 1997. "The Unlikely Abolitionists: The Russian Struggle against the Slave Trade in the Caucasus, 1800–1864." PhD diss., SUNY Binghamton.

Derounian-Stodola, Kathryn, and James Arthur Levernier. 1993. *The Indian Captivity Narrative, 1550–1900.* New York: Twayne.

Ditchev, Ivalyo. 2002. "Communism: Between Ideological Gift and the Gift in Everyday Life." *Diogenes* 49 (2): 86–94.

Dixon, Robyn. 2000. "Chechnya's Grimmest Industry: Thousands of People Have Been Abducted by the War-Torn Republic's Kidnapping Machine. Tales of Survivors Read Like Relics from a Barbaric Past." *Los Angeles Times,* September 18, A1.

Dmitriev, V. A. 2001. "Nasil'stvennye deistviia i ikh proiavleniia v traditsionnom i sovremennom sotsiore adygov." In *Antropologiia nasiliia,* edited by V. V. Bocharov and V. A. Tishkov, 332–381. St. Petersburg: Nauka.

Dorfman, Ariel, and Armand Mattelart. 1975. *How to Read Donald Duck: Imperialist Ideology in the Disney Comic.* New York: International General.

Dostoevskii [Dostoevsky], Fedor M. [1881] 1999. *Sobranie sochinenii.* Tom 20, *Dnevnik pisatelia.* Moscow: Terra.

Dragadze, Tamara. 1988. *Rural Families in Soviet Georgia: A Case Study in Ratcha Province.* London: Routledge.

Duchemin, Jacqueline. 2000. *Prométhée: Histoire du mythe, de ses origines orientales à ses incarnations modernes.* Paris: Belles Lettres.

Dudayev, Umalt. 2003. "Chechnya: Disappearances Mount." *Caucasus Reporting Service* 178. http://www.iwpr.net (accessed May 9, 2003).

Dumézil, George. 1979. *Mariages indo-européens: Suivi de quinze questions romaines.* Paris: Payot.

Duve, Freimut, and Heidi Tagliavini, eds. 2000. *Zashchita budushchego: Kavkaz v poiskakh mira.* Moscow: Glagol.

Dzhimov, B. M. 1995. "Politika vedushchikh derzhav i ee otrazhenie v khode Kavkazskoi voiny (konets XVIII–pervaia polovina XIX v.)." In *Kavkazskaia voina: Uroki istorii i sovremennost',* edited by V. N. Ratushniak, 5–24. Krasnodar: Kubanskii gosudarstvennyi universitet.

Edgar, Adrienne. 2004. *Tribal Nation: The Making of Soviet Turkmenistan.* Princeton: Princeton University Press.

Egorova, E. B. 1997. "175 let so vremeni vykhoda v svet poemy A. S. Pushkina 'Kavkazskii plennik.'" *Stavropol'skii khronograf na 1997 god,* edited by L. P. Durenko, 101–103. Stavropol': Biblioteka.

Eisenstein, Sergei. 1998. *Planirovka mesta deistviia na materiale "Kavkazskogo Plennika" (Lektsii S. M. Eizenshteina vo VGIKe).* Moscow: Muzei Kino.

Ekel'n, Lev. 1841. "Iz zapisok russkago, byvshago v plenu u Cherkesov." *Otechestvennye zapiski* 19 (12): 91–96.

Emerson, Ralph Waldo. [1844] 1997. "Gifts." In *The Logic of the Gift: Toward an Ethic of Generosity,* edited by Alan D. Schrift, 25–28. New York: Routledge.

Engels, Friedrich. 1902. *The Origin of the Family, Private Property, and the State.* Chicago: Kerr.

Enikolopov, I. K. 1938. *Pushkin na Kavkaze.* Moscow: Zaria Vostoka.

Ergushov, P. 1929. *Kavkazskii plennik: Povest' iz vremen grazhdanskoi voiny.* Prague: Izdanie avtora.

Esadze, S. [1914] 2004. *Pokorenie zapadnogo kavkaza i okonchanie kavkazskoi voiny.* Moscow: Gosudarstvennaia publichnaia istoricheskaia biblioteka.

Eschment, Beate, and Hans Harder, eds. 2004. *Looking at the Coloniser: Cross-Cultural Perceptions in Central Asia and the Caucasus, Bengal, and Related Areas.* Würzburg: Ergon.

Fabian, Johannes. 1983. *Time and the Other: How Anthropology Makes It Object.* New York: Columbia University Press.

Fasmer, Maks. 1971. *Etimologicheskii slovar' russkogo iazyka.* Tom 3. Moscow: Progress.

Feldman, Allen. 1991. *Formations of Violence: The Narrative of the Body and Political Terror in Northern Ireland.* Chicago: University of Chicago Press.

Ferdowsi [Fîrdawsi]. 1998. *The Lion and the Throne: Stories from the Shahnameh of Ferdowsi,* Vol. I. Translated from the Persian by Dick Davis. Washington, DC: Mage.

———. 2000. *Fathers and Sons: Stories from the Shahnameh of Ferdowsi,* Vol. II. Translated from the Persian by Dick Davis. Washington, DC: Mage.

———. 2004. *Sunset of Empire: Stories from the Shahnameh of Ferdowsi,* Vol. III. Translated from the Persian by Dick Davis. Washington, DC: Mage.

Ferguson, Kennan. 2007. "The Gift of Freedom." *Social Text* 25 (2): 39–52.

Filipov, David. 2000. "Kidnappers of All Stripes Thrive on Chaos in Chechnya." *Boston Globe,* July 4, A1.

Fischer-Tiné, Harald, and Michael Mann, eds. 2004. *Colonialism as a Civilizing Mission: Cultural Ideology in British India.* London: Anthem.

Foucault, Michel. 1997. "Power, Right, Truth." In *Contemporary Political Philosophy: An Anthology,* edited by Robert E. Goodin and Philip Pettit, 543–550. Oxford: Blackwell.

Freygang, Frederika von, and Wilhelm von Freygang. 1816. *Lettres sur le Caucase et la Géorgie. Suivies d'une relation d'un voyage en Perse en 1812.* Hamburg: Perthes and Besser.

Freud, S. [1919] 1959. "The Uncanny." In *Sigmund Freud: Collected Papers,* 4:368–407. New York: Basic Books.

———. 1950. *Totem and Taboo.* New York: Norton.

Friedrich, Paul. 2003. "Tolstoy and the Chechens: Problems in Literary Anthropology." *Russian History/Histoire russe* 30 (1–2): 113–143.

Gadjiev, Murtuzali, Philip L. Kohl, and Rabadan G. Magomedov. 2007. "Mythologizing the Remote Past for Political Purposes in the Northern Caucasus." In *Caucasus Paradigms: Anthropologies, Histories, and the Making of a World Area,* edited by Bruce Grant and Lale Yalçın-Heckmann, 119–141. Berlin: LIT.

Gadzhiev, Bulach. 2005. *Khadzhi-Murat v istoriiakh i legendakh.* Makhachkala, Russ.: Epokha.

Gadzhiev, V. G. 1998. "Nereshennye i spornye voprosy istorii kavkazskoi voiny." In *Kavkazskaia voina: Spornye voprosy i novye podkhody,* edited by A. I. Osmanov, 3–8. Makhachkala, Russ.: Akademiia nauk.

Gagieva, M. A. 1973. *Zhenshchiny gor.* Ordzhonikidze, Russ.: Ir.

Gagloiti, Z. D. 1974. *Ocherki po etnografii osetin.* Vol. 1, *Obshchestvennyi byt osetin v XIX v.* Tbilisi: Metsniereba.

Gaguev, U. K. 1977. "O sootnoshenii prava i obychaev." In *Novyi byt—novye obychai: Formirovanie progressivnykh traditsii u narodov Karachaevo-Cherkesii,* edited by S. M. Arutiunian, 74–84. Stavropol': Karachaevo-Cherkesskii Nauchno-Issledovatel'skii Institut ekonomiki, istorii, iazyka i literatury.

Gammer, Moshe. 1993. "'The Conqueror of Napoleon' in the Caucasus." *Central Asian Survey* 12 (3): 253–265.

———. 1994. *Muslim Resistance to the Tsar: Shamil and the Conquest of Chechnia and Daghestan.* London: F. Cass.

———. 2006. *The Lone Wolf and the Bear: Three Centuries of Chechen Defiance of Russian Rule.* Pittsburgh: University of Pittsburgh Press.

Gamzatov, Rasul. 1970. *My Dagestan.* Moscow: Progress.

———. 1999. "Pushkin i Kavkaz." In *Pushkin i Kavkaz,* edited by G. I. Kusov. Moscow: Menedzher.

Garsoian, Nina G. 1996. "Iran and Caucasia." In *Transcaucasia, Nationalism, and Social Change: Essays in the History of Armenia, Azerbaijan, and Georgia,* edited by Ronald Suny, 7–24. Ann Arbor: University of Michigan Press.

Geraci, Robert. 2001. *Window on the East: National and Imperial Identities in Late Tsarist Russia.* Ithaca: Cornell University Press.

Gillespie, David. 1999. "New Versions of Old Classics: Recent Cinematic Interpretations of Russian Literature." In *Russia on Reels: The Russian Idea in Post-Soviet Cinema,* edited by Birgit Beumers, 114–126. London: I. B. Tauris.

Gilsenan, Michael. 1996. *Lords of the Lebanese Marches: Violence and Narrative in an Arab Society.* Berkeley: University of California Press.

Godelier, Maurice. 1999. *The Enigma of the Gift.* Translated by Nora Scott. Chicago: University of Chicago Press.

Gordin, Iakov. 2000. *Kavkaz: Zemlia i krov'.* St. Petersburg: Zvezda.

Gordon, Michael. 2000. "Freed in Chechnya: A Kidnap Victim Serves Russia's Needs." *New York Times,* January 4, A3.

Goscilo, Helena. 2003. "Casting and Recasting the Caucasian Captive." In *Two Hundred Years of Pushkin.* Vol. 1, *'Pushkin's Secret': Russian Writers Reread and Rewrite Pushkin,* edited by Joe Andrew and Robert Reid, 195–207. Amsterdam: Rodopi.

Gould, Rebecca. 2007. "Transgressive Sanctity: The Abrek in Chechen Culture." *Kritika* 8 (2): 271–306.

Gould, Stephen Jay. 1994. "The Geometer of Race." *Discover* 15 (11): 65–69.

Graeber, David. 2001. *Toward an Anthropological Theory of Value: The False Coin of Our Own Dreams.* New York: Palgrave.

Grant, Bruce. 1993. "Siberia Hot and Cold: Reconstructing the Image of Siberian Indigenous Peoples." In *Between Heaven and Hell: The Myth of Siberia in Russian Culture,* edited by Galya Diment and Yuri Slezkine, 227–253. New York: St. Martin's.

———. 1995. *In the Soviet House of Culture: A Century of Perestroikas.* Princeton: Princeton University Press.

———. 2004. "An Average Azeri Village (1930): Remembering Rebellion in the Caucasus Mountains." *Slavic Review* 63 (4): 705–731.

Greenleaf, Monika. 1991. "Pushkin's Journey to Arzrum." *Slavic Review* 50 (4): 940–953.

Greenhouse, Carol. 2006. "Lear and Law's Doubles: Identity and Meaning in a Time of Crisis." *Law, Culture, and the Humanities* 2 (2): 239–258.

Griffith, Mark. 1983. "Commentary" in Aeschylus, *Prometheus Bound,* edited by Mark Griffith, 79–280. Cambridge: Cambridge University Press.

Grosheva, E., and A. Il'in. 1949. *Pushkin na stsene Bol'shogo Teatra.* Moscow: Muzgiz.

Haase-Dubosc, Danielle. 1999. *Ravie et enlevée: De l'enlèvement des femmes comme stratégie matrimoniale au XVIIe siècle.* Paris: Albin Michel.

Hansen, Thomas Blom, and Finn Stepputat. 2006. "Sovereignty Revisited." *Annual Review of Anthropology* 35:295–315.

———, eds. 2005. *Sovereign Bodies: Citizens, Migrants, and States in the Postcolonial World.* Princeton: Princeton University Press.

Harkins, Anthony. 2004. *Hillbilly: A Cultural History of an American Icon.* New York: Oxford University Press.

Harrison, Simon. 2003. "Cultural Difference as Denied Resemblance: Reconsidering Nationalism and Ethnicity." *Comparative Studies in Society and History* 45 (2): 343–361.

Hauner, Milan. 1990. *What Is Asia to Us?: Russia's Asian Heartland Yesterday and Today.* Boston: Unwin Hyman.

Hellie, Richard. 1979. "Muscovite Slavery in Comparative Perspective." *Russian History/Histoire Russe* 6, pt. 2: 133–209.

Hesiod. 1983. *Theogony, Works and Days, Shield.* Translated by Apostolos N. Athanassakis. Baltimore: Johns Hopkins University Press.

Herzfeld, Michael. 1987. "'As In Your Own House': Hospitality, Ethnography, and the Stereotype of the Mediterranean Society." In *Honor and Shame in the Unity of the Mediterranean,* edited by David Gilmore, 75–89. Washington, DC: American Anthropological Association.

Hirsch, Francine. 2005. *Empire of Nations: Ethnographic Knowledge and the Making of the Soviet Union.* Ithaca: Cornell University Press.

Hobsbawm, Eric. 1969. *Bandits.* London: Weidenfeld and Nicolson.

Hokanson, Katya. 1994. "Literary Imperialism, Narodnost' and Pushkin's Invention of the Caucasus." *Russian Review* 53 (July): 336–352.

Humphrey, Caroline. 2004. "Sovereignty." In *A Companion to the Anthropology of Politics,* edited by David Nugent and Joan Vincent, 418–436. Oxford: Blackwell.

Inal-Apa, Sh. 1954. *Ocherki po istorii braka i sem'i u abkhazov.* Sukhumi, Abkhaziia: Abgiz.

Irigaray, Luce. 1985. *This Sex Which Is Not One.* Translated by Catherine Porter with Carolyn Burke. Ithaca: Cornell University Press.

Iskander, Fazil'. 1979. *Sandro iz Chegema.* Ann Arbor: Ardis, 1979.

———. 1993. "Ballada ob ukradennom kozle." In *Stikhotvoreniia,* 23–27. Moscow: Moskovskii rabochii.

Jersild, Austin. 2002. *Orientalism and Empire: North Caucasus Mountain Peoples and the Georgian Frontier, 1845–1917.* Montreal: McGill-Queens' University Press.

Kan, Sergei. 1989. *Symbolic Immortality: The Tlingit Potlatch of the Nineteenth Century.* Washington, DC: Smithsonian Institution Press.

Kandelaki, Marina Bidzinovna. 1987. *Iz obshchestvennogo byta gortsev Gruzii: Institut amanatstva.* Tbilisi: Metsniereba.

Kant, Emmanuel. 1980. *Essai pour introduire en philosophie le concept de grandeur néga-tive.* Translated by Roger Kempf. Paris: Librairie philosophique J. Vrin.

Karagezov, Rauf. 2005. *Metamorfozy kollektivnoi pamiati v Rossii i na tsentral'nom Kavkaze.* Baku: Nurlan.

Karakashly, K. T. 1970. "A Contribution to the History of the Social Structure of the Lesser Caucasus." *Soviet Anthropology and Archaeology* 8 (4): 304–354.

Karpeev, Igor'. 2000. "Bog dal mne silu i terpenie." *Rodina* 1–2: 58–60.

Karpov, Iu. Iu. 1996. *Dzhigit i volk: Muzhskie soiuzy v sotsiokul'turnoi traditsii gortsev Kavkaza.* St. Peterburg: Muzei antropologii i etnografii.

Kavkaz. 1846. "Ostatki khristianstva mezhdu zakubanskimi plemenami, proshedshee i nyneshnee sostoianie ikh nravov i obychaev." October 19, 166–167.

"'Kavkazskii nerv,' ili pozhelaem im dobra." 2000. *Rodina* 1–2:12–19 (roundtable discussion).

Kazemzadeh, Firuz. 1951. *The Struggle for Transcaucasia (1917–1921).* New York: Philosophical Library.

———. 1974. "Russian Penetration of the Caucasus." In *Russian Imperialism from Ivan the Great to the Revolution,* edited by Taras Hunczak. New Brunswick: Rutgers University Press.

Kemal, Y. [1900] 1961. *Memed My Hawk.* New York: Pantheon.

Kerashev, A. T. 1991. "Sotsial'naia sushchnost' adygskogo naezdnichestva." In *Kul'tura i byt adygov (Etnograficheskie issledovaniia).* Vol. VIII, edited by M. A. Mererutkov and L. T. Solov'eva, 167–186. Maikop, Russ.: Adygeiia.

Khaibulaev, Magomedrasul Kh. 2002. *Khadzhi Murat v pamiati potomkov.* Makhachkala, Russ.: Khunzakh.

Khan-Girei. 1847. "Beslnyi Abat'—Iz sochinenii pod zaglaviem: Biografiia znameni-tykh cherkesov i ocherki cherkesskikh nravov i predanii, pokoinago fligel'-adiutanta Xan'-Gireia. Chast II." *Kavkaz,* October 23, 170–171.

———. 1893. "Kniaz' Pshs'koi Akhodiagoko." *Sbornik materialov dlia opisaniia mestno-stei plemen Kavkaza* 17:1–43.

Khodarkovsky, Michael. 2002. *Russia's Steppe Frontier: The Making of a Colonial Empire, 1500–1800.* Bloomington: Indiana University Press.

King, Charles. 2006. "Across the Black Sea." Paper presented to the Eurasian Connections Working Group, New York University, March.

———. 2008. *The Ghost of Freedom: A History of the Caucasus.* New York: Oxford University Press.

Kisliakov, Nikolai Andreevich. 1959. *Sem'ia i brak u tadzhikov po materialam kontsa XIX–nachala XX veka.* Moscow-Leningrad: Akademiia nauk.

Klinger, Ivan. 1860. "Dva s polovinoiu goda v plenu u chechentsev." *Russkii arkhiv* 6:964–1006.

Kobychev, V. P., and A. I. Robakidze. 1969. "Basic Typology and Mapping of Dwell-ings of the Caucasian Peoples: Materials for the Caucasian Historical-Ethnographic Atlas." *Soviet Anthropology and Archeology* 7 (4): 13–28.

Kohl, Philip, and Gocha Tsetskhladze. 1995. "Nationalism, Politics and the Practice of Archaeology in the Caucasus." In *Nationalism, Politics and the Practice of Archae-ology,* edited by Philip L. Kohl and Gocha R. Tsetskhladze, 149–174. New York: Cambridge University Press.

Kolodny, Annette. 1993. "Among the Indians: The Uses of Captivity." *Women's Studies Quarterly* 3–4:184–195.

Konovalova, Evgeniya. 2006. "Russia: Out with the Yan. Thousands of Armenians Have Changed their Names to Avoid the 'Foreigner' Label." *Transitions Online,* December 6. http://www.tol.cz (accessed June 5, 2008).

Kostiukovskii, Iakov, Moris Slobodskii, and Leonid Gaidai. 1998. "Kavkazskaia plennitsa: Literaturnyi stsenarii." In *Zhit' khorosho. A khorosho zhit'—eshche luchshe,* 95–147. Moscow: Pik and Soglasie.

Kosven, M. O. 1961. *Etnografiia i istoriia Kavkaza.* Moscow: Vostochnaia literatura.

Kotkin, Stephen. 2007. "Mongol Commonwealth? Exchange and Governance across the Post-Mongol Space." *Kritika* 8 (3): 487–531.

Koval'skaia, Galina. 1998. "Kavkaz i plenniki." *Itogi,* March 24, 60–62.

Kravtsova, T. Iu., and B. M. Rosenfel'd. 1999. *A. S. Pushkin i Severnyi Kavkaz: Bibliograficheskii ukazatel' literatury.* Stavropol': Stavropol'skaia kraevaia nauchnaia biblioteka.

Kucherskaia, Maiia. 2004. "Fazil' Iskander: Ochelovechivanie cheloveka." *Rossiiskaia Gazeta,* March 4, 8.

Kudaev, M. Ch. 1988. *Karachaevo-balkarskii svadebnyi obriad.* Nal'chik, Russ.: El'brus.

Kudriashev, P. M. 1826. "Kirgizskii plennik. Byl' Orenburgskoi linii." *Otechestvennye zapiski* 28 (79).

Kurbatov, V. 1999. "Azbuka russkoi pravdy: 'Kavkazskii Plennik' i 'Khadzhi-Murat' L'va Tolstogo." *Literatura v shkole* 7:35–42.

Kuznetsov, A. B. 1986. *Diplomaticheskaia bor'ba Rossii za bezopasnost' iuzhnykh granits (pervaia polovina XVI veka).* Minsk: Universitetskoe.

Laidlaw, James. 2000. "A Free Gift Makes No Friends." *Journal of the Royal Anthropological Institute* 6:617–634.

Lakoff, George. 2006. *Whose Freedom? The Battle over America's Most Important Idea.* New York: Farrar, Straus and Giroux.

Lambton, A. 1981. *State and Government in Medieval Islam.* Oxford: Oxford University Press.

Laroui, Abdallah. 1997. *The History of the Maghrib: An Interpretive Essay.* Translated by Ralph Manheim. Princeton: Princeton University Press.

Layton, Susan. 1992a. "Eros and Empire in Russian Literature about Georgia." *Slavic Review* 51 (2): 195–213.

———. 1992b. "Marlinsky's 'Ammalat-Bek' and the Orientalisation of the Caucasus in Russian Literature." In *The Golden Age of Russian Literature and Thought,* edited by Derek Offord, 34–57. New York: St. Martin's.

———. 1994. *Russian Literature and Empire: Conquest of the Caucasus from Pushkin to Tolstoy.* New York: Cambridge University Press.

———. 1997a. "Nineteenth-Century Russian Mythologies of Savagery." In *Russia's Orient: Imperial Borderlands and Peoples, 1700–1917,* edited by Daniel R. Brower and Edward J. Lazzerini, 80–100. Bloomington: Indiana University Press.

———. 1997b. "A Russian Reverie: Chechnya's Literary Legacy." *History Today* 47 (2): 6–9.

———. 1999. "Aleksandr Polezhaev and Remembrance of War in the Caucasus: Constructions of the Soldier as Victim." *Slavic Review* 58 (3): 559–583.

———. 2001. "Colonial Mimicry and Disenchantment in Alexander Druzhinin's 'A Russian Circassian' and Other Stories." *Russian Review* 60:56–71.

———. 2004. Imagining a Chechen Military Aristocracy: The Story of the Georgian Princesses Held Hostage by Shamil." *Central Asian Survey* 23 (2): 183–203.

Lazarev, M. S. 1990. "Da, Aziaty my." Preface to *Byt' mozhet za khrebtom Kavkaza,* by Natan Ia. Eidelman, 3–18. Moscow: Nauka.

Lehmann, John. 1938. *Prometheus and the Bolsheviks.* New York: Alfred Knopf.

Leibov, Roman. 2000. "K genealogii kavkazskikh plennikov." *Ruthenia Online.* http://www.ruthenia.ru/document/175347.html (accessed September 2003).

Leighton, Lauren. 1975. *Alexander Bestuzhev-Marlinsky.* Boston: Twayne.

Leontovich, F. I. [1882] 2002. *Adaty kavkazskikh gortsev: Materialy po obychnomu pravu severnogo i vostochnogo Kavkaza.* Nal'chik, Russ.: El'fa.

Lepselter, Susan. 2005. "The Flight of the Ordinary: Narrative, Poetics, Power and UFOs in the American Uncanny." PhD diss., University of Texas at Austin. Archived online at http://hdl.handle.net/2152/397 (accessed June 2008).

Lermontov, Mikhail Iur'evich. 1948. *Polnoe sobranie sochinenii.* Vol. 2. Moscow-Leningrad: OGIZ.

———. 1983. *Mikhail Lermontov's Major Poetical Works.* Translated by Anatoly Liberman. Minneapolis: University of Minnesota Press.

LeVine, Steve. 1997. "Get Rich in Chechnya: Kidnap Your Neighbors." *New York Times,* September 5, A4.

Lévi-Strauss, Claude. 1963. *Totemism.* Translated by Rodney Needham. Boston: Beacon.

———. 1969. Elementary Structures of Kinship. Boston: Beacon.

———. 1976. *Structural Anthropology.* Vol. 2. Translated by Monique Layton. New York: Basic Books.

Likhachev, B. S. 1927. *Kino v Rossii (1896–1926).* Leningrad: Academia.

Lipovetsky, Mark. 2000. "Znamenitoe chegemskoe lukavstvo: Strannaia idilliia Fazilia Iskandera." *Kontinent* 103:280–291.

Lomsadze, Giorgi. 2002. "Georgian Kidnapping: A Deadly Trend." *Caucasus Reporting Service* 135. http://www.iwpr.net (accessed June 27, 2002).

Lomsadze, Sh. V. 1973. *Iuzhnaia Gruziia (Samtskhe-Dzhavakheti) s serediny XVII v. po piatidesiatye gody XIX v.* Tbilisi: Metsniereba.

Lotman, Iurii. 1984. "'Agreement' and 'Self-Giving' as Archetypal Models of Culture." In *The Semiotics of Russian Culture,* edited by Iurii Lotman and Boris Uspenskii, 125–140. Ann Arbor: Michigan Slavic Contributions.

———. 1985. "Problema Vostoka i Zapada v tvorchestve pozdnego Lermontova." In *Lermontovskii sbornik,* edited by I. S. Chistova, 5–22. Leningrad: Nauka.

Lunochkin, Andrei, and Andrei Mikhailov. 1994. "Grigorii Zass i Iakov Baklanov." *Rodina* 3–4:91–96.

Luzbetak, Louis J. 1951. *Marriage and Family in Caucasia.* Vienna: St. Gabriel's Mission Press.

Makanin, Vladimir. 1995. "Kavkazskii plennyi." *Novyi Mir* 840 (4): 3–19.

Maksimova, M. I. 1965. "Mif o pokhishchenii Ganimeda v peredache Bosporskogo mastera." *Kratkie soobshcheniia o dokladakh i polevykh issledovaniiakh Instituta Arkheologii* 103:23–27.

Malinowski, Bronislaw. [1922] 1961. *Argonauts of the Western Pacific: An Account of Native Enterprise and Adventure in the Archipelagoes of Melanesian New Guinea.* New York: Dutton.

Mal'sagov, Akhmet. 1989. *Pritchi o gorskom etikete.* Nal'chik, Russ.: El'brus.

Mamedov, Mikhail. 1999. "Massovye stereotipy i predrassudki v national'nykh istoriiakh i predstavleniiakh o proshlom (na primere 'litsa kavkazskoi natsional'nosti')." In *Natsional'nye istorii v sovetskom i postsovetskikh gosudarstvakh,* edited by K. Aimermakher and G. Bordiugov, 104–114. Moscow: AIRO-XX.

Mann, Robert. 1990. "Pushkin's Kavkazskij Plennik." *Russian Language Journal* 147–149:109–126.

Manning, Paul. 2007. "Love Khevsur Style: The Romance of the Mountains and Mountaineer Romance in Georgian Ethnography." In *Caucasus Paradigms: Anthropologies, Histories, and the Making of a World Area,* edited by Bruce Grant and Lale Yalçın-Heckmann, 23–46. Berlin: LIT.

Markelov, N. V. 2002. "'Where Martial Plunder Prowls the Mountains' (Prisoners of the Caucasus)." *Russian Studies in History* 41 (2): 21–38.

Marlinskii [Bestuzhev, Bestuzhev-Marlinskii], Aleksandr. 1837. *Russkie povesti i razskazy A. Marlinskago. Chast' sed'maia.* St. Petersburg: Vingeberg.

———. 1892. *Razskaz ofitsera, byvshago v plenu u gortsev. Krasnoe pokryvalo. Noch' na korable. Osada.* St. Petersburg: Suvorin.

Marlinsky, Alexander. 1843. "Ammalat-Bek." 4 parts, translated by Thomas B. Shaw. *Blackwood's Edinburgh Magazine* 53, no. 329 (March): 281–301; no. 330 (April): 464–483; no. 331 (May): 568–589; no. 332 (June): 746–761.

Martin, Terry. 2001. *The Affirmative Action Empire: Nations and Nationalisms in the Soviet Union, 1923–1939.* Ithaca: Cornell University Press.

Martin, Virginia. 2000. *Law and Custom in the Steppe: The Kazakhs of the Middle Horde and Russian Colonialism in the Nineteenth Century.* Richmond, Surrey: Curzon.

Maslova, Elena. 2001. "Presentatsiia: Mudrets iz Chegema." *Slovo,* July 27, 15.

Matveev, Vladimir. 1995. "K voprosu o posledstviiakh kavkazskoi voiny i vkhozhdenii severokavkazskikh narodov v sostav Rossii (novoe kontseptual'noe osveshchenie problemy)." In *Kavkazskaia voina: Uroki istorii i sovremennost',* edited by V. N. Ratushniak, 188–198. Krasnodar: Kubanskii gosudarstvennyi universitet.

———. 2002. "Severnyi kavkaz: Abreki, kachagi i drugie." *Orientir* 4:9–11.

Mauss, Marcel. [1925] 1990. *The Gift: Form and Functions of Exchange in Archaic Societies.* Translated by Ian Cunnison. New York: Norton.

———. [1925] 2000. *The Gift: The Form and Reason for Exchange in Archaic Societies.* Translated by W. D. Halls. New York: Norton.

Mbembe, Achille. 2003. "Necropolitics." *Public Culture* 15:11–40.

Mel'ts, M. Ia. 2000. "Pesni i romansy na stikhi A. S. Pushkina v lubochnykh kartinakh." *Etnograficheskoe obozrenie* 2:140–147.

Merzabekov, M. 1990. "Vstrechi v Bashkirii, rabochaia poezdka B. N. El'tsina po Rossii." *Sovetskaia Rossiia,* August 14, 1.

Michaels, Paula. 2004. "Prisoners of the Caucasus." *Russian Studies in Literature* 40 (2): 52–77.

Moores, Ralph Kerney. 1992. "Tolstoy's Kavkazskii Plennik through the Prism of the Iuzhnaia Poema: Transcending Russian Orientalism." Master's thesis, Ohio State University.

Morgan, Lewis Henry. [1870] 1997. *Systems of Consanguinity and Affinity.* Lincoln: University of Nebraska Press.

Morozov, Petr. 1912. "Lichnyia nastroeniia Pushkina pred sozdaniem 'Kavkazskogo Plennika.'" In *Aleksandr Sergeevich Pushkin: Ego zhizn' i sochineniia,* edited by V. Pokrovskii, 391–394. Moscow: Spiridonov and Mikhailov.

Mostashari, Firouzeh. 2006. *On the Religious Frontier: Tsarist Russia and Islam in the Caucasus.* London: I. B. Tauris.

Murray, David. 2000. *Indian Giving: Economies of Power in Indian-White Exchanges.* Amherst: University of Massachusetts Press.

Musaeva, Faniya. 2001. "Trafficking in Persons as a Modern Kind of Slavery." Central Asia Caucasus-Analyst. http://www.cacianalyst.org/July_18_2001/July_18_2001_Trafficking_in_persons.htm (accessed August 4, 2001).

Nancy, Jean-Luc. 1993. *The Birth to Presence.* Translated by Brian Holmes and others. Stanford: Stanford University Press.

Nandy, Ashis. "The Discreet Charms of Indian Terrorism." *Journal of Commonwealth and Comparative Politics* 28 (1): 25–43.

Nazpary, Joma. 2002. *Post-Soviet Chaos: Violence and Dispossesion in Kazakhstan.* London: Pluto.

Ortabaev, Batyrbek Khadzeumarovich, and F. V. Totoev. 1988. "Eshche raz o kavkazskoi voine: O ee sotsial'nykh istokakh i sushchnosti." *Istoriia SSSR* 4:78–96.

Oushakine, Serguei. 2009. *The Patriotism of Despair: Nation, War, and Loss in Russia.* Ithaca: Cornell University Press.

Pagden, Anthony. 1995. *Lords of All the World. Ideologies of Empire in Spain, Britain, and France c. 1500–1800.* New Haven: Yale University Press.

Patterson, Orlando. 1982. *Slavery and Social Death: A Comparative Study.* Cambridge: Harvard University Press.

Pavlova, I. K. 2004. "K chitateliu." Preface to *Noveishiia izvestiia o Kavkaze, sobrannyia i popolnennyia Semenom Bronevskim,* by Semen Bronevskii, 5–21. St. Petersburg: Peterburgskoe vostokovedenie.

Pearce, Roy Harvey. 1947. "The Significances of the Captivity Narrative." *American Literature* 19 (1): 1–20.

"Perevernutyi mir beskonechnoi voiny." 1994. *Rodina* 3–4:17–23 (roundtable discussion).

Pershits, Abram Isaakovich. 1982. "Pokhishchenie nevest: Pravilo ili iskliuchenie." *Sovetskaia etnografiia* 4:121–127.

Pesmen, Dale. 2000. *Russia and Soul: An Exploration.* Ithaca: Cornell University Press.

Platz, Stephanie. 1996. "Pasts and Futures: Space, History and Armenian Identity, 1988–1994." PhD diss., University of Chicago.

Pokrovskii, M. N. 1924. *Diplomatiia i voiny tsarskoi Rossii v XIX stoletii.* Moscow: Krasnaia nov'.

Pollock, Sean. 2006. "Empire by Invitation? Russian Empire-Building in the Caucasus in the Reign of Catherine II." PhD diss., Harvard University.

Potapova, G. E., and Iu. A. Tsyganova. 1998. "Kavkazskii plennik ot Pushkina do Leskova." *Nachalo,* no. 4:71–86.

Potto, V. A. [1885–1887] 1994. *Kavkazskaia voina: Ot drevneishikh vremen do Ermolova.* 5 vols. Stavropol': Kavkazskii krai.

Prokhorov, Aleksandr. 2003. "Cinema of Attractions versus Narrative Cinema: Leonid Gaidai's Comedies and El'dar Riazanov's Satires of the 1960s." *Slavic Review* 62 (3): 455–472.

Propp, Vladimir. 1968. *Morphology of the Folktale.* Translated by Laurence Scott. Austin: University of Texas Press.

Proskurin, Oleg. 2006. "Pushkin and Politics." In *The Cambridge Companion to Pushkin,* edited by Andrew Kahn, 105–117. Cambridge: Cambridge University Press.

Pushkin, Aleksandr. [1822] 1997. "Captive of the Caucasus." In *Alexander Pushkin,* edited by A. D. P. Briggs, 57–75. London: J. M. Dent.

———. 1938. *Polnoe sobranie sochinenii.* Tom 8, *Romany i povesti, puteshestviia.* Moscow: Akademiia nauk.

———. 1958. *Polnoe sobranie sochinenii v desiati tomakh.* Tom 10, *Pis'ma.* Moscow: Akademiia nauk.

Ram, Harsha. 1998. "Russian Poetry and the Imperial Sublime." In *Russian Subjects: Empire, Nation, and the Culture of the Golden Age,* edited by Monika Greenleaf and Stephen Moeller-Sally, 21–49. Evanston, IL: Northwestern University Press.

———. 1999. "Prisoners of the Caucasus: Literary Myths and Media Representations of the Chechen Conflict." Working paper, Berkeley Program in Soviet and Post-Soviet Studies Working Paper Series.

———. 2003. *The Imperial Sublime: A Russian Poetics of Empire.* Madison: University of Wisconsin Press.

Ramazanov, Khidir Kh. 1961. *K voprosu o rabstve v Dagestane.* Makhachkala, Russ.: Akademiia nauk.

Ratushniak, Valerii N. 1995. *Kavkazskaia voina: Uroki istorii i sovremennost'.* Krasnodar: Kubanskii gosudarstvennyi universitet.

Rayfield, Donald. 1994. *The Literature of Georgia: A History.* London: Curzon.

Reynolds. Michael. 2005. "Myths and Mysticism: A Longitudinal Perspective on Islam and Conflict in the North Caucasus." *Middle Eastern Studies* 41 (1): 31–54.

Ries, Nancy. 1997. *Russian Talk: Culture and Conversation during Perestroika.* Ithaca: Cornell University Press.

Romanovskii, D. [1860] 2004. *Kavkaz i kavkazskaia voina.* Moscow: Gosudarstvennaia publichnaia istoricheskaia biblioteka.

Rubin, Gayle. 1975. "The Traffic in Women." In *Toward an Anthropology of Women,* edited by Rayna Reiter, 157–210. New York: Monthly Review.

Sahlins, Marshall. [1978] 1996. "On the Sociology of Primitive Exchange." In *The Gift: An Interdisciplinary Perspective,* edited by Aafke E. Komter, 26–38. Amsterdam: Amsterdam University Press.

Sahni, Kalpana. 1997. *Crucifying the Orient: Russian Orientalism and the Colonization of the Caucasus and Central Asia.* Bangkok: White Orchid Press.

Sakharov, Vsevolod. 1994. "Gvardeiskii Prometei, ili Kavkaz A. A. Bestuzheva-Marlinskogo." *Rodina* 3–4:104–107.

Sanders, Thomas, Ernest Tucker, and Gary Hamburg, eds. 2004. *Russian-Muslim Confrontations in the Caucasus: Alternative Visions of the Conflict between Imam Shamil and the Russians, 1830–1859.* London: RoutledgeCurzon.

Sandler, Stephanie. 1989. *Distant Pleasures: Alexander Pushkin and the Writing of Exile.* Stanford: Stanford University Press.

Sandrygailo, I. Ia. 1899. *Adaty Dagestanskoi oblasti i Zakatal'skago okruga: Sudoustroistvo i sudoproizvodstvo v chastiakh kraia voenno-narodnago upravleniia.* Tbilisi: Kantseliariia glavnonachal'stva grazhdanskoi chasti na Kavkaze.

Savushkina, Nina I. 1988. *Russkaia narodnaia drama.* Moscow: Narodnyi universitet.

Schmitt, Carl. 1985. *Political Theology: Four Chapters on the Concept of Sovereignty.* Cambridge: MIT Press.

Schulze, Wolfgang. 1999. "Affinal Kin Terms in the East Caucasus: Inheritance v. Borrowing?" *Diachronica* 16 (1): 97–122.

Sergeenko, A. P. 1983. *"Khadzhi-Murat" L'va Tolstogo: Istoriia sozdaniia povesti.* Moscow: Sovremennik.

Sertel, Ayse K. 1969. "Kidnapping and Elopement in Rural Turkey." *Hacettepe Bulletin of Social Sciences and Humanities* 1 (2): 96–104.

Shalikashvili, Dimitri. 1954. "Gruzinsko-russkie vzaimootnosheniia." Typescript. Hoover Institution Archive. Box 1, folder 8.

———. 1956. "Vospominaniia." Typescript. Hoover Institution Archive. Box 2.

———. n.d. "The Bright Days of Our Independence," translated by Maria Shalikashvili. Typescript. Hoover Institution Archive. Box 1, folder 4.

Shami, Seteney. 1999. "Islam in the Post-Soviet Space: Imaginative Geographies of the Caucasus and Central Asia." *Bulletin of the Royal Institute for Inter-Faith Studies* 1 (1): 181–195.

———. 2000. "Prehistories of Globalization." *Public Culture* 12 (1): 177–204.

Sheliga-Pototskii, V. A. [Wassily Potocki]. 1848. "Posledniia minuty Marlinskago." *Illiustratsiia* 6 (156): 376–378.

Shnirel'man, Viktor. 2001. *The Value of the Past: Myths, Identity, and Politics in Transcaucasia.* Osaka, Japan: National Museum of Ethnology.

———. 2006. *Byt' alanami: Intellektualy i politika na severnom kavkaze v XX veke.* Moscow: Novoe literaturnoe obozrenie.

Shternberg, Lev Iakovlevich. 1910. "Inorodtsy." In *Formy natsional'nogo dvizheniia v sovremennykh gosudarstvakh,* edited by A. P. Kastelianskii, 529–574. St. Petersburg: Obshchestvennaia Pol'za.

Simmel, Georg. [1907] 1971. "Exchange." In *On Individuality and Social Forms,* edited by Donald N. Levine, 43–69. Chicago: University of Chicago Press.

Slezkine, Yuri. 1994a. *Arctic Mirrors: Russia and the Small Peoples of the North.* Ithaca: Cornell University Press.

———. 1994b. "The USSR as Communal Apartment, or, How a Socialist State Promoted Ethnic Particularism." *Slavic Review* 53 (2): 414–452.

———. 2000. "Imperialism as the Highest Form of Socialism." *Russian Review* 59 (2): 227–234.

Slonimskii, Iu. I. 1938. "'Kavkazskii plennik' Didlo." In *Kavkazskii plennik: Balet v trekh aktakh,* edited by G. Ia. Tarasenko, 37–54. Leningrad: Malyi opernyi teatr.

Slotkin, Richard. 1973. *Regeneration through Violence: The Mythology of the American Frontier, 1600–1860.* Norman: University of Oklahoma Press.

Smal-Stocky, Roman. 1947. "The Struggle of the Subjugated Nations in the Soviet Union for Freedom: Sketch of the History of the Promethean Movement." *Ukrainian Quarterly* 3 (4): 324–344.

Smirnova, Iaroslava Sergeevna. 1979. "K tipologii obychaev umykaniia (po materialam narodov Severnogo i Zapadnogo Kavkaza)." In *Problemy tipologii v etnografii,* edited by Iu. V. Bromlei, 265–269. Moscow: Nauka.

——. 1983. *Sem'ia i semeinyi byt narodov Severnogo Kavkaza: Vtoraia polovina XIX–XX v.* Moscow: Nauka.

Smith, Adam. [1759] 1790. *A Theory of Moral Sentiments.* London: A. Millar.

Sokolov, Nikita. 2005. "Kavkazskaia zagogulina." *Otechestvennye zapiski* 2 (23): 338–344 (archival documents compiled by Nikita Sokolov).

Solzhenitsyn, Aleksandr. 1990. *Kak nam obustroit' Rossiiu? Posil'nye soobrazheniia.* Paris: YMCA.

Specter, Michael. 1996. "Updating Tolstoy, A Russian Director Faces War's Anguish." *New York Times,* July 22, C17.

Ssorin-Chaikov, Nikolai. 2006. "On Heterochrony: Birthday Gifts to Stalin, 1949." *Journal of the Royal Anthropological Institute,* no. 12:355–275.

Stankevich and Mel'gunov. 1832. "Kalmytskii plennik." *Molva* 75 (16 September): 1–2.

Statiev, Alexander. 2005. "The Nature of Anti-Soviet Armed Resistance, 1942–44: The North Caucasus, the Kalmyk Autonomous Republic, and Crimea." *Kritika* 6 (2): 285–318.

Stefanovich, Vera N. 1927. "Iz istorii 'Kavkazskogo plennika' Pushkina." In *Tvorcheskaia istoriia: Issledovaniia po russkoi literature,* edited by N. K. Piksanov, 7–42. Moscow: Nikitinskie subbotniki.

Stewart, Susan. 1991. "Notes on Distressed Genres." *Journal of American Folklore* 104: 5–28.

Strathern, Marilyn. 1984. "Subject or Object? Women and the Circulation of Valuables in Highlands New Guinea." In *Women and Property, Women as Property,* edited by R. Hirschon, 158–175. London: Croom Helm.

——. 1988. *The Gender of the Gift: Problems with Women and Problems with Society in Melanesia.* Berkeley: University of California Press.

Strong, Pauline Turner. 1999. *Captive Selves, Captivating Others: The Politics and Poetics of Colonial American Captivity Narratives.* Boulder: Westview.

Strukov, D. P. 1906. *Avgusteishii general-fel'dtseikhmeister velikii kniaz' Mikhail Nikolaevich.* St. Petersburg: Soikin.

Sugar, Peter. 1971. "The Ottoman Professional Prisoner." *Études balkaniques* 7 (2): 82–91.

Sultanov, Kazbek Kamilovich. 2004. "Mezhdu svobodoi i sud'boi: Kavkazskaia voina v zerkale literatur Severnogo Kavkaza." Paper presented to the American Association for the Advancement of Slavic Studies, Boston.

Suny, Ronald G. 1988. *The Making of the Georgian Nation.* Bloomington: Indiana University Press.

——. 1993. *The Revenge of the Past: Nationalism, Revolution, and the Collapse of the Soviet Union.* Stanford: Stanford University Press.

——. 1995. "Ambiguous Categories: States, Empires, and Nations." *Post-Soviet Affairs* 11 (2): 185–196.

Suny, Ronald G., and Terry Martin, eds. 2001. *A State of Nations: Empire and Nation-Making in the Age of Lenin and Stalin.* New York: Oxford University Press.

Svirin, N. 1934. "Russkaia kolonial'naia literatura." *Literaturnyi kritik* 9: 51–79.

——. 1935. "K voprosu o baironizme Pushkina." *Literaturnyi sovremennik* 7: 184–210.

Swietochowski, Tadeusz. 1995. *Russia and Azerbaijan: A Borderland in Transition.* New York: Columbia University Press.

Tarasenko, G. Ia. 1938. *Kavkazskii plennik: Balet v trekh aktakh.* Leningrad: Malyi opernyi teatr.

Taussig, Michael. 1986. *Shamanism, Colonialism, and the Wild Man: A Study in Terror and Healing.* Chicago: University of Chicago Press.

———. 1995. "The Sun Gives without Receiving: An Old Story." *Comparative Studies in Society and History* 37 (2): 368–398.

Ter-Sarkisiants, A. E. 1989. "Brak i svadebnyi tsikl u armian (vtoraia polovina XIX–nachalo XX v.)." In *Kavkazskii etnograficheskii sbornik IX. Voprosy istoricheskoi etnografii Kavkaza,* edited by N. G. Volkova and V. K. Gardanov, 246–284. Moscow: Nauka.

Thomson, George. 1972. *Aeschylus and Athens: A Study in the Social Origins of Drama.* New York: Haskell.

Tillett, Lowell. 1969. *The Great Friendship: Soviet Historians on the Non-Russian Nationalities.* Chapel Hill: University of North Carolina Press.

Tishkov, Valery. 2004. *Chechnya: Life in a War-Torn Society.* Berkeley: University of California Press.

Todorova, Maria. 1997. *Imagining the Balkans.* New York: Oxford University Press.

———. 2009. *Bones of Contention: The Living Archives of Vasil Levski and the Making of Bulgaria's National Hero.* Budapest: Central European University Press.

Toledano, Ehud. 1982. *The Ottoman Slave Trade and Its Suppression, 1840–1890.* Princeton: Princeton University Press.

Tolmachev, E. P. 2002. "Russia's Annexation of the Caucasus (Some Conclusions and Consequences)." *Russian Studies in History* 41 (2): 16–20.

Tolstoi [Tolstoy], Lev N. [Leo]. "Kavkazskii plennik." *Zaria* (February): 7–33.

———. 1977. "A Prisoner of the Caucasus: A True Story." In *Master and Man and Other Stories,* translated by Ronald Wilks and Paul Foote, 117–142. New York: Penguin.

———. 2003. *Hadji Murad.* Translated by Aylmer Maude. New York: Modern Library.

Tolstoy, Aleksei. [1923] 1985. *Aelita, or The Decline of Mars.* Ann Arbor: Ardis.

Tomkeev, V. 1898. *Kavkazskii sbornik* 19: 168–218.

Trubitsyn, Nikolai. 1912. *O narodnoi poezii v obshchestvennom i literaturnom obikhode pervoi treti XIX veka.* St Petersburg: Glavnoe upravlenie udelov.

Tsing, Anna. 2005. *Friction: An Ethnography of Global Connection.* Princeton: Princeton University Press.

Tsivian, Yuri. 1991. "Early Russian Cinema: Some Observations." In *Inside the Film Factory: New Approaches to Russian and Soviet Cinema,* edited by Richard Taylor and Ian Christie, 7–30. New York: Routledge.

Tsvizhba, Larisa. 2000. "Plennik." *Rodina* 1–2:88–89.

Tuite, Kevin. 1998a. "Achilles and the Caucasus." *Journal of Indo-European Studies* 26 (3–4): 289–343.

———. 1998b. "Evidence for Prehistoric Links between the Caucasus and Central Asia: The Case of the Burushos." In *The Bronze Age and Early Iron Age Peoples of Eastern Central Asia,* edited by Victor Mair, 448–475. Washington, DC: Institute for the Study of Man.

Uehling, Greta. 2004. *Beyond Memory: The Crimean Tatars' Deportation and Return.* New York: Palgrave.

Umanets, F. M. 1912. *Prokonsul Kavkaza.* St. Petersburg: I. G. Vatsar.

Uslar, Petr. 1868. "Koe-chto o slovesnykh proizvedeniiakh gortsev." *Sbornik svedenii o kavkazskikh gortsakh.* Tbilisi.

Vakhitov, Rustem. 2004. "Komu srodni Saakhov?" *Sovetskaia Rossiia,* August 14, 4.

Vedeneev, Dmitrii. 2000. "77 tysiach chelovek poteriala Rossiia v kavkazskikh voinakh." *Rodina* 1–2:108–110.

Velichko, Vasilii L'vovich. 1904. *Polnoe sobranie publitsisticheskikh sochinenii V. L. Velichko.* St. Petersburg: Artel' pechatnogo dela.

Verderevskii, Evgenii Aleksandrovich. 1856. *Plen u Shamilia: Pravdivaia povest' o vos'mimesiachnom i shestidnevnom (v 1854–1855 g.) prebyvanii v plenu u Shamilia semeistv: Pokoinago General-Maiora Kniazia Orbeliani i Podpolkovnika Kniazia Chavchavadze, osnovannaia na pokazaniiakh lits, uchastvovavshikh v sobytii.* St. Petersburg: Korolev.

Verdery, Katherine. 1999. *The Political Lives of Dead Bodies: Reburial and Postsocialist Change.* New York: Columbia University Press.

Vernant, Jean-Pierre. 1989. "At Man's Table: Hesiod's Foundation Myth of Sacrifice." In *The Cuisine of Sacrifice among the Greeks,* edited by Marcel Detienne and Jean-Pierre Vernant, translated by Paula Wissing, 21–86. Chicago: University of Chicago Press.

Vinogradov, Viktor Vladimirovich. 1929. *Slovar' iazyka Pushkina.* Tom 3. Moscow: Inostrannye natsional'nye slovari.

Vishnevskii, Veniamin. 1945. *Khudozhestvennye fil'my dorevoliutsionnoi Rossii.* Moscow: Goskinoizdat.

Volkov, Anatolii. 2003. "Kavkazskaia plennitsa, ili novye prikliucheniia Shurika." In *Rossiiskii Illiuzion,* edited by Liudmila M. Budiak, 405–410. Moscow: Materik.

Von Busack, Richard. 1997. "Pondering Prisoner." *Metroactive Movies.* http://www.metroactive.com (accessed March 2005).

Von Hagen, Mark. 2004. "Empires, Borderlands, and Diasporas: Eurasia as an Anti-Paradigm for the Post-Soviet Era." *American Historical Review* 109 (2): 445–468.

Wagner-Pacifici, Robin. 2005. *The Art of Surrender: Decomposing Sovereignty at Conflict's End.* Chicago: University of Chicago Press.

Weiner, Annette. 1976. *Women of Value, Men of Reknown: New Perspectives in Trobriand Exchange.* Austin: University of Texas Press.

———. 1992. *Inalienable Possessions: The Paradox of Keeping-While-Giving.* Berkeley: University of California Press.

Werner, Cynthia. 2004. "Women, Marriage, and the Nation-State: The Rise of Consensual Bride Kidnapping in Post-Soviet Kazakhstan." In *The Transformation of Central Asia: States and Societies from Soviet Rule to Independence,* edited by Pauline Jones Luong, 59–89. Ithaca: Cornell University Press.

Werth, Paul. 2002. *At the Margins of Empire: Mission, Governance, and Confessional Politics in Russia's Volga-Kama Region, 1827–1905.* Ithaca: Cornell University Press.

White, Richard. [1947] 1991. *The Middle Ground: Indians, Empires, and Republics in the Great Lakes Region, 1650–1815.* New York: Cambridge University Press.

Whitman, Walt. 1980. "A Song of the Rolling Earth," In *Leaves of Grass: A Textual Variorum of the Printed Poems.* Vol. 1, *Poems, 1855–1856,* edited by Sculley Bradley, Harold W. Blodgett, Arthur Golden, and William White, 265–272. New York: New York University Press.

Wiesehöfer, Josef. 2001. "Gift-Giving." In *Encyclopaedia Iranica,* 10:604–617. Boston: Routledge.

Wilhelm, Christopher. 1998. "Prometheus and the Caucasus: The Origins of the Prometheus Myth," in *Proceedings of the Ninth Annual UCLA Indo-European Conference,* edited by Karlene Jones-Bley, Angela Della Volpe, Miriam Robbins Dexter, and Martin E. Huld, 142–157. Washington, DC: Institute for the Study of Man.

Yalçın-Heckmann, Lale. 1991. *Tribe and Kinship among the Kurds.* New York: Peter Lang.

———. 2001. "The Political Economy of an Azeri Wedding." Working Paper 28, Max Planck Institute for Social Anthropology, Halle (Salle).

Zagorskii, Ivan. 1898. "Vosem' mesiatsev v plenu u gortsev." *Kavkazskii sbornik* 19 (191): 221–247.

Zakharov, P. 1949. "Dushoi ispolnennyi polet." *Isskustvo* 6:94–95.

Zakharov, V. A., and I. A. Nastenko. 2000. "Kavkazskii uzel." In *Sbornik russkogo istoricheskogo obshchestva,* edited by O. M. Rapov, 2:8–14. Moscow: Russkaia panorama.

Zamotin, I. I. 1913. *Romantizm dvadtsatykh godov XIX stol. v russkoi literature.* Vol. 2. St. Petersburg: Vol'f.

Zhemukhov, S. N. 1997. *Mirovozzrenie Khan-Gireia.* Nal'chik, Russ: Nauchnoe izdanie.

Zhirmunskii, V. 1923. "Vokrug 'Kavkazskogo plennika' Pushkina (K stoletnei godovshchine—avgust 1822)." *Literaturnaia mysl'* 2: 110–123.

———. 1924. *Bairon i Pushkin: Iz istorii romanticheskoi poemy.* Leningrad: Academia.

Ziolkowski, Margaret. 2005. *Alien Visions: Chechens and Navajos in Russian and American Literature.* Newark: University of Delaware Press.

Ziolkowski, Theodore. 2000. *The Sin of Knowledge: Ancient Themes and Modern Variations.* Princeton: Princeton University Press.

Zorkaia, Neia Markovna. 1994. *Fol'klor, lubok, ekran.* Moscow: Isskustvo.

Zubov, Platon. 1834. *Kartina Kavkazskogo kraia prinadlezhashchego Rossii i sopredel'nykh emu zemel'.* 2 vols. St. Petersburg: Vingeber.

Zvanba, Solomon T. 1955. *Etnograficheskie etiudy.* Sukhumi, Abkhaziia: Abkhazskoe gosudarstvennoe izdatel'stvo.

Index